# Effective Instruction for Struggling Readers, K–6

## Barbara M. Taylor
## James E. Ysseldyke

EDITORS

TEACHERS
COLLEGE
PRESS

Teachers College, Columbia University
New York and London

Published by Teachers College Press, 1234 Amsterdam Avenue, New York, NY 10027

Copyright © 2007 by Teachers College, Columbia University

Portions of Chapter 5 appeared previously in *Developing Literacy in Second-Language Learners: Report of the National Literacy Panel on Language Minority Children and Youth* (2006), Diane August and Timothy Shanahan, Eds. Used with the permission of Lawrence Erlbaum Associates.

*Library of Congress Cataloging-in-Publication Data*

Effective instruction for struggling readers, K–6 / edited by Barbara M. Taylor and James E. Ysseldyke.
    p. cm. — (Language and literacy series)
    Includes bibliographical references and index.
    ISBN 978-0-8077-4821-3 (pbk.) — ISBN 978-0-8077-4822-0 (hardcover)
    1. Reading—Remedial teaching—United States.   2. Reading (Elementary)—United States.   3. Effective teaching—United States.   I. Taylor, Barbara M.
II. Ysseldyke, James E.
    LB1050.5.E336 2007
    372.430973—dc22                                                    2007019531


ISBN: 978-0-8077-4821-3 (paper)
ISBN: 978-0-8077-4822-0 (hardcover)

Printed on acid-free paper
Manufactured in the United States of America

14  13  12  11  10  09  08  07      8  7  6  5  4  3  2  1

---

(Continued)

# Contents

**PART III    Effective Instruction to Develop
Students' Comprehension**

**PART IV    Effective Schoolwide Practices
to Improve All Students' Reading**

# Acknowledgments

This book is the outgrowth of the third Guy Bond Commemorative Reading Conference, held at the University of Minnesota on October 10–11, 2005.

For 29 years, from 1937–1966, Guy Bond served the University of Minnesota and children and teachers throughout the nation as one of the foremost reading educators of his time. He authored a host of articles on reading instruction and diagnosis of reading problems, coauthored the leading reading diagnosis text of the time—*Reading Difficulties*—and served as the principal author of a major basal reading series. He also served as principal investigator of the largest investigation of beginning reading instruction ever conducted—the First Grade Studies—and as the advisor and mentor of a group of students who themselves became national leaders in reading education.

Guy Bond died in 1980, but his contributions to the field of reading continue to be felt. In 1994, through the generosity of Fredericka Bond, the University of Minnesota College of Education and Human Development established the Guy Bond Chair in Reading, a perpetual endowment to promote the cause of literacy and literacy instruction. The Guy Bond Commemorative Reading Conference, which served as the impetus for this volume, was one of the first activities of the endowment. We are very thankful to Dr. Bond for being who he was and doing what he did for children, and we are very thankful to Fredericka Bond for giving us the opportunity to continue to pursue Dr. Bond's goal of literacy for all children.

# CHAPTER 1

# Understanding the Factors That Allegedly Contribute to Students' Reading Difficulties

James E. Ysseldyke
Barbara Taylor

While recent efforts to "leave no child behind" have focused largely on improving student reading scores, illiteracy continues to be a problem in United States schools. According to the most recent data from the National Assessment of Educational Progress (NAEP, 2005), only 31% of fourth-grade students tested at or above "Proficiency" at grade level in reading. In addition, the percentage of 4th graders reading at or above the "Basic" level has not changed significantly from the percentages reported in 1992. This lack of progress in young readers becomes even more distressing when we consider the findings of the National Institute of Child Health and Human Development (1999), which indicated that 74% of children who fail to read by third grade are still unable to read well by ninth grade.

With more than 18% of students in the United States experiencing reading difficulties in their first three years of school, and with nearly half of special education students being diagnosed as having reading disabilities, we must admit that we are not successfully meeting the challenge of teaching our children to read (National Reading Panel [NRP], 2000; U.S. Department of Education [USED], 2001). This is a text on effective instruction for struggling readers in elementary and middle school settings, and in this opening chapter we briefly review the magnitude of the challenge and alternative explanations for why so many young children struggle to acquire reading skills. We also establish the focus of this volume—the need for multiple, effective instructional approaches within schools to support elementary and middle school students who are struggling to read well—and provide an overview of the chapters to follow.

# WHY DO STUDENTS STRUGGLE WITH READING?

Reading difficulties typically have been attributed to three main causes: internal student factors, environmental factors, and instructional factors. A brief discussion of the internal factors and environmental factors traditionally considered to be related to students' reading difficulties is included here, but most of this chapter is devoted to reviewing instructional factors that contribute to students' success since the focus of the book is on what schools must do to ensure that all students, especially those who are struggling, learn to read well.

## Internal Student Factors

Any deficits, disorders, and dysfunctions that are innate or acquired (e.g., traumatic brain injury) aspects of a student's makeup are considered internal factors. Some educators believe that such factors explain why certain students struggle with reading, and why those students do not respond to the same reading instruction techniques as their peers. When Ysseldyke, Christenson, Algozzine, and Thurlow (1983) surveyed regular classroom teachers about their attributions for student difficulties in school, they found that, regardless of the type of student behavior, over 85% of students' difficulties were attributed to these within-child characteristics.

### Processing Deficits

Those who attribute reading failure to internal factors often theorize that students who struggle with reading have processing difficulties. More specifically, it is believed that such students do not process letter and word sequences efficiently, or that they are unable to coordinate the components of processing effectively (Bradley, Danielson, & Hallahan, 2005). Students who have processing difficulties are often subsequently diagnosed as learning disabled. In fact, students with reading disabilities compose at least 80% of the population of students with learning disabilities (Lerner & Kline, 2006).

While the existence of processing difficulties often leads people to think there is a need for the remediation of process deficits, this conclusion has not been substantiated in the research literature. Instead, the remediation of process deficits has failed to result in reading improvements (Arter & Jenkins, 1979; Ysseldyke, 1973). As such, the exact nature of this proposed deficit remains unclear (Ysseldyke, Algozzine, & Thurlow, 2000).

### Deficient Neuropsychological Functioning

Another explanation for students' reading difficulties is the presumption that these students have deficiencies in neuropsychological functioning. For instance, some researchers have suggested that students with "laterality confusions" between the two hemispheres of the brain might have more difficulty reading (Taylor & Pearson, 2002). Another theory suggests that minimal brain damage could lead to reading difficulties (Taylor & Pearson, 2002). However, neither of these theories has been supported by the research literature (Chalfant & Sheffelin, 1970).

## Environmental Factors

The second of the three main causes to which reading failure is attributed are environmental factors, including student experiences, family characteristics, and early education. A number of these factors will be discussed below to invite educators to acknowledge their possible contribution to some students' reading challenges, and to move beyond these factors since they are out of educators' control. Throughout the chapter we encourage teachers to focus their efforts on alterable variables (e.g., specific skill deficits, instructional setting) rather than on environmental factors that are difficult or impossible to alter (e.g., who the child's parents are, prior negative home or community experiences). The intended consequence of such a discussion is for educators to appreciate the importance of what can be done within schools to help struggling readers achieve success in reading.

It is well recognized that some environmental factors act, in general, to impact reading achievement. Students from high poverty environments, in general, acquire reading skills at rates slower than those from more affluent environments; in general, there is a gap in achievement between students from high-income and low-income environments. We stress "in general" because there are specific individuals for whom, or instances in which, this generalization does not hold.

### Student Experience

Many children in the United States come to school lacking the kinds of experiential backgrounds that are often considered crucial to academic success. Some reading experts have used the term *deficiency* as an explanation for lack of such experiences. Although students with less rich experiences may have no innate learning problems, some may have a limited behavioral repertoire because they have not had opportunities to develop the verbal, conceptual, attentional, and learning skills necessary for success in reading and other academic areas (Ysseldyke, Algozzine, & Thurlow, 2000).

## Home Literacy Environment

Researchers and educators alike often consider the home literacy environment of vital importance to a student's success. In fact, children who are exposed to similar values in the home as at school are more likely to experience success in the school environment overall (Taylor & Pearson, 2002). In addition, families who teach the importance of academic achievement are more likely than others to see their children value the intrinsic reward of education, rather than extrinsic incentives such as grades and teacher praise (Taylor & Pearson, 2002).

More specific to the area of reading, family members who value the importance of education are likely to encourage children to engage in home-based practices that promote literacy. In fact, there is a significant body of research that is used to support the notion that home support for learning can have an impact on a student's ability to read successfully. Researchers consistently find that children who are read to frequently by family members are significantly more likely to display beginning literacy skills (Nord, Lennon, Banning, & Chaudler, 1999). A longitudinal study of kindergartners also revealed that "the differences in children's reading skills and knowledge usually seen in later grades appear to be present as children begin school, and persist after 1 and 2 years of school" (National Center for Education Statistics [NCES], 2003). For instance, children who work with their parents in the home on literacy activities (e.g., recognizing letters, reading aloud) experience improved language skills and heightened interest in books (Primavera, 2000). Also, a large-scale study by the National Assessment of Educational Progress (2000) indicates that, while the relationship between home literacy environment and reading scores is small ($r = .21$), the relationship is, in fact, significant.

## Preprimary Education

Researchers have shown that the reading scores of young children are also affected by their preprimary educational experiences (Schweinhart, Montie, Xiang, Barnett, Belfield, & Nores, 2005). The results of a large-scale longitudinal study of the Chicago Child-Parent Centers' preschool program showed that preschool participation was significantly correlated with high school completion. In fact, the group of children who had participated in the preschool program graduated at a rate of 9–11% higher than their counterparts who had not attended preschool (Clements, Reynolds, & Hickey, 2004). At the international level, students who attended preschool for more than 2 years were the highest achievers in reading, while those who did not attend preschool achieved the lowest reading scores (International Reading Association [IRA], 2004). The impact of preprimary education on reading achievement becomes even more significant when we consider the fact that children in poverty are less likely to receive preprimary education experiences than their wealthier counterparts (Federal Interagency Forum on Child and Family Statistics, 2001; USED, 2002).

## Home Language Environment

With an ever-increasing population of students who are English-language learners (ELL) in our schools, home language environment continues to be an extremely salient factor in academic success. While the effects of language differences on success in learning to read English have not been fully determined, ELL students in the United States are clearly not performing at the level of their peers who are native speakers of English. In fact, the most recent Nation's Report Card from the NAEP reports that, while 34% of non-ELL students achieved reading proficiency at grade level, only 7% of ELL students achieved reading proficiency at grade level (NAEP, 2005).

## Parent Education

The exact nature of the relationship between a parent's education level and their child's reading success is unclear. Perhaps parents who are less educated are less able to provide their children with a supportive home literacy environment. Perhaps parents with a lower level of education also experience lower socioeconomic status and are less likely to have the means to provide their children with the academic tools and experiences they require. Quite possibly, the relationship results from a combination of these factors plus a number of others.

Whatever the reason for the relationship, a parent's education level does correlate with children's reading success. For example, in one large-scale study it was demonstrated that the ability to recognize letters proficiently at kindergarten entry varies as a function of the mother's education level. Thirty-eight percent of children with mothers who had not completed high school were proficient at this skill, while 86% of children whose mothers had a bachelor's degree or more were proficient. This same study also revealed that "the higher the mother's education level, the better the child performs on tests and in school" (NCES, 2000).

### Homework Participation

The contribution of experiential factors does not cease to exist once a child begins attending school, nor once a child successfully learns the basics of reading. Factors that arise later in schooling have also been shown to impact a student's ability to read. One such factor is homework participation. Researchers in a study conducted by the U.S. Department of Education (1996) revealed that the amount of homework completed correlates positively with reading achievement, and students who read 11 or more pages of reading as homework per day were more proficient readers than students who read fewer than five pages. The study also showed that 17-year-olds who spent more than 2 hours per day doing homework were better readers than those who did less than 1 hour of homework per day (USED, 1996).

## Instructional Factors

A third set of factors shown to be related to acquisition of reading skills involves the actual instruction a student receives (NRP, 2000); this is the subject of this book. When considering students' reading difficulties, this is the dimension around which educators within schools can collaborate to substantially improve struggling readers' chances of success.

There is a well-confirmed knowledge base on effective instruction. Some have argued that children's reading problems are due, to a large degree, to failure on the part of professionals to apply what we know about effective instruction. For example, in 1998 the National Research Council Panel on Preventing Reading Difficulties stated:

> Most reading difficulties can be prevented (p. 13). The critical importance of providing excellent reading instruction to all children is at the heart of the committee's recommendations. We recommend attention to ensuring high-quality preschool and kindergarten environments, teachers who are well prepared, highly knowledgeable and receive ongoing support. Home languages should be taken into account in designing reading instruction. (Snow, Burns, & Griffin, 1998, pp. 5–6)

Below we briefly review research on components of effective reading instruction, effective reading interventions for struggling readers, and effective teaching of reading. It is our position that all of these factors within schools need to be addressed when teachers and administrators are working together to substantially improve all students' reading abilities.

### Research-Based Components of Effective Reading Instruction

Effective teachers of reading provide explicit instruction in the basic components of reading and also provide students with many teacher-guided opportunities to engage in and apply strategies to the reading of and writing and talking about texts (Pressley, 2006; Taylor, Pearson, Peterson, & Rodriguez, 2003, 2005). Research-based instructional practices in the basic components of reading, including development in phonemic awareness, phonics, fluency, vocabulary, and comprehension, are briefly described below.

*Phonemic awareness instruction.* Phonemic awareness, which involves hearing and manipulating the *phonemes*, or sounds, in spoken words, has been found to be one of the strongest predictors, when measured in kindergarten or at the beginning of first grade, of how well children will learn to read (NRP, 2000). Furthermore, explicit, systematic instruction in phonemic awareness has been found to be effective (Adams, 1990; NRP, 2000). The National Reading Panel concluded that phonemic awareness instruction in small groups was most effective and that the focus should be on segmentation and blending of individual phonemes. Focusing on multiple aspects of phonemic awareness was less effective than focusing on just a few aspects. Having students manipulate letters while working on segmentation and blending was found to be helpful. Also, the amount of training in phonemic awareness found to be most effective was 5–18 hours per week; more time spent on phonemic awareness was not found to be as effective.

*Phonics instruction.* Explicit, systematic phonics instruction has been found to be more effective than unsystematic phonics instruction or no phonics instruction. (NRP, 2000). Letter-by-letter, larger-unit (e.g., onset and rime), and miscellaneous approaches were all found to be effective. Furthermore, phonics instruction in kindergarten and Grade 1 was found to be more effective than phonics instruction after first grade. Phonics instruction had a moderate effect on decoding measures for reading disabled, but not low achieving students, in Grades 2–6. There were insufficient data to draw conclusions about the effects of phonics instruction with normally developing readers above first grade (NRP, 2000). The NRP concluded that teachers should also help children apply their phonics knowledge accurately and fluently in daily reading and writing activities and that systematic phonics instruction should be integrated with other aspects of reading instruction to create a balanced reading program.

*Fluency instruction.* The NRP (2000) reported that oral reading procedures with guidance or support from a teacher or peers had a significant impact on students' reading. Repeated reading with feedback and assisted reading with support from a teacher or a skilled reader were both found to be effective. Oral reading fluency, commonly measured in words read correctly in one minute, has also been found to be highly correlated to other reading measures, such as decoding and comprehension ability, especially in the primary grades.

*Vocabulary.* The National Reading Panel (2000) concluded that vocabulary instruction leads to gains in reading comprehension and that there is a need for explicit instruction in vocabulary. Prereading vocabulary instruction, learning word meanings in rich contexts, repeated exposures to words in authentic contexts, active engagement in learning words, and incidental learning of word meanings were all found to be beneficial. Effective vocabulary instruction involves students' learning individual words, learning to use strategies to unlock the meanings of words, developing word consciousness, and engaging in wide reading.

*Comprehension.* The National Reading Panel (2000) reported that reading comprehension was the essence of reading and was essential for lifelong learning. Active and interactive strategic processes by students are necessary for the development of good reading comprehension abilities. Fortunately, the explicit teaching of reading comprehension strategies can improve reading comprehension. The NRP concluded that the following types of comprehension strategy instruction were most effective: comprehension monitoring, use of graphic and semantic organizers, use of story structure, question answering, question generation, summarizing important ideas, and flexible use of multiple comprehension strategies in naturalistic contexts. Besides instruction in comprehension strategies, engaging students in high-level talk and writing about text has also been found to enhance students' reading comprehension abilities (Taylor et al., 2003, 2005).

### Reading Interventions

Snow, Burns, and Griffin (1998) concluded that good classroom reading instruction was a pivotal force in the prevention of reading failure. However, they also acknowledged the importance of good reading interventions as well. In the last 20 years the educational community has made substantial progress in the prevention of reading failure through the careful development and implementation of early reading intervention programs (Hiebert & Taylor, 2000; Pikulski, 1994). Research on successful programs has documented that educators can teach almost all first-grade children to learn to read, including those who enter school with low levels of literacy and who in the past would have failed to learn to read in first grade.

Early reading intervention programs have received a considerable amount of attention from educators, legislators, and policy makers because such programs can be very successful in preventing reading failure in first- and second-grade children. The important components of successful early reading intervention programs are not revolutionary: repeated reading, systematic word recognition instruction, carefully selected texts, guided writing, one-on-one reading practice, home connections, and ongoing staff development. However, in these programs explicit, fast-paced instruction and ongoing assessment are delivered consistently, and children spend extra time in meaningful reading and writing activities. Furthermore, teachers receive additional training and support in how to effectively teach children to read who have historically met with little success in learning to read in Grades 1 and 2. The programs also appear to operate with high expectations and from the belief that all children can learn to read well in the primary grades.

### Effective Teaching

Four components of effective instruction include planning, managing, delivering, and evaluating instruction. These components are described elsewhere by Algozzine and Ysseldyke (2006); Algozzine, Ysseldyke, and Elliott (1997); and Ysseldyke and Christenson (2002), but will be briefly reviewed in Figure 1.1.

## CHARACTERISTICS OF EFFECTIVE TEACHERS OF READING AND THEIR SCHOOLS

Research over the past 30 years on the characteristics of effective teachers has highlighted the importance of a strong academic focus, explicit instruction, high levels of pupils on task, and supportive classroom environments (Hoffman, 1991). Recent studies on effective teachers of reading have highlighted the importance of instructional balance, high-level thinking, and motivating instruction that fosters active pupil involvement (Pressley, 2006; Taylor et al., 2003). Effective teachers of reading provide scaffolded instruction in which they model a strategy and then release responsibility to their students over time. For example, they coach their students to apply word recognition and comprehension skills as strategies that can help them successfully read and write authentic texts. Effective teachers of reading have

**Figure 1.1.** Instructional support for learning components

**Instructional Planning**: Decisions are made about what to teach and how to teach the student. Realistic expectations are communicated to the student.
- *Instructional Match:* The student's needs are assessed accurately, and instruction is matched appropriately to the results of the instructional diagnosis.
- *Instructional Expectations:* There are realistic, yet high, expectations for both the amount and accuracy of work to be completed by the student, and these are communicated clearly to the student.

**Instructional Managing**: Effective instruction requires managing the complex mix of instructional tasks and student behaviors that are part of every classroom interaction. This means making decisions that control and support the orderly flow of instruction. To do this, teachers make decisions about classroom rules and procedures, as well as how to handle disruptions, how to organize classroom time and space to be most productive, and how to keep classrooms warm, positive, and accepting places for the student with different learning preferences and performances.
- *Classroom Environment:* The classroom management techniques used are effective for the student; there is a positive, supportive classroom atmosphere; and time is used productively.

**Instructional Delivering**: Decisions are made about how to present information, as well as how to monitor and adjust presentations to accommodate individual differences and enhance the learning of the student.
- *Instructional Presentation:* Instruction is presented in a clear and effective manner; the directions contain sufficient information for the student to understand the kinds of behaviors or skills that are to be demonstrated; and, the student's understanding is checked.
- *Cognitive Emphasis:* Thinking skills and learning strategies for completing assignments are communicated explicitly to the student.
- *Motivational Strategies:* Effective strategies for heightening student interest and effort are used with the student.
- *Relevant Practice:* The student is given adequate opportunity to practice with appropriate materials and experience a high success rate. Classroom tasks are clearly important to achieving instructional goals.
- *Informed Feedback:* The student receives relatively immediate and specific information on his/her performance or behavior; when the student makes mistakes, correction is provided.

**Instructional Evaluating**: Effective instruction requires evaluating. Some evaluation activities occur during the process of instruction (i.e., when teachers gather data during instruction and use those data to make instructional decisions). Other evaluation activities occur at the end of instruction (e.g., when the teacher administers a test to determine whether a student has met instructional goals).
- *Academic Engaged Time:* The student is actively engaged in responding to academic content; the teacher monitors the extent to which the student is actively engaged and redirects the student when the student is unengaged.
- *Adaptive Instruction:* The curriculum is modified within reason to accommodate the student's unique and specific instructional needs.
- *Progress Evaluation:* There is direct, frequent measurement of the student's progress toward completion of instructional objectives; data on the student's performance and progress are used to plan future instruction.
- *Student Understanding:* The student demonstrates an accurate understanding of what is to be done and how it is to be done in the classroom.

Source: Ysseldyke, J.E. & Christenson, S.L. (2002). *Functional Assessment of Academic Behavior.* Longmont, CO: Sopris West.

good classroom management skills as well as high expectations for their students' behavior and their reading growth. Finally, effective teachers of reading communicate well with their students' parents or guardians.

Research on schools that are effective in teaching children to read stress strong, collaborative leadership (Bryk, Sebring, Kerbow, Rollow, & Easton, 1998; Puma et al., 1997), and collaboration in both teaching and professional development (Puma et al., 1997; Taylor et al., 2005; Taylor, Pressley, & Pearson, 2002). Successful schools also foster parent partnerships, respect for cultural differences, and community involvement.

The principal in successful schools is a strong leader who fosters collaborative leadership. Teachers and administrators work together to make improved student learning a schoolwide priority with sustained, strategic educational planning.

Teachers in successful schools have a sense of collective responsibility for increasing students' reading achievement (Goddard, Hoy, & Hoy, 2000). They also feel they collectively have the ability to succeed. These teachers have a strong sense of professional community and collaboration. They collaborate in their teaching of reading and in ongoing, building-level professional development that focuses on research-based reading practices (Taylor et al., 2002).

Successful schools regularly monitor student progress and use multiple data sources to guide their change process and to impact their instruction. Successful schools also provide balanced reading instruction. Teachers instruct students in basic skills as needed, but they also challenge students with cognitively demanding reading activities (Taylor et al., 2002).

## CONCLUSION AND OVERVIEW
## OF VOLUME CHAPTERS

As we noted earlier in this chapter, when asked what caused academic problems, 85% of the teachers asked attributed the problems to internal student deficits, dysfunctions, or disabilities. However, in this volume contributors share research-based practices about how to successfully teach all students to read, especially struggling readers. The chapters focus on multiple approaches to providing good instruction from diverse perspectives.

Will these instructional interventions work? Yes and no. Each of the interventions described will work to improve reading performance with some students under some conditions. There are no interventions that are universally successful, that work with all students under all conditions.

However, it is also important to note that intervention integrity is critical. Researchers consistently observe that specific reading interventions are implemented with differing degrees of integrity. Sometimes the interventions are implemented precisely as their developers intended. Most of the time they are changed as they are implemented. Schmoker (1999) noted that teachers are confronted with "initiatives du jour," and unless there is support for and monitoring of implementation, and some form of recognition for those who implement the initiatives well, teachers may not do so. This same phenomenon was observed by Goodlad and his colleagues more than 30 years ago. Goodlad, Klein, and associates (1970) reported that "innovation is not enough, behind the classroom door even teachers who think they are implementing an innovation are often only twisting it right back into what they have always done" (p. 72).

As educators look for evidence that specific kinds of instructional interventions impact student performance, it is critical that they take into account intervention integrity. Just as it is important in drug studies to demonstrate that those in the experimental group actually took their drug(s) in the manner and at the rate prescribed, so to it is critical to demonstrate that students we assume participated in an intervention actually did so.

Each of the following chapters in this volume begins with a set of framing questions and ends with follow-up activities. It is hoped that this framework will foster discussion and help educators translate research-based ideas into practice.

Part I focuses on effective practices to foster first-grade students' success in learning to decode. In Chapter 2 Darrell Morris discusses the valuable contributions that one-on-one tutoring approaches have made to the reduction in number of children suffering from reading difficulties. He makes recommendations for ways in which such approaches need to evolve to remain viable.

In Chapter 3 Chambers, Cheung, Madden, Slavin, and Gifford describe the impact of a promising multimedia intervention that has been incorporated into the Success for All reading program. The components, relevant also to schools not using that program, include multimedia puppet skits and animations to enhance teachers' lessons as well as a computer-assisted intervention program.

Part II focuses on effective instructional strategies to improve students' vocabulary. In Chapter 4 Michael Graves has conceptualized four dimensions of effective vocabulary instruction for all students. Dimensions include providing rich, varied, and extensive language experiences; teaching individual words; teaching word-learning strategies; and fostering word consciousness. In Chapter 5 Diane August and Catherine Snow review research on effective vocabulary instruction for second-language learners. They break their review into the four dimensions of effective vocabulary instruction conceptualized by Graves.

Part III focuses on effective instruction to develop students' comprehension. In Chapter 6 Edwards, Santoro, Baker, Chard, and Howard describe a classroom intervention designed to increase primary-grade students' comprehension and vocabulary. Teachers use read-alouds to engage students in comprehension conversations about text-based discourse, text structure, metacognitive self-monitoring, and interactive vocabulary learning.

In Chapter 7 Carol Sue Englert and associates describe a program designed to improve middle-grade special education students' reading and writing of informational text. Students learn concrete strategies that will assist them beginning, during, and after reading and writing of expository texts. Although designed for special education students, the program would be beneficial to intermediate-grade students in general.

Part IV focuses on effective schoolwide practices to improve all students' reading in high-poverty, diverse elementary schools. In Chapter 8 Sharon Vaughn and associates describe a three-tier model of providing interventions to students with reading/learning disabilities. Different levels of intervention consider screening and ongoing progress-monitoring results, provide differentiated instruction targeted to students' specific needs through small groups or one-on-one tutoring, and vary in terms of intensity and duration.

In Chapter 9 Russell Gersten and associates describe an observation tool designed to give teachers feedback on effective comprehension and vocabulary instruction for second-language learners. The tool was developed to assess the extent to which teachers are implementing research-based approaches to teaching comprehension and vocabulary on which they have received professional development.

In Chapter 10 Barbara Taylor and associates describe a schoolwide reading reform model that has been found to be effective in high-poverty schools. The model is based on the premise that by working collaboratively and relentlessly and by seriously reflecting on and improving practice, teachers within schools can significantly improve students' reading abilities.

In the final chapter of the book, based on Taylor and Peterson's school change work, the authors discuss possible steps a school could go through to look at the assessments, interventions, classroom reading instruction, and the schoolwide plan for delivery of reading instruction with an eye for coherence, collaboration, completeness, and effectiveness. They also discuss steps for developing productive, ongoing professional learning experiences.

## Follow-up Activities

1. Develop a timetable for reading and discussing the remainder of the chapters in the book that will add to your knowledge base about

effective reading instruction and lead to possible action steps. Assign a discussion leader for each of the chapters.

2. In the above timetable, include plans to learn more about and discuss aspects of research-based components of effective reading instruction, effective reading interventions, effective teaching generally, and effective schools that are not covered in the chapters in this book. (See the list of resources in the appendix at the end of Chapter 11.) Assign teams who will be responsible for each of these topics.

## REFERENCES

Adams, M. J. (1990). *Beginning to read: Thinking and learning about print.* Cambridge, MA: MIT Press.

Algozzine, B., & Ysseldyke, J. (2006). *Effective instruction for students with special needs: A practical guide for every teacher.* Thousand Oaks, CA: Corwin Press.

Algozzine, B., Ysseldyke, J. E., & Elliott, J. L. (1997). *Strategies and tactics for effective instruction* (2nd ed.). Longmont, CO: Sopris West.

Arter, J., & Jenkins, J. R. (1979). Differential diagnosis–prescriptive teaching: A critical appraisal. *Review of Educational Research, 49,* 517–556.

Bradley, R., Danielson, L. & Hallahan, D. P. (Eds.). (2005). *Identification of learning disabilities: Research to practice.* Mahwah, NJ: Erlbaum.

Bryk, A. S., Sebring, P. B., Kerbow, D., Rollow, S., & Easton, J. Q. (1998). *Charting Chicago school reform: Democratic localism as a lever for change.* Boulder, CO: Westview.

Chalfant, J. C., & Sheffelin, M. A. (1970). *Central processing dysfunction in children: A review of the research.* Bethesda, MD: U.S. National Institutes of Health.

Clements, M. A., Reynolds, A. J., & Hickey, E. (2004). Site-level predictors of children's school and social competence in the Chicago Child-Parent Centers. *Early Childhood Research Quarterly, 19,* 273–296.

Federal Interagency Forum on Child and Family Statistics. (2001). *America's children: Key national indicators of well-being, 2001.* Washington, DC: Author.

Goddard, R. D., Hoy, W. K., & Hoy, A. W. (2000). Collective teacher efficacy: Its meaning, measure, and impact on student achievement. *American Educational Research Journal, 37,* 479–507.

Goodlad, J., Klein, M. F., & associates. (1970). *Behind the classroom door.* Worthington, OH: Charles A. Jones.

Hiebert, E. H., & Taylor, B. M. (2000). Beginning reading instruction: Research on early interventions. In M. Kamil, P. Mosenthal, P. D. Pearson, & R. Barr (Eds.), *Handbook of reading research, Vol. 3* (pp. 455–482). Mahwah, NJ: Erlbaum.

Hoffman, J. V. (1991). Teacher and school effects in learning to read. In R. Barr, M. L. Kamil, P. B. Mosenthal, & P. D. Pearson (Eds.), *Handbook of reading research, Vol. 2* (pp. 911–950). New York: Longman.

International Reading Association. (2004). *Teaching and learning in preschool.* Newark, DE: Author.

Lerner, J., & Kline, F. (2006). *Learning disabilities and related disorders* (10th ed.). Boston: Houghton-Mifflin.

National Assessment of Educational Progress (NAEP). (2000). *The nation's report card.* Retrieved August 2005 from http://nces.ed.gov/nationsreportcard/reading/

National Assessment of Educational Progress (NAEP). (2005). *The nation's report card.* Retrieved October 2005 from http://nces.ed.gov/nationsreportcard/reading/

National Center for Education Statistics (NCES). (2003). *Early childhood longitudinal study: Kindergarten class of 1998–99.* Retrieved July 2005 from http://nces.ed.gov/ecls/kinderdatainformation.asp

National Institute for Child Health and Human Development. (1999). *Keys to successful learning.* Washington, DC: Author.

National Reading Panel (NRP). (2000). *Report of the National Reading Panel: Teaching children to read* (NIH Publication No. 00-4769). Washington, DC: National Institute of Child Health and Human Development, National Institutes of Health.

Nord, C. W., Lennon, J., Banning, L., & Chaudler, K. (1999). Home literacy activities and signs of children's emerging literacy. *Educational Statistics Quarterly,* 2(1), 69–77.

Pikulski, J. J. (1994). Preventing reading failure: A review of five effective programs. *The Reading Teacher,* 48, 30–39.

Pressley, M. (2006). *Reading instruction that works: The case for balanced teaching* (3rd ed.). New York: Guilford Press.

Primavera, J. (2000). Enhancing family literacy competence through literacy activities. *Journal of Prevention and Intervention in the Community,* 20, 85–101.

Puma, M. J., Karweit, N., Price, C., Ricciuiti, A., Thompson, W., & Vaden-Kiernan, M. (1997). *Prospects: Final report on student outcomes.* Washington, DC: U.S. Department of Education, Planning, and Evaluation Services.

Schmoker, M. (1999). *Results: The key to continuous school improvement.* Alexandria, VA: Association for Supervision and Curriculum Development.

Schweinhart, L. J., Montie, J., Xiang, Z., Barnett, W. S., Belfield, C. R., & Nores, M. (2005). *Lifetime effects: The High/Scope Perry Preschool study through age 40.* Ypsilanti, MI: High/Scope Press.

Snow, C., Burns, S., & Griffin, M. (Eds.). (1998). *Preventing reading difficulties in young children: Committee on the prevention of reading difficulties in young children.* Washington, DC: National Academy Press.

Taylor, B. M., & Pearson, D. P. (2002). *Teaching reading: Effective schools, accomplished teachers.* Mahwah, NJ: Erlbaum.

Taylor, B. M., Pearson, P. D., Peterson, D. S., & Rodriguez, M. C. (2003). Reading growth in high-poverty classrooms: The influence of teacher practices that encourage cognitive engagement in literacy learning. *The Elementary School Journal,* 104, 3–28.

Taylor, B. M., Pearson, D. P., Peterson, D. S., & Rodriguez, M. C. (2005). The CIERA school change framework: An evidence-based approach to professional development and school reading improvement. *Reading Research Quarterly*, *40*(1), 40–69.

Taylor, B. M., Pressley, M., & Pearson, P. D. (2002). Research-supported characteristics of teachers and schools that promote reading achievement. In B. M. Taylor & P. D. Pearson (Eds.), *Teaching reading: Effective schools, accomplished teachers* (pp. 361–374). Mahwah, NJ: Erlbaum.

U.S. Department of Education (USED). (1996). *The condition of education*. Washington, DC: National Center for Education Statistics.

U.S. Department of Education (USED). (2001). *The condition of education*. Washington, DC: National Center for Education Statistics.

U.S. Department of Education (USED). (2002). *The condition of education*. Washington, DC: National Center for Education Statistics.

Ysseldyke, J. E. (1973). Diagnostic-prescriptive teaching: The search for aptitude-treatment interactions. In L. Mann & D. A. Sabatino (Eds.), *The first review of special education* (pp. 1–37). New York: Grune & Stratton.

Ysseldyke, J. E., Algozzine, B., & Thurlow, M. L. (2000). *Critical issues in special and remedial education* (3rd ed.). Boston: Houghton-Mifflin.

Ysseldyke, J. E., & Christenson, S. L. (2002). *Functional assessment of academic behavior*. Longmont, CO: Sopris West.

Ysseldyke, J. E., Christenson, S. L., Algozzine, B., & Thurlow, M. L. (1983). *Classroom teachers' attributions for students exhibiting different behaviors*. Minneapolis: University of Minnesota Institute for Research on Learning Disabilities.

# PART I

**Effective Practices to Foster Students' Success in Learning to Decode**

# CHAPTER 2

# One-to-One Reading Intervention in the Primary Grades: An Idea That Must Evolve to Survive

## Darrell Morris

In addressing the problem of early reading failure, historically there has been tension between advocates of programmatic interventions and teacher-training interventions. This chapter clearly comes down on the side of intensive teacher training. It advocates increasing the theoretical and applied knowledge of all those who teach struggling beginning readers, be they reading specialists, classroom teachers, or paraprofessionals.

### Questions for Reflection and Discussion

- Why might a supervised, one-to-one tutoring experience be the best way for a teacher of beginning readers to develop needed expertise?
- What are the key components in a lesson plan for a struggling beginning reader?
- Can reading problems be solved in the 1st grade with early identification and intensive intervention?

The history of beginning reading instruction over the past 50 years has been one of contention and change. In search of the "best" teaching approach, we had "The Great Debate" of the 1960s (Bond & Dykstra, 1967; Chall, 1967) and "The Reading Wars" of the 1990s (Goodman, 1986; Liberman & Liberman, 1990). First-grade reading materials in the 1970s and 1980s were characterized by repetition of a core sight vocabulary and phonics drill. In the 1990s, these components were de-emphasized in favor of more authentic stories written in natural, rhythmic language. Finally, in the basal readers of the 2000s, phonics, along with formulaic decodable text, reemerged with a vengeance (Hoffman, Sailors, & Patterson, 2002; Morris, 1999). It is unclear how these radical programmatic changes have affected the plight of struggling beginning readers; however, it is surely clear that they reflect the ongoing search for something new and better—a methodological "silver bullet" that will somehow reduce the occurrence of reading failure in our schools.

My purpose in this chapter is not to advance a new solution but rather to defend an old one: the idea of careful, one-to-one intervention for at-risk beginning readers. In a sense, I am a little late in mounting this defense, because first-grade tutorial intervention—extremely popular in the 1990s (see Shanahan & Barr, 1995)—seems currently to be on the decline, replaced by a federal initiative to use "scientifically based" reading programs in the classroom to prevent reading failure (U.S. Department of Education, 2001). Nonetheless, history has a way of repeating itself in our applied discipline, and it is my hope that in the not-too-distant future the idea of careful tutorial intervention will reemerge with even greater force.

## THE EMERGENCE OF ONE-TO-ONE TUTORING INTERVENTION IN THE UNITED STATES

One-to-one tutoring, as an early reading intervention strategy, came to the United States in 1985. That was the year that Marie Clay brought her Reading Recovery program to Columbus, Ohio. There was a great deal of enthusiasm and anticipation in this country regarding Reading Recovery because of the program's successful field trials in New Zealand (Clay, 1979) and because of Clay's international reputation as a beginning reading scholar. Several years earlier she had published *Reading: The Patterning of Complex Behavior* (Clay, 1972), a widely read monograph that provided important insight into the developmental progression of beginning reading.

Clay's Reading Recovery intervention was based on three premises. First, it is important to intervene early. The longer we wait, the further at-risk readers fall behind their average-achieving classmates (see Figure 2.1). The knowledge gap between low and average readers is smallest at the beginning of first grade; therefore, intervene at this point. Second, the intervention needs to be intensive. To catch up, low readers actually have to move faster than children who start out with more reading-related knowledge. Given this challenging circumstance, Clay maintained that intensive one-to-one, as opposed to small-group, instruction was necessary. Third, expert training is required for intervention teachers. This training, which includes both theory and hands-on practice, should occur over a year's time so that teachers can acquire a developmental understanding of the beginning reading process.

**Figure 2.1.** Achievement trajectories of readers with high (H), middle (M), and low (L) readiness across 1st and 2nd grades

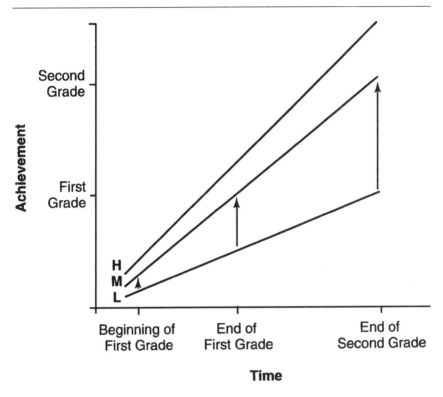

These notions of intervening early in first grade, using one-to-one instruction, and providing expert training to the teacher were quite novel in the American context. In the 1980s low readers in U.S. schools were not usually identified until the second grade, remedial instruction was provided in a small-group context, and there was no special training for the teacher (Slavin, 1989).

The initial field trials of Reading Recovery in Columbus, Ohio (Pinnell, Huck, & DeFord, 1986), were quite promising, and under the direction of Gay Su Pinnell and her colleagues, the program spread rapidly throughout the United States. To assure fidelity to the Reading Recovery model, potential trainers had to come to Ohio for a full year to be trained by the Ohio State University staff, who themselves had been directly trained by Clay. Once these educators (many of them college professors) had completed their training in Ohio, they went back and set up Reading Recovery training centers in their respective geographic areas (e.g., New York, South Carolina, Illinois,

Texas). This was the genius of the Reading Recovery program in the United States—the ability to spread or upscale the intervention on a national level while maintaining program integrity.

## SUCCESS AND CRITICISM
## OF READING RECOVERY

The effectiveness of Reading Recovery has been documented in many studies (e.g., Center, Wheldall, Freeman, Outhred, & McNaught, 1995; Pinnell, Lyons, DeFord, Bryk, & Seltzer, 1994; Schwartz, 2005). Overall, it appears that approximately two out of three low-reading first graders benefit from the program and begin to close the achievement gap between them and their average-achieving classmates. (Keep in mind that this two out of three success rate pertains to the lowest quartile of first-grade readers.) Moreover, with the program's widespread implementation over a 20-year period, thousands of teachers who received Reading Recovery training have improved their knowledge of beginning reading and their ability to help children who struggle with the process.

Still, success and influence inevitably bring scrutiny, and Reading Recovery has had its share of critics. In a broad-ranging and, I believe, objective critique of Reading Recovery, Shanahan and Barr (1995) raised many issues, three of which I mention below:

- *Reading Recovery is very expensive.* The yearlong training of a tutor is costly, but this is a one-time expense. What is cost-prohibitive for many schools is allowing a certified teacher to tutor only four children during a 2.5 hour period each day. In a low-income urban or rural school, with 20 or more at-risk first graders, how does one determine who receives the tutoring and who does not?
- *Reading Recovery proponents contend that reading problems can be "fixed" in first grade.* That is, Reading Recovery–tutored children are thought to develop a "self-improving" system that enables them to catch up and then keep up with their average-achieving peers. If this were true, the high cost of the first-grade tutoring would be offset by a greatly diminished need for remediation services (e.g., Title I, Special Education) in later grades. However, Shanahan and Barr (1995) conclude that the evidence does not support such a strong claim:

Stability is likely to be maintained only if students receive classroom instruction that is responsive to the accelerated progress of these children, or if additional maintenance interventions are provided. That the effects of Reading

Recovery and other early interventions are apparent for so long without such support is a testimonial to their quality. Despite the claims of many Reading Recovery advocates, however, it is unreasonable to expect this program to entirely do away with the need for later special assistance for low-achieving children. (p. 982)

- *Reading Recovery does not include systematic instruction in the alphabetic code.* The tutor does provide incidental letter-sound or pattern instruction as a specific need arises in the child's contextual reading or writing (e.g., a minilesson in consonant digraphs [*ch, sh, th*] or rhyming patterns [*-at* or *-ake*]). However, Reading Recovery instruction does not include systematic, step-by-step coverage of basic phonics elements (e.g., beginning consonants and consonant blends; short, long, and r-controlled vowel patterns). Although Shanahan and Barr mentioned this as a possible weakness in their 1995 review, the issue has assumed more importance in recent years, given the emphasis placed on systematic, explicit phonics instruction in the National Reading Panel report (2000).

To these criticisms of the Reading Recovery model, I wish to add two more that I have not come across in the literature.

- *In most cases only the reading teacher in a given elementary school was trained.* This got expert knowledge into a school, but the knowledge was often encapsulated. That is, only one teacher had been trained, and this teacher was not free to share the training, in any detail, with other educators within the school (e.g., classroom teachers, special education teachers, or teacher assistants). This is a significant flaw in a program that claims to be a systemic intervention. Knowledge of how to help struggling beginning readers is a rare and precious commodity. When such knowledge enters an elementary school—via expert training of one teacher—it needs to be shared in substantive ways.
- *Strict implementation fidelity, an often-cited strength of Reading Recovery, exacted a cost.* On the one hand, maintaining close adherence to Reading Recovery standards and procedures ensured an element of quality control in the tutoring. On the other hand, it tended to reduce the program's flexibility or adaptability. For example, over a 15-year period, there was limited experimentation with the lengthy, cumbersome training program, with elements of the lesson plan (particularly phonics instruction), or with who could be trained to implement the program (e.g., reading teachers, classroom teachers, teacher assistants).

## REVIEW OF READING RECOVERY'S
## ORIGINAL PREMISES

Although I believe the aforementioned criticisms of Reading Recovery are valid, they in no way lead me to denigrate the program. To the contrary, along with many others (e.g., Allington, 2001; Hoffman & Pearson, 2000; Wasik & Slavin, 1993), I believe that Reading Recovery has made unique and lasting contributions—both conceptual and practical—to the prevention of reading failure. The program's original premises were insightful—indeed, revolutionary. I wish to review them before moving forward:

1. *To prevent reading failure, it is important to intervene early*. At the start of first grade, a child has not fallen too far behind his or her peers in reading. Moreover, effective instruction at this point will strengthen not only the child's reading skill but also his or her academic self-concept at a critical point in development.

2. *Intensive, one-to-one instruction is called for*. Although the authors of a recent meta-analysis (Elbaum, Vaughn, Hughes, & Moody, 2000) asserted that small-group instruction is just as effective as tutoring, there is actually little research to back up this claim. Such a research study would have to take a quality, beginning-reading instructional model (e.g., Reading Recovery; Early Steps [Santa & Hoien, 1999]) and apply it in both a one-to-one and small-group context. Everything held equal (e.g., entry-level ability of students, teacher quality, instructional time), it is difficult to see how the small-group instruction would be as effective as tutoring. Issues of behavior management, time-on-task, instructional level, and immediate corrective feedback are all more easily resolved in a one-to-one context (Wasik & Slavin, 1990, 1993). This is not to say that small-group, beginning reading instruction cannot be effective; however, it is probably not as effective as one-to-one tutoring.

3. *Tutors who work with struggling beginning readers require careful training*. Clay's idea that apprentice-like training for tutors should extend across the course of reading acquisition (i.e., a full year) is an important one. The reading process changes as a child progresses from an emergent to a beginning to a halting to a semifluent reader at the end of first grade. Any serious, teacher-training initiative must take into account these phases or transitions across the first year of reading development.

Finally, it should be acknowledged that the Reading Recovery *lesson plan* was a novel and elegant contribution to beginning reading instruction (see Figure 2.2). The ideas of (1) having beginners reread carefully leveled texts

**Figure 2.2.** Reading Recovery lesson plan

---

1. **Rereading familiar books.** The child rereads three, short, natural-language books with the tutor offering support as is needed. During the reading, the tutor encourages the child to use strategies (e.g., multiple cues [beginning letter, syntax, and picture] for word identification, self-correction, prediction) that will eventually lead to self-control of the reading process.

2. **Sentence writing.** Each day the child writes a sentence of his or her own choice. At the beginning of the year, the tutor supports the child in "hearing" sounds in words and forming letters. As the child improves in these areas, the tutor lessens the amount of assistance provided. In this part of the lesson, the tutor may also stop and teach a given letter sound, sight word, or spelling pattern that the child needs to learn.

3. **Introduction of a new book.** The tutor and the child preview the new book, identifying difficult vocabulary and surveying the pictures in order to predict the story line. Then the child returns to the first page and attempts to read the new story, the tutor providing assistance as needed. The new book is then reread in Part 1 of the next day's lesson.

---

to develop sight vocabulary, decoding skill, and fluency and (2) using guided sentence writing to develop phoneme awareness and letter-sound knowledge have proven their effectiveness. Innovative at the time (mid-1980s), these Reading Recovery instructional strategies have since become part of conventional practice in teaching beginning reading.

Its contributions to theory and practice notwithstanding, Reading Recovery's influence has waned in the United States since the year 2000. In my own state of North Carolina, several large school districts (e.g., Charlotte, Greensboro, and Raleigh) have discontinued the program, and others have cut back on its use. In addition, start-up Reading Recovery sites have diminished over the past few years. Cost has been cited as a major reason, but the fickleness and contentiousness of the field of beginning reading must also be factored in. In any case, I find the weakening support for Reading Recovery (and similar early reading intervention initiatives) to be problematic—indeed, a step backward in the ongoing effort to reduce reading failure. In the pages that follow, I consider some directions in which early reading intervention models may have to evolve if they are to survive in the future.

## HOW TUTORIAL INTERVENTION MODELS MIGHT EVOLVE

As a young reading professor in the Chicago area in the mid-1980s, I was greatly influenced by Clay's Reading Recovery model. Although I did not pursue direct training in the model at Ohio State University, I borrowed liberally from Reading Recovery in developing my own first-grade intervention program, Early Steps. To this end, I readily accepted Clay's three premises: Intervene early, intervene intensively (one-to-one), and provide careful training for the tutor. I also adopted the basic elements in her lesson plan (e.g., rereading leveled books, guided sentence writing, and introducing a new book each day). However, I deviated from the Reading Recovery model by (1) adding a systematic phonics component to the lesson plan and (2) changing the nature and intensity, if not the length, of the tutor training (see Morris, Tyner, & Perney, 2000). Perhaps I should point out that although Reading Recovery is a copyrighted program, ideas are not copyrighted. From my perspective, pedagogical ideas are the property of the professional community, to be referenced for sure, but then to be shared, applied in various contexts, refined, and reshared.

I learned about early reading intervention in the best way possible—by doing it. For 17 years (1987–2004), I crisscrossed the nation, helping school districts in eight states (Illinois, New York, North Carolina, Montana, Tennessee, Utah, Virginia, and Pennsylvania) set up first-grade reading intervention programs. Consulting in urban schools, rural schools, high-poverty schools, and middle-class schools, I never tired of working with reading teachers and first-grade teachers, and watching their neediest students learn how to read.

Early Steps may not be as powerful as Reading Recovery (there is no research on that question), but it has proven to be an effective intervention. Two matched control-group studies have been conducted: the first in Kalispell, Montana (Santa & Hoien, 1999); the second in Chattanooga, Tennessee (Morris et al., 2000). In both studies, the Early Steps–tutored children outperformed the control group on end-of-grade measures of word recognition and passage reading. Effect sizes were moderate to large (see Table 2.1). Similar to Reading Recovery, Early Steps seems to be effective with approximately two thirds of the tutored children. In the Chattanooga study, for example, 63% of the Early Steps group attained an end-of-year reading level of Primer or higher, compared to only 30% of the control group (see Table 2.2).

**Table 2.1.** Effect sizes for Woodcock's Word Attack and Comprehension subtests in two Early Steps studies

|  | Word Attack | Comprehension |
| --- | --- | --- |
| Montana | 1.2 | 1.0 |
| Tennessee | .9 | .8 |

*Note.* Effect size is the proportion of a standard deviation by which the tutored students exceeded controls. An effect size of .20 is considered small, .50, moderate, and .80, large. Subtests were taken from *Woodcock Reading Mastery Tests—Revised (Form G)* (Woodcock, 1987).

**Table 2.2.** Number of children achieving various passage-reading levels at the end of first grade (Tennessee study: Morris, Tyner, & Perney, 2000)

| | Group | |
|---|---|---|
| Passage-reading level | Early Steps | Comparison |
| | $n = 43$ | $n = 43$ |
| Nonreader | 2 | 9 |
| Emergent | 1 | 6 |
| Preprimer | 13 | 15 |
| Primer | 14 | 7 |
| Late-first grade | 8 | 5 |
| Early-second grade | 2 | 1 |
| Late-second grade | 3 | 0 |

*Note.* These are the results of the Chattanooga, TN study that appears in "Early Steps: Replicating the Effects of a First-Grade Reading Intervention Program," by D. Morris, B. Tyner, and J. Perney, 2000, *Journal of Educational Psychology, 92,* pp. 681–693.

My purpose here is not to compare Early Steps with Reading Recovery in terms of effectiveness, but rather to show how Early Steps modified the Reading Recovery training model. These four modifications, discussed below, offer a view of how one-to-one reading intervention might evolve in the future.

## Adding Systematic Word Study

The first modification involved adding a systematic word study (or phonics) component to the Reading Recovery lesson plan (see also, Iversen & Tumner, 1993). One fourth of each Early Steps lesson is devoted to helping the child learn basic letter-sound relationships and spelling patterns (e.g., beginning consonants; short-vowel word families; short, long, and *r*-controlled vowel patterns; see Figure 2.3). Word sorts, games, and spelling checks are the vehicles for phonics instruction that is developmentally paced to the needs of the individual child (Morris, 2005a). The emphasis is on mastery at one level (e.g., short-vowel word families) before moving to the next level (e.g., vowel patterns).

Posttests in two studies (Santa & Hoein, 1999; Morris et al., 2000) showed that Early Steps–tutored students outperformed a control group not only in passage comprehension, but also in pseudoword reading, a pure measure of decoding skill. This is an interesting finding because it shows that

**Figure 2.3.** Sequence of word study instruction

| Beginning consonants | Word families | Short vowel | One-syllable vowel patterns |
|---|---|---|---|
| b | -at | (ă) hat | (a) mat |
| c | -an | | lake |
| d | -ap | | park |
| f | -ack | | tall |
| g | | | |
| h | -it | (ĭ) big | (i) kid |
| | -in | | ride |
| j | -ig | | bird |
| k | -ick | | light |
| (and so on) | | | |
| | -ot | (ŏ) top | (o) job |
| ch | -op | | rope |
| sh | -ob | | coat |
| th | -ock | | born |
| wh | | | |
| | -ed | (ĕ) pet | (e) leg |
| | -et | | seed |
| | -ell | | meat |
| | | | he |
| | -ut | (ŭ) rub | (u) bug |
| | -ug | | mule |
| | -ub | | burn |
| | -uck | | suit |

*Note.* Consonant blends *(bl, dr, st,* and so on) are introduced at the word-family and short-vowel levels.

struggling readers can be taught with leveled, natural-language books (as opposed to decodable text) and still become good decoders, if their instruction includes a systematic phonics component.

## Changing the Teacher Training

Of necessity, we changed the amount and type of teacher training. In Reading Recovery, teachers attend weekly training sessions throughout the school year. However, because I, the Early Steps trainer, was living in North Carolina and training a group of teachers in Tennessee (or Utah or Pennsylvania), we obviously could not have weekly training sessions. After a few years of experimentation, I found that I could provide adequate Early Steps training by making nine site visits spread across the school year (five visits before the winter break, four visits after the break).

In these training sessions, the tutors taught, I observed, and then we immediately discussed the lessons. A one-hour seminar at the end of the day served to relate theory to practice and to anticipate instructional issues the tutors might face before the trainer's next visit. Overall, the training sessions had three purposes. First, they allowed the trainer to explain and model teaching techniques, which led to refinement in the Early Steps tutors' performance. Second, the trainer was able to provide feedback on instructional pacing; that is, whether or not to move a child forward in contextual reading or word study. (Such pacing advice was always accompanied by a reason why.) And third, the training sessions helped the participating teachers develop a practice-informed theory of how reading acquisition unfolds across the first-grade year. This theory—shaped by the lesson plan, informed by the tutoring experience— would eventually allow the Early Steps tutors to apply their new pedagogical knowledge in other contexts, for example, in small-group or individual instruction in the classroom or resource room.

## Including Both Reading Specialists and First-Grade Teachers

We began to include first-grade classroom teachers in the Early Steps training. During the first few years of the program, only reading teachers were trained. However, when a curriculum coordinator in a rural North Carolina system asked if her first-grade teachers could participate in the training, I quickly said yes. There were logistical problems. The first grade teachers had to find 30 minutes each day—before, during, or after school—to tutor a low reader. In addition, the school system had to provide a half-day release for the teachers nine times during the year so that they could participate in the Early Steps training.

Nonetheless, the training of first-grade classroom teachers paid off in several ways. First, through the supervised tutoring experience, the teachers grasped the importance of providing instruction at the appropriate level (i.e., challenge but do not frustrate the child). This made clear the need for a carefully leveled set of reading materials in the first-grade classroom. Second, they learned to use invented spelling to track the development of phonemic and orthographic awareness in their beginning readers. And third, the teachers learned to teach phonics systematically, looking for mastery at one level (e.g., short vowels) before moving to the next level (e.g., long vowels). Each of these understandings applied directly to the classroom context. How well the transfer was made, of course, depended on the skill and industriousness of the individual first-grade teacher.

One final advantage of training a school's reading teacher and first-grade teachers together is that this left behind a "team" of educators who had a shared set of experiences (i.e., Early Steps training) and a common language to describe these experiences. This in many cases led to useful dialogue among the teachers and ultimately to coordination of instruction for low readers in that school.

## Extending the Tutoring Into Second Grade

The fourth modification involved extending the tutoring into second grade. I mentioned earlier that in several school districts Early Steps–tutored children made it only to the Primer reading level by the end of first grade. Teachers who work in challenging settings (e.g., low-income rural or urban schools) realize that this is no small accomplishment. To help children, who enter first grade with incomplete alphabet knowledge and little phoneme awareness, attain a Primer reading level in just one year is not easy. At the same time, we realized that such children would be entering second grade reading 2 to 3 months below grade level. Without additional support, they might founder in a second-grade reading curriculum.

Having some prior experience with a volunteer-staffed, second-grade tutoring program (see Morris, 2005b; Morris, Shaw, & Perney, 1990), I realized that the teaching strategies the Early Steps tutors had learned to use during the last 2 to 3 months of first grade were exactly what was needed in second grade. That is, when an Early Steps–tutored child attained the Primer reading level, perhaps in March of first grade, we modified his or her lesson plan (see Figure 2.4). Instead of rereading leveled books and writing a sentence each day, the child (1) read a new Primer-level story each day, (2) continued to study short- and long-vowel patterns, and (3) began to work on

**Figure 2.4.** Modification of Early Steps lesson plan when child attains the Primer reading level

| Original Lesson Plan | Modified Lesson Plan* |
|---|---|
| 1. Child rereads two or three leveled books (10 min.). | 1. Child reads a new, longer Primer-level story (or book), focusing on comprehension (15 min.). |
| 2. Child sorts, reads, and spells short-vowel word families (7 min.). | 2. Child sorts, reads, and spells short-vowel patterns (8 min.). |
| 3. Child writes a sentence of his or her own choice (7 min.). | 3. Child reads an easy book or rereads a favorite book to work on fluency (7 min.). |
| 4. Child reads a new book with tutor's assistance (6 min.). | |

*In the modified lesson plan, sentence writing is omitted.

reading fluency or phrasing. Common sense dictated that this same plan would be appropriate in second grade; that is, pick the child up where he or she left off in first grade, and adjust the book difficulty level according to the child's ability.

I explained to the reading teachers that they possessed the knowledge and skills to direct a "follow-up" tutoring program in second grade. They would have to find tutors (community volunteers or paraprofessionals), and they would need to closely supervise the twice-weekly lessons of these tutors. However, if they did so, I argued, the Early Steps children, having established a reading foundation in first grade (Primer level), would continue to make "catch-up" progress in second grade. This argument is represented by the dotted line in Figure 2.5.

Several reading teachers in my home county in North Carolina accepted the challenge. They had seen the power of one-to-one instruction and wanted

**Figure 2.5.** Impact of a 2-year tutorial intervention on (see dotted line) on the reading achievement of low-readiness children

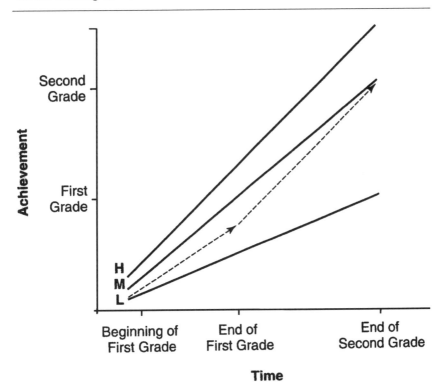

to extend the tutoring into second grade. Each reading teacher recruited six to eight tutors for her school (a mix of teacher assistants, college students, and community volunteers), provided some initial training, and then supervised the work of tutors. That is, the reading teacher planned the lessons for each tutor-child pair (guided reading, word study, reading for fluency) and observed the actual tutoring. This was possible because all the tutors at a given school tutored at the same time (e.g., 8:00–8:45 a.m. or 12:15–1:00 p.m.). The twice-weekly tutoring lessons added up to approximately 40 hours of one-to-one instruction over the course of the school year.

Focused instruction of this kind should produce achievement gains, and it did. Table 2.3 shows the results in one of the schools (Morris, 2005b). All

**Table 2.3.** Reading achievement levels for 12 low-reading, Title I children across three years—1st grade through 3rd grade (Morris, 2005b)

| Students | End of 1st Grade Reading Level | End of 2nd Grade Reading Level | End of 3rd Grade Reading Level |
|----------|-------------------------------|-------------------------------|-------------------------------|
| E. B. | Primer | 2-2 | 5th (53%)* |
| D. N. | Primer | 2-2 | 4th (60%) |
| K. W. | Primer | 1-2 | 4th (56%) |
| A. W. | Primer | 2-1 | 4th (56%) |
| J. M. | Primer | 2-2 | 4th (56%) |
| A. K. | 1–2 | 2-2 | 3rd (41%) |
| L. S. | Primer | 2-1 | 4th (80%) |
| D. B. | Primer | 2-1 | 2-2 (49%) |
| B. B. | Preprimer | Primer | 2-1 (18%) |
| L. M. | Preprimer | Primer | 1-2 (–) |
| D. C. | below Preprimer (retained in 1st grade) Preprimer | 1-2 | –(–) |
| M. P. | Preprimer | Primer (retained in 2nd grade) 1-2 | –(–) |

*Percentile score is from North Carolina end-of-grade reading test (a standardized measure of silent reading comprehension).

*Note.* These are the results of the study in "A Title I Success Story," by D. Morris, 2005, *Reading Research and Instruction, 45,* pp. 1–15.

12 children in Table 2.3 were identified as "at-risk" at the beginning of first grade. All 12 received Early Steps tutoring during first grade (five times per week with a teacher or teacher assistant), 10 received follow-up tutoring during second grade, and 5 during third grade (two times per week with a college student or community volunteer). Notice that whereas only 1 of the 12 children reached grade level in reading (1-2) by the end of first grade, 7 more attained the Primer level. At the end of second grade, 4 of the 12 students had reached grade level in reading (2-2) and 3 more could read at a mid-second-grade level (2-1). The reading teacher in this school decided to continue the twice-weekly tutoring in third grade for the children who still needed it. At the end of third grade, 7 of the original 12 at-risk students read at grade level (3rd) or higher.

The results shown in Table 2.3 represent a success story. Far too often, at-risk readers fall behind in first grade and remain behind throughout the elementary grades (Clay, 1991; Juel, 1988; Stanovich, 1986). However, in this school, 12 rural, working-class children entered first grade with marginal alphabet knowledge and very limited phoneme awareness. Three years later, 7 of these 12 children read at grade level or higher, having improved their reading status each consecutive year. Moreover, the other 5 children, 3 of whom qualified for special education services, also learned to read by the end of third grade, achieving reading levels ranging from late-first grade (1-2) to late-second grade (2-2). It seems clear that all 3 years of tutoring were necessary to attain these results. The intensive, Early Steps tutoring in first grade allowed the children to establish a foundation (Primer-level reading skill). Then the less intensive, twice-weekly tutoring in second and third grades built on this foundation, enabling most of the children to eventually become grade-level readers.

## CONCLUSION

Reading Recovery ushered in the important concept of early, tutorial-based reading intervention some 20 years ago. In the United States, hundreds of thousands of children have benefited from this innovation, as have their teachers who received specialized training in how to teach struggling beginning readers. My purpose in this chapter has been twofold; first, to point out the undeniable strengths of the Reading Recovery model (early identification, one-to-one context, balanced instruction, and careful teacher training), and second, to point out ways in which Reading Recovery and similar intervention programs may need to evolve if they are to survive in the turbulent field of beginning reading. The modifications of Reading Recovery that I have suggested address issues of (1) systematic phonics instruction, (2) cost,

(3) involvement of more school-based educators in the intervention training, and (4) maintenance of achievement gains in later grades.

These modifications create a less complex intervention program, which I see as an advantage. Less complexity means that classroom teachers and paraprofessionals can be trained as tutors; certain lesson components (e.g., word study) can transfer directly into classroom use; and a school-based reading teacher, who masters the intervention model, can train others to use it in future years. But note that Clay's three basic premises are still present: early identification of at-risk readers, one-to-one instruction, and careful, yearlong training for the teacher.

The teacher training component is crucial. Educators at all levels talk endlessly about the need for quality inservice training for teachers, but it is seldom provided. Teacher training of the kind described in this chapter is expensive, time-consuming, and sometimes difficult to obtain. However, such training enables teachers to learn and grow as problem-solving professionals. It also brings expertise into a school system—expertise that if properly nurtured can adapt and spread within a local context (school or district).

We fool ourselves when we think that better reading materials or programs—even so-called scientifically based programs—can solve the reading problem. Good materials and a balanced instructional routine (e.g., guided reading, phonics, and writing) are necessary. However, teacher expertise is, and always has been, the key to reducing the incidence of reading failure in the primary grades. One way to develop such expertise, as I have tried to show in this chapter, is through carefully supervised one-to-one reading intervention efforts.

## Follow-up Activities

1. Discuss ways that a given school could secure "expert" knowledge about how to teach struggling beginning readers (e.g., by purchasing a well-known program; by hiring a reputable intervention consultant; by sending a teacher back for advanced graduate training).
2. What are the advantages (or disadvantages) of using paraprofessionals to work with struggling readers? What type of training (preservice and ongoing) for the paraprofessionals would be required? Who would provide this training and supervision?
3. Discuss how a supervised tutoring experience for primary-grade teachers might influence their classroom reading instruction.
4. Discuss how the introduction of a first-grade reading intervention program in a school might influence future reading intervention initiatives in kindergarten and second grade.

# REFERENCES

Allington, R. (2001). *What really matters for struggling readers.* New York: Longman.

Bond, G., & Dykstra, R. (1967). The cooperative program in first-grade reading instruction. *Reading Research Quarterly, 2,* 5–141.

Center, Y., Wheldall, K., Freeman, L., Outhred, L., & McNaught, M. (1995). An experimental evaluation of Reading Recovery. *Reading Research Quarterly, 30,* 240–263.

Chall, J. (1967). *Learning to read: The great debate.* New York: McGraw-Hill.

Clay, M. (1972). *Reading: The patterning of complex behavior.* Auckland, New Zealand: Heinemann.

Clay, M. (1979). *The early detection of reading difficulties.* Auckland, New Zealand: Heinemann.

Clay, M. (1991). *Becoming literate: The construction of inner control.* Portsmouth, NH: Heinemann.

Elbaum, B., Vaughn, S., Hughes, M. T., & Moody, S. W. (2000). How effective are one-to-one tutoring programs in reading for elementary students at risk for reading failure: A meta-analysis of the intervention research. *Journal of Educational Psychology, 92,* 605–619.

Goodman, K. (1986). *What's whole in whole language.* Portsmouth, NH: Heinemann.

Hoffman, J., & Pearson, P. D. (2000). Reading teacher education in the next millennium: From what your grandmother's teacher didn't know that your granddaughter's teacher should. *Reading Research Quarterly, 35,* 28–44.

Hoffman, J., Sailors, M., & Patterson, E. (2002). Decodable texts for beginning reading instruction: The year 2000 basals. *Journal of Literacy Research, 34,* 269–298.

Iversen, S., & Tumner, W. (1993). Phonological processing skills and the Reading Recovery program. *Journal of Educational Psychology, 85,* 112–126.

Juel, C. (1988). Learning to read and write: A longitudinal study of 54 children from first through fourth grades. *Journal of Educational Psychology, 80,* 437–447.

Liberman, I., & Liberman, A. (1990). Whole language versus code emphasis: Underlying assumptions and their implications for reading instruction. *Annals of Dyslexia, 40,* 51–76.

Morris, D. (1999). Preventing reading failure in the primary grades: Annual review of research. *National Reading Conference Yearbook, 48,* 17–38.

Morris, D. (2005a). *The Howard Street tutoring manual: Teaching at-risk readers in the primary grades* (2nd ed.). New York: Guilford Press.

Morris, D. (2005b). A Title I reading success story. *Reading Research and Instruction, 45,* 1–15.

Morris, D., Shaw, B., & Perney, J. (1990). Helping low readers in grades 2 and 3: An after-school volunteer tutoring program. *Elementary School Journal, 91,* 133–150.

Morris, D., Tyner, B., & Perney, J. (2000). Early Steps: Replicating the effects of a first-grade reading intervention program. *Journal of Educational Psychology, 92,* 681–693.

National Reading Panel (NRP). (2000). *Report of the National Reading Panel: Teaching children to read* (NIH Publication No. 00-4769). Washington, DC: National Institute of Child Health and Human Development, National Institutes of Health.

Pinnell, G., Huck, C., & DeFord, D. (1986). *The Reading Recovery Project in Columbus, Ohio Studies, Vol. 3* (Year 1, 1985–86). Columbus: Ohio State University.

Pinnell, G., Lyons, C., DeFord, D., Bryk, A., & Seltzer, M. (1994). Comparing instructional models for the literacy education of high-risk first graders. *Reading Research Quarterly, 29,* 8–39.

Santa, C., & Hoien, T. (1999). An assessment of Early Steps: A program for early intervention of reading problems. *Reading Research Quarterly, 34,* 54–79.

Schwartz, R. (2005). Literacy learning of at-risk first-grade students in the Reading Recovery early intervention. *Journal of Educational Psychology, 97,* 257–267.

Shanahan, T., & Barr, R. (1995). Reading Recovery: An independent evaluation of the effects of an early instructional intervention for at-risk readers. *Reading Research Quarterly, 30,* 958–996.

Slavin, R. (1989). Students at risk of school failure: The problem and its dimensions. In R. Slavin, N. Karweit, & N. Madden (Eds.), *Effective programs for students at risk* (pp. 3–19). Boston: Allyn & Bacon.

Stanovich, K. (1986). Matthew effects in reading: Some consequences of individual differences in the acquisition of literacy. *Reading Research Quarterly, 21,* 360–406.

U.S. Department of Education. (2001). *No Child Left Behind Act.* Washington, DC: Author. Retrieved March 6, 2007, from www.ed.gov/policy/elsec/leg/esea02/index.html

Wasik, B., & Slavin, R. (1990, April). *Preventing early reading failure with one-to-one tutoring: A best-evidence synthesis.* Paper presented at the annual meeting of the American Educational Research Association, Boston.

Wasik, B., & Slavin, R. (1993). Preventing early reading failure with one-to-one tutoring: A review of five programs. *Reading Research Quarterly, 28,* 178–200.

Woodcock, R. (1987). *Woodcock Reading Mastery Tests—Revised* (Form G). Circle Pines, MN: American Guidance Service.

# CHAPTER 3

# Embedded Multimedia: Using Video to Enhance Reading Outcomes in Success for All

Bette Chambers

Alan Cheung

Nancy A. Madden

Robert E. Slavin

Richard Gifford

For more than 50 years, educators and policy makers have been expectantly waiting for the video revolution in education. However, video is still typically used only as a Friday afternoon reward or filler. This chapter describes an innovative application of video in classrooms that has significant potential in reading instruction. This application involves threading brief video segments throughout teachers' lessons.

## Questions for Reflection and Discussion

- How might video content be used more effectively in your classrooms to enhance students' reading achievement?
- What strategies might you employ to have your students actively engage with the video content that you use in your classes?

Research on educational programs such as *Sesame Street* (Bogatz & Ball, 1971; Fisch & Truglio, 2000; Rice, Huston, Truglio, & Wright, 1990) and

*Between the Lions* (Linebarger, Kosanic, Greenwood, & Doku, 2004) has shown positive effects of educational television for the reading and language development of young children. Yet video has remained a minor medium in the classroom, where it has been seen as a replacement for teacher instruction rather than a tool for teachers. (Throughout this chapter the term *video* is assumed to include DVD and CD formats as well as VHS unless otherwise noted.)

In recent years, however, video has begun to appear in educational practice in a new form that has great potential for education reform. Video is one example of what Mayer (2001) calls "multimedia," instructional formats that combine words and pictures. Instead of replacing instruction, multimedia can be embedded in classroom instruction to enhance teachers' lessons. This "embedded multimedia" application is not widely known or used, but research on the practice has shown initial promise. In embedded multimedia, brief multimedia segments are threaded throughout teachers' lessons. In one sense, embedded multimedia should at least share the impacts on achievement found in studies of the use of pictures, illustrations, diagrams, and other graphic content to enhance the effects of class lessons and text (see Carney & Levin, 2002; Schnotz, 2002; Shah, Mayer, & Hegarty, 1999; Vekiri, 2002). Yet well-designed embedded multimedia using video has properties that go beyond static graphics. First, video can model skills or content for students, giving them clear demonstrations of proficient performance. For example, videos can show children modeling advanced problem-solving strategies, sounding out words, thinking out loud about their creative writing, or working through a scientific investigation. Further, any multimedia that models for children also models for teachers, providing "just-in-time" professional development. For example, showing children working in cooperative groups to solve particular kinds of problems may provide teachers with a clear idea of what cooperative learning should look like, just as it would for students.

## DRAWING ON THEORETICAL PRINCIPLES

The theoretical basis for embedded multimedia begins with Paivio's dual coding theory (Clark & Paivio, 1991), which demonstrated that information held both in verbal memory and in visual memory is retained better than information held in only one memory system. For example, Mayer and his colleagues carried out a series of experiments in which students were taught how lightning works (Mayer, 2001). Teaching about lightning using narration alone or text alone teaches only to verbal memory. Adding diagrams or moving pictures to illustrate the concept teaches to visual memory. Adding the pictures to narration or text greatly increased initial learning of the concept, as well as both retention and transfer, as long as the pictures and text or narration were closely aligned with each other and focused on the instructional objective (Mayer & Moreno, 2003).

Another key concept in multimedia learning is cognitive load. It has long been known that working memory places a severe limitation on the amount of information that can be absorbed at any given time (Solso, 2001). Each learning objective has a given intrinsic cognitive load, and if this exceeds the working memory capacity of children of a given age or level of knowledge, the objective must be broken into components that fit within the child's working memory capacity (Paas, Renkl, & Sweller, 2003). However, each memory system has its own limitations, which may be fairly independent of the other; that is, a learner has a limited working memory capacity for words and a limit for pictures, but "using up" the word limit does not "use up" the picture limit. Therefore, Mayer and Moreno (2003) suggest that instructors or designers can "off-load" meaningful information from one channel to the other, by using fewer words and more pictures when verbal working memory would otherwise be overloaded. Again, this "off-loading" only works if the pictures and words directly support each other. Pictures that are interesting but irrelevant to the words, containing "seductive details," can be detrimental because they fill limited working memory with the irrelevant content (Mayer, 2001).

The complementary nature of words and moving pictures has been demonstrated in a series of studies in which instructional video material was broken into audio and silent video components and compared to the full video with audio (see Kozma, 1991, for a review). In most cases children learned significantly more from the video-audio presentations, and in no case did they learn less. This supports the concept that narrative and picture information do not interfere with each other, but instead support each other.

When both memory systems are in danger of overload, Mayer and Moreno's (2003) research suggests segmentation of combined word-picture content, organizing content in "bite-size segments" with opportunities to integrate and organize new information between segments (Mayer & Chandler, 2001).

Embedded multimedia takes advantage of these theoretical principles, combining verbal and visual content (words and moving pictures) to give learners multiple pathways to retention and comprehension and interspersing "bite-sized segments" with opportunities to practice and apply new learnings. For example, a key problem in early reading instruction is teaching associations between letter shapes and letter sounds. The embedded multimedia strategy described in this chapter contains a series of animations designed to link the letter shape and letter sound in a brief, memorable story.

In introducing the /p/ sound, for instance, a parrot eats some watermelon, and then spits out the seeds, making the sound /p/, /p/, /p/. The seeds fall in the shade of the letter *p*. This 30-second story, which 5-year-olds readily learn and remember, gives them a link in their visual memory between the shape *p* and the sound /p/ that they can easily access, adding to the verbal and tactile learning the teacher provides by having children look at a picture of the parrot in the shape of the letter *p* and having them make the /p/ sound and noticing how their lips form when they do so.

In English reading, children must learn 44 phonemes represented by more than 60 graphemes (Adams, 1990). In order to quickly and automatically recognize each, and avoid confusions among them, children need to practice them separately and in words and sentences. Practice in cooperative groups working with the teacher and practice in other formats is necessary to solidify learnings from "bite-sized segments," which is why the multimedia segments by themselves are insufficient.

Similar theories underlie other multimedia applications in beginning reading (see Pailliotet & Mosenthal, 2000). To teach sound blending, the strategy described in this chapter used video skits showing puppets sounding out words, creating both visual and auditory representations in memory. To teach vocabulary, live-action skits acted out the meanings of key words, both in context and then out of context. Again, students were expected to recall the skits (in their visual memories) to gain access to word meanings (needed in their verbal memories).

## ENHANCING SUCCESS FOR ALL
## WITH EMBEDDED MULTIMEDIA

In 2001 researchers and developers at the nonprofit Success for All Foundation and Johns Hopkins University began a project to enhance the Success for All reading program with embedded multimedia. Success for All teaches beginning reading using a systematic phonics approach (see Slavin & Madden, 2001, for a program description). Fifty experimental-control comparisons of one or more years' duration have found, on average, positive effects of Success for All on children's reading achievement (see Borman, Hewes, Overman, & Brown, 2003; Herman, 1999; Slavin & Madden, 2001). A review by the Comprehensive School Reform Quality Center at the American Institutes of Research (CSRQ, 2005) identified Success for All as one of only two programs to qualify for the highest category awarded for "strength of evidence of positive effects." In addition, a recent national randomized evaluation involving 35 schools found significant positive impacts on reading performance (Borman, Slavin, Cheung, Chamberlain, Madden, & Chambers, 2005; in press).

The addition of embedded multimedia to Success for All's beginning reading program was intended to enhance the effectiveness of the program by giving children compelling, memorable demonstrations of letter sounds, sound-blending strategies, vocabulary, and comprehension strategies. We chose to focus mostly on phonics skills for two reasons. First, these skills are critical in helping beginning readers crack the code and start sounding out simple words. Second, these skills are most amenable to creating the mnemonic images that animation and puppet skits can create. A particular focus was on the needs of English-language learners, who were felt to be in particular need of visual models for vocabulary and sound blending.

A preliminary study of the embedded multimedia strategy was carried out by Chambers, Slavin, Madden, Cheung, and Gifford (2004). In that study, four schools primarily serving Hispanic students were compared with four matched schools with similar demographics and achievement histories. The experimental schools used Success for All with embedded multimedia, while the control schools used traditional basal approaches. After a one-year implementation, students in the Success for All/embedded multimedia treatment scored significantly higher than those in the matched control group, controlling for Peabody Picture Vocabulary Test (PPVT) pretests (Dunn & Dunn, 1997), on the Woodcock Word Identification, Word Attack, and Passage Comprehension scales of the Woodcock Reading Mastery Test Revised (WRMT-R) (Woodcock, McGrew, & Mather, 2001). There were no differences on Letter Identification.

The Chambers et al. (2004) experiment established the combined effect of Success for All reading and embedded multimedia on reading achievement, but it did not allow for a test of the unique contribution of the embedded multimedia content.

## THE DEFINITIVE STUDY

Chambers, Cheung, Madden, Slavin, and Gifford (2006) carried out the definitive study of embedded multimedia. This study controlled the instructional content by including only schools using Success for All reading. Experimental and control schools differed only in the use or nonuse of the multimedia content. All schools were in the same district, the Hartford (Connecticut) Public Schools, further ensuring similarity between experimental and control schools on all factors other than the embedded multimedia treatment. In addition, schools were randomly assigned to the embedded multimedia or control treatments. Random assignment in studies of promising programs is critical because it eliminates all differences between experimental and control groups other than the treatment. In this case, it increases certainty that the differences in the outcomes are due to differences between the programs, not to other differences between the groups (see Mosteller & Boruch, 2002). All schools had an equal chance of being assigned to the experimental or control groups. All school staffs were willing to implement the embedded multimedia program; those randomly assigned to the control group were given the materials and training in the year following the experiment, as a delayed treatment control procedure.

Details about the methods and analyses of the Chambers et al. (2006) study are provided in Appendix A at the end of the chapter.

## Multimedia Content

The experimental group used multimedia content embedded in teachers' daily 90-minute Success for All reading lessons. This material consisted of 30-second to 3-minute skits and other demonstrations integrated with teachers' lessons. No additional time was added to the lessons to accommodate the multimedia. The purpose of the multimedia content was to directly present to students compelling demonstrations of key elements of beginning reading: letter sounds, sound-blending strategies, and vocabulary. In addition, it was hoped that by showing multimedia content in class, teachers would have constant reinforcement of effective teaching strategies.

The embedded multimedia materials were developed to be particularly beneficial to English-language learners. In particular, the vocabulary skits demonstrating the vocabulary emphasized in each story children are about to read were designed to ensure that all children know the vocabulary in advance so that they can focus on the decoding and comprehension tasks required to master and enjoy each book. The alphabet and sound-blending segments are also designed to build children's language skills as well as their reading skills.

The multimedia materials created for the experimental program were called Reading Reels, which included the components described below.

### The Animated Alphabet

Animations teach and reinforce sound-symbol relationships. For example, the animation introducing the short /e/ sound features an elephant pushing a rock with an *e* on it up a hill, making an /e/ sound with each push. At the top, the rock rolls down, and the exhausted elephant says "ehhhh" in frustration. The pairing of the memorable images, the letter sound, and the letter shape gives students many mental pathways to link the letter with its sound. There are animations for 58 different graphemes that comprise most of the phonemes used in the English language. Each animation is between 30 and 60 seconds long.

### The Sound and the Furry

Multimedia skits, using puppet characters, model the word-blending process, phonemic awareness, spelling, fluency, reading strategies, and co-operative learning routines. For example, a puppet sees a sign, "Watch out for stick." He sounds out the word *stick* phonetically. Then he notices a stick, which he picks up. The stick sticks to his fur, and in trying to get it off he bites it—and then realizes he's in real trouble. After the skit, the sounding-out section is repeated, and children sound out the word along with the puppets. More than a hundred such vignettes illustrate sound blending strategies from simple consonant-vowel-consonant (CVC) words to multisyllable words. The average puppet skit is about 2 minutes long.

### Word Plays

Live action multimedia skits dramatize important vocabulary concepts from the Success for All beginning reading texts. These skits are particularly designed to help English-language learners build the specific vocabulary for the books they will be reading. For example, when children are going to read a story about China, they first see a skit that introduces words such as *chopsticks*, *fireworks*, *beautiful*, and *ugly*. The average Word Play is about 3 minutes long.

### Between the Lions

Puppet skits and animations from the award-winning PBS program help teach phonemic awareness, sound-symbol correspondence, and sound blending. *Between the Lions* segments are about one minute long.

## Results

### Pretests

Pretests showed that experimental and control schools were well matched on the PPVT, but the control schools scored higher at pretest on the Word Identification pretest than the experimental schools, with an effect size of –0.35. This was statistically significant at the individual level ($p < .01$), but was not significant at the school level.

### Hierarchical Linear Modeling (HLM)

For the hierarchical linear analyses, we developed two-level hierarchical models that nested students within schools to test differences between posttests, with pretests as covariates. The experimental group scored significantly higher than the control group on the Word Attack subtest. Using the treatment coefficient of 6.21 for the mean achievement outcome and dividing this value by the unadjusted standard deviation for the Word Attack posttest, we estimated the magnitude of this school-level effect at $ES = +0.47$. Although the experimental group also scored higher than the control on Word Identification ($ES = +0.23$), Passage Comparison ($ES = +0.20$), and DIBELS ($ES = +0.29$), these differences were not statistically significant in the HLM analysis. Individual-level ANCOVAs found significant differences on Word Attack ($p < .001$) and Word Identification ($p < .02$), but not Passage Comprehension or DIBELS. Analyses for the Hispanic subsample produced results very similar to those of the whole sample. No interactions between ethnicity and treatment were found.

## A Second Study

A second study evaluating the effects of embedded multimedia was carried out by Chambers et al. (in press). This study used random assignment of individual students to conditions in two high-poverty Success for All schools. Low-achieving first graders who qualified for tutoring received a computer-assisted tutoring intervention in addition to embedded multimedia in their regular reading classes. However, students who did not qualify for tutoring were randomly assigned to embedded multimedia or control conditions. Details about the methods and analyses of the Chambers et al. (2005) study are provided in Appendix B at the end of the chapter.

### Results

Pretest scores for experimental and control students were similar ($p < .21$). On adjusted posttests, effect sizes and $p$ values were as follows: Letter-Word Identification ($ES = +0.35, p < .03$), Word Attack ($ES = +0.27, p < .10$.), Fluency ($ES = +0.27, p < .07$), Comprehension ($ES = +0.04$, n.s.), and the Gray Oral Reading Test (GORT) Total ($ES = +0.22, p < .02$).

School-level implementation reports, completed by trainers after their technical support visits, indicated a high level of implementation. Anecdotal observations conducted by the research team indicate that while most teachers threaded the approximately 5 minutes of multimedia throughout their 90-minute lessons as they were designed to be used, some teachers showed them all together, usually at the end of the lesson. Because we do not have data at the individual teacher or tutor level, we cannot determine whether these different ways of displaying the multimedia influenced student outcomes. Future studies should include structured observations of implementation fidelity that would permit correlation of teacher implementation quality and outcomes.

## CONCLUSION

The results of the two Chambers et al. studies (2006, in press) partially support the expectation that the addition of embedded multimedia content to a beginning reading program would enhance children's reading achievement. In both studies, schools were randomly assigned to conditions and all schools used the same Success for All reading strategies, so the use of embedded multimedia content was the only factor differentiating experimental and control conditions. In the Chambers et al. (2006) study, a conservative HLM analysis found that only one of the four outcome measures, Word Attack, showed significant experimental-control differences, but this is in line with theoretical expectations. Three of the four multimedia segments dealt primarily with letter sounds and sound blending, which are key components of Word Attack. The fourth, Word Plays, focused on vocabulary. The other measures, especially Passage Comprehension and DIBELS, are more logically related to reading of connected text, which was emphasized equally in both treatments. In the Chambers et al. (in press) study, positive effects were found on Letter-Word Identification, Word Attack, and Fluency, but not Comprehension.

Because of the use of Word Plays and the visual content in all of the Reading Reels materials, it was expected that Hispanic children would benefit disproportionately from the embedded multimedia treatment. However, this was not the case. Effects for Hispanic children in the Chambers et al. (2006) study were nearly identical to those for other children (mostly African American). However, no measures of English vocabulary were used, and we were unable to obtain data on children's initial English proficiency, so it may be that there were undetected differential positive effects for the subgroup of children with limited English proficiency.

These studies build on laboratory studies and theory-building work by Mayer (2001) and others, and applies the use of embedded multimedia to beginning reading instruction. Threading multimedia content throughout class lessons and tutoring sessions appears to help make concepts clear and memorable to children, taking advantage of the well-established finding that linked visual and auditory content is retained better than either type of content alone. The findings of the Chambers et al. (2005, 2006) studies and of Chambers et al. (2004) suggest that the use of embedded multimedia has potential to enhance the effectiveness of beginning reading instruction for disadvantaged children. The individual-level effect size of +0.32 for Word Attack in Chambers et al. (2006) and +0.27 in Chambers et al. (in press) is educationally important, particularly given the minimal cost of the intervention. Adding the DVDs to an existing Success for All school costs $129 per classroom (plus the cost of a DVD player and television) and occupies an average of less than 5 minutes per day out of a 90-minute reading period.

The effects of the computer-assisted tutoring in the Chambers et al. (2006) study provide more positive support for the use of computers in teaching reading than reviews of computer-aided instruction have found (Kulik, 2003). Perhaps the role of assistant to the tutor, rather than a replacement for the tutor, is a more effective application of the technology. Much further work is needed, comparing similar programs used alone and with adult mediation, to ascertain this.

Much research remains to be done to further understand these effects. It would be important to study the program's effects on teachers' practices in order to assess the validity of the theory that multimedia modeling of effective teaching practices would improve teachers' implementations of the reading program and their overall teaching skill. Further, small-scale studies are needed to examine the separate impacts of the multimedia components and to vary elements of the interventions. Such studies could help build a theoretical base for embedded multimedia in reading instruction and suggest design principles for further development. Future studies should include fidelity measures to determine the effects of different levels of implementation and to assess factors that can improve implementation fidelity.

Research on multimedia learning (e.g., Mayer, 2001) shows that specific design elements matter a great deal in determining learning outcomes. However, using design principles known to contribute to learning, multimedia embedded in literacy instruction may have significant potential to improve reading outcomes for children.

## Follow-up Activities

1. This chapter suggests several mechanisms by which embedded video might improve students' reading ability: providing mnemonic cues for the skills, providing for dual coding of content, providing interaction with the video, and improving instruction by providing models for teachers. Discuss which mechanisms you think are most responsible for the effects.
2. Discuss how embedded multimedia might be employed to enhance other literacy skills, such as comprehension or fluency.
3. Using data from recent reading assessments, determine in which areas (e.g., phonics, fluency) your struggling readers need the most help. Decide upon strategies that you could employ that would best target those areas.

# APPENDIX A: THE CHAMBERS ET AL. (2006) STUDY

## Method

### Design

This study employed a cluster randomized trial (CRT) design, with random assignment of schools to treatments. A total of 10 elementary schools were identified. Five were randomly assigned to standard Success for All (control) and five to Success for All with embedded multimedia.

### Participants

Subjects were 450 first graders, of whom 394 completed pre- and posttests. The students attended 10 schools in inner-city Hartford, Connecticut. Almost all students qualified for free- or reduced-price lunches, and 62% of students were Hispanic and 35% African American. The two groups were well matched on the percentage of students eligible for free- or reduced-price lunch, ethnicity, and the percentage of limited English proficient students in the school. Pretests were used as covariates in the main analyses to adjust for any initial difference between the two groups and to increase statistical power. Because the unit of random assignment and treatment was the school, the school was also the unit of analysis.

### Treatments

*Experimental.* The experimental group used multimedia content embedded in teachers' daily 90-minute Success for All reading lessons. This material consisted of 30-second to 3-minute skits and other demonstrations integrated with teachers' lessons. No additional time was added to the lessons to accommodate the multimedia. The purpose of the multimedia content was to directly present to students compelling demonstrations of key elements of beginning reading: letter sounds, sound-blending strategies, and vocabulary. In addition, it was hoped that by showing multimedia content in class, teachers would have constant reinforcement of effective teaching strategies. The multimedia materials ultimately created for the program were called Reading Reels.

*Control.* Control schools used the regular 90-minute Success for All reading program without the embedded multimedia content. In place of the multimedia content, teachers used picture cards to illustrate the letter shapes and vocabulary in the student books. Demonstrations and games were used to teach word-level blending.

## Measures

Participants were pretested in early October 2003, and posttested in early May 2004. The pretests were the Peabody Picture Vocabulary Test (Dunn & Dunn, 1997) and the Word Identification subtest from the Woodcock Reading Mastery Test—Revised (WRMT—R; Woodcock et al., 2001). On average, each testing session took approximately 30 minutes per child.

The posttests included the reading fluency test from the Dynamic Indicators of Basic Early Literacy Skills (DIBELS; Good & Kaminski, 2002) and three scales from the WRMT—R: Word Identification, Word Attack, and Passage Comprehension. Testing sessions required, on average, 42 minutes per child.

The DIBELS fluency test is a standardized, individually administered test of accuracy and fluency with connected text. Student performance is measured by having students read a passage aloud for one minute. The WRMT—R test requires the subject to identify isolated words that appear in large type on the subject pages in the test book. The Word Attack test requires the subject to read nonsense words (letter combinations that are not actual words). The test measures the subject's ability to apply phonic and structural analysis skills in order to pronounce words with which he or she is unfamiliar. The Passage Comprehension test measures the subject's ability to read a short passage—usually two to three sentences long—and to identify a key word missing from the passage.

## Analyses

The data were analyzed using Hierarchical Linear Modeling (HLM; Raudenbush, 1997), with students nested within schools. Classroom-level analyses could not be done because, as part of the Success for All design, children routinely change reading teachers over the course of the year. HLM is the appropriate analysis for cluster randomized designs of this kind. Condition was the independent variable and the WRMT—R subtests and the DIBELS fluency test were the dependent measures. The PPVT and Word Identification pretests were used as covariates to adjust for initial differences between the treatment and control groups and to increase statistical power. Analyses were carried out both for the overall sample and for a Hispanic subsample.

# APPENDIX B: THE CHAMBERS ET AL. (IN PRESS) STUDY

## Method

### Design

The study took place in two large, multitrack year-round schools that had been implementing Success for All for several years. In each school, each student was part of a "track" that followed a schedule of four sessions over the year with vacation time between sessions (i.e., time usually allocated to summer vacation was instead divided into four minivacations). Multitrack schools of this kind are not uncommon in growing areas of the West, and are primarily intended to utilize buildings all year, to reduce the need for school construction. For researchers, multitrack schools of this kind offer an opportunity to randomly assign students to one of four "minischools" (i.e., the tracks), in a situation in which an essentially random process is used by the schools themselves to make the tracks equivalent to each other in student characteristics.

On entry to first grade, children in the two schools were assigned at random to one of the four tracks. Then tracks were randomly assigned to treatments (technology or no technology). Teachers assigned to the no-technology control group were given the technology and training at the end of the year-long study, so this was a delayed-treatment control group comparison.

There were a few children who could not be randomly assigned to tracks because they had a sibling in a given track and their parents wanted both children in the same track so they could take family vacations together. These children were nonrandomly assigned to their sibling's track. A test for differences between these students and those who were randomly assigned found nearly identical scores, so these children were included in the analyses.

### Participants

Subjects for the complete experiment were 159 first graders in two multi-track, year-round schools. One was a charter school of 1,487 students in Los Angeles, in which 94% of students received free lunch and 97% were Mexican American. The other was a public elementary school of 756 students in Las Vegas, in which 81% of students received free lunch and 69% were Mexican American, 17% were White, 7% were Asian American, and 6% were African American. Within the sample, the 60 lowest achieving students received tutoring, and were therefore not included in the study of embedded multimedia alone. The remaining 99 students (43 experimental, 56 control) were the subjects for the multimedia study.

## Treatments

*Experimental.* In the experimental group, all students were instructed in reading using Success for All with embedded multimedia, as described previously.

*Control.* Students in the control treatment experienced Success for All without the multimedia content. The use or nonuse of the videos was the only factor differentiating experimental and control treatments.

## Measures

Participants were individually pretested in September 2004 and posttested in May 2005. Specially trained testers, unaware of children's experimental assignments, administered the tests. The measures were as follows:

1. *Woodcock Letter-Word Identification.* (Pre, post). The Letter-Word Identification scale of the Woodcock-Johnson III Tests of Achievement was used as a pretest and again as a posttest. It requires subjects to identify isolated letters and words (Woodcock et al., 2001).
2. *Woodcock Word Attack.* (Post). Word Attack asks subjects to read nonsense words as an assessment of phonetic skills (Woodcock et al., 2001).
3. *Gray Oral Reading Test—Fluency.* (Post). GORT—Fluency asks subjects to read connected text, and scores them on rate and accuracy (Gray & Robinson, 2001).
4. *Gray Oral Reading Test—Comprehension.* (Post). GORT—Comprehension is a multiple-choice test based on questions asked of subjects after they read the passages used in the Fluency test (Gray & Robinson, 2001).
5. *Gray Oral Reading Test—Total.* (Post). GORT—Total subsumes the Fluency and Comprehension subscales (Gray & Robinson, 2001).

## Analyses

The data were analyzed using analyses of covariance, controlling for Letter-Word Identification pretests.

*Acknowledgment.* This research was funded by the Interagency Educational Research Initiative (IERI), a collaboration among the National Science Foundation, the Institute of Education Sciences, and the National Institute of Child Health and Human Development (Grant No. REC 0115659). However, any opinions expressed are those of the authors and do not necessarily represent the positions or policies of our funders.

## REFERENCES

Adams, M. J. (1990). *Beginning to read: Thinking and learning about print.* Cambridge, MA: MIT Press.

Bogatz, G. A., & Ball, S. (1971). *The second year of "Sesame Street."* Princeton, NJ: Educational Testing Service.

Borman, G. D., Hewes, G. M., Overman, L. T., & Brown, S. (2003). Comprehensive school reform and achievement: A meta-analysis. *Review of Educational Research, 73*(2), 125–230.

Borman, G., Slavin, R. E., Cheung, A., Chamberlain, A., Madden, N. A., & Chambers, B. (2005). The national randomized field trial of Success for All: Second-year outcomes. *American Educational Research Journal, 42*(4), 673–696.

Borman, G., Slavin, R. E., Cheung, A., Chamberlain, A., Madden, N. A., & Chambers, B. (in press). Final reading outcomes of the national randomized field trial of Success for All. *American Educational Research Journal.*

Carney, R. N., & Levin, J. R. (2002). Pictorial illustrations still improve students' learning from text. *Educational Psychology Review, 14*(1), 5–26.

Chambers, B., Cheung, A., Madden, N. A., Slavin, R. E., & Gifford, G. (2006). Achievement effects of embedded multimedia in a Success for All reading program. *Journal of Educational Psychology, 42,* 673–696.

Chambers, B., Slavin, R. E., Madden, N. A., Abrami, P., Tucker, B., Cheung, A., et al. (in press). *Technology infusion in Success for All: Reading outcomes for first graders.* Baltimore: Success for All Foundation.

Chambers, B., Slavin, R. E., Madden, N. A., Cheung, A., & Gifford, R. (2004). *Effects of Success for All with embedded video on the beginning reading achievement of Hispanic children.* Manuscript submitted for publication.

Clark, J. M., & Paivio, A. (1991). Dual coding theory and education. *Educational Psychology Review, 3*(3), 149–210.

Comprehensive School Reform Quality Center (CSRQ). (2005). *CSRQ Center report on elementary school comprehensive school reform models.* Washington, DC: American Institutes for Research.

Dunn, L., & Dunn, L. (1997). *Peabody Picture Vocabulary Test: Examiner's Manual* (3rd ed.). Circle Pines, MI: American Guidance System.

Fisch, S., & Truglio, R. (2000). G is for growing: 30 years of research on *Sesame Street.* New York: Lea's Communications Series.

Good, R., & Kaminski, R. (Eds.). (2002). *Dynamic indicators of basic early literacy skills* (6th ed.). Eugene, OR: Institute for the Development of Educational Achievement.

Gray, W. S., & Robinson, H. (2001). *Gray Oral Reading Tests* (4th ed.). Austin, TX: PRO-ED.

Herman, R. (1999). *An educator's guide to schoolwide reform.* Arlington, VA: Educational Research Service.

Kozma, R. (1991). Learning with media. *Review of Educational Research, 61*(2), 179–211.

Kulik, J. A. (2003). *Effects of using instructional technology in elementary and secondary schools: What controlled evaluation studies say* (SRI Project Number P10446.001). Arlington, VA: SRI International.

Linebarger, D. L., Kosanic, A. Z., Greenwood, C. R., & Doku, N. S. (2004). Effects of viewing the television program *Between the Lions* on the emergent literacy skills of young children. *Journal of Educational Psychology, 96,* 297–308.

Mayer, R. E. (2001). *Multimedia learning.* Cambridge: Cambridge University Press.

Mayer, R. E., & Chandler, P. (2001). When learning is just a click away: Does simple user interaction foster deeper understanding of multimedia messages? *Journal of Educational Psychology, 93,* 390–397.

Mayer, R. E., & Moreno, R. (2003). Nine ways to reduce cognitive load in multimedia learning. *Educational Psychologist, 38*(1), 43–52.

Mosteller, F., & Boruch, R. (Eds.). (2002). *Evidence matters: Randomized trials in educational research.* Washington, DC: Brookings Institution.

Paas, F., Renkl, A., & Sweller, J. (2003). Cognitive load theory and instructional design: Recent developments. *Educational Psychologist, 38*(1), 1–4.

Pailliotet, A. W., & Mosenthal, P. B. (Eds.). (2000). *Reconceptualizing literacy in the age of media, multimedia, and hypermedia.* Norwood, NJ: JAI/Ablex.

Raudenbush, S. W. (1997). Statistical analysis and optimal design for cluster randomized trials. *Psychological Methods, 2,* 173–185.

Rice, M. L., Huston, A. C., Truglio, R., & Wright, L. C. (1990). Words from *Sesame Street:* Learning vocabulary while viewing. *Developmental Psychology, 26,* 421–428.

Schnotz, W. (2002). Towards an integrated view of learning from text and visual displays. *Educational Psychology Review, 14*(1), 101–120.

Shah, P., Mayer, R., & Hegarty, M. (1999). Graphs as aids to knowledge construction: Signaling techniques for guiding the process of graph comprehension. *Journal of Educational Psychology, 91*(4), 690–702.

Slavin, R. E., & Madden, N. A. (Eds.). (2001). *One million children: Success for All.* Thousand Oaks, CA: Corwin Press.

Solso, R. L. (2001). *Cognitive psychology* (6th ed.). Boston: Allyn & Bacon.

Vekiri, I. (2002). What is the value of graphical displays in learning? *Educational Psychology Review, 14*(3), 261–312.

Woodcock, R. W., McGrew, K. S., & Mather, N. (2001). *Woodcock-Johnson III Tests of Achievement.* Itasca, IL: Riverside.

# PART II

# Effective Instructional Strategies to Improve Students' Vocabulary

# CHAPTER 4

# Conceptual and Empirical Bases for Providing Struggling Readers with Multifaceted and Long-Term Vocabulary Instruction

## Michael F. Graves

As Jeanne Chall and her colleagues pointed out in their pioneering book *The Reading Crisis: Why Poor Children Fall Behind* (Chall, Jacobs, & Baldwin, 1990) and as we now clearly understand, vocabulary knowledge is absolutely crucial to success in reading and many struggling readers lack vocabulary knowledge.

### Questions for Reflection and Discussion

- We know that vocabulary knowledge is crucial to comprehension, but what exactly is the relationship between the two? Is vocabulary knowledge a direct cause of reading comprehension? Will teaching vocabulary to struggling readers necessarily result in better comprehension?
- Teaching vocabulary means more than teaching individual words. It means teaching word-learning strategies such as using context to infer word meanings and using word parts to deduce word meanings. What are some other ways of helping struggling readers build strong vocabularies?

Strangely, vocabulary has not always received the attention it deserves. Throughout most of the last century, interest in vocabulary repeatedly waxed and waned. Between 1920 and about 1960, Edward Thorndike's research on vocabulary, most notably his work on the *Teacher's Wordbook* (Thorndike, 1921, 1932; Thorndike & Lorge 1944), had a huge influence on the vocabulary used in basal reading series (Clifford, 1978), the texts with which almost all children entering school between 1920 and 1960 learned to read. Between 1940 and about 1970, a series of studies on the components of reading comprehension (Davis, 1944, 1968, 1972; Spearritt, 1972; Thorndike, 1973–74) showed vocabulary to be a central component of reading comprehension and resulted in vocabulary continuing to receive some attention. However, despite receiving some attention, during the 1970s the frequency of vocabulary research declined sharply (Calfee & Drum, 1978)). In fact, the first edition of the *Handbook of Reading Research* (Pearson, Barr, Kamil, & Mosenthal, 1984) failed to include a chapter on vocabulary.

This inattention was short lived. In the 1980s, Anderson and Nagy and their colleagues (e.g., Anderson & Freebody, 1981; Nagy & Anderson, 1984) and Beck and McKeown and their colleagues (e.g., Beck, Perfetti, & McKeown, 1982; McKeown, Beck, Omanson, & Pople, 1985) undertook programs of vocabulary research that once more made vocabulary a vital part of reading research. And when the second edition of the *Handbook of Reading Research* (Barr, Kamil, Mosenthal, & Pearson, 1991) was released, it had two chapters on vocabulary. Once again, though, interest waned, and by the mid-1990s, vocabulary was not a central concern of reading researchers.

In recent years the situation has once again changed, primarily because of five factors:

1. Hart and Risley's *Meaningful Differences in the Everyday Experience of Young American Children* (1995) revealed the huge vocabulary deficit faced by children of poverty.
2. Growing numbers of English-language learners in U.S. classrooms require assistance in developing their English vocabularies.
3. The Report of the National Reading Panel (National Reading Panel, 2000) identified vocabulary as one of the five central components of reading instruction.
4. The report of the RAND Reading Study Group (2002) identified vocabulary as crucial to reading comprehension.
5. The No Child Left Behind (NCLB) legislation identified vocabulary instruction as one of the five required components of Reading First programs (NCLB, 2002).

Testimony to the current interest in vocabulary can be found in the fact that 75% of the respondents to the International Reading Association's (IRA) most recent poll of "What's Hot, What's Not" in reading (Cassidy & Cassidy, 2005/06) agreed that vocabulary should be a "very hot" topic. Testimony can further be found in the recent publication of three research-based books on vocabulary—Hiebert and Kamil's *Teaching and Learning Vocabulary*

(2005), Stahl and Nagy's *Teaching Word Meanings* (2006), and my own, *The Vocabulary Book* (Graves, 2006).

Throughout the past 20 years of this waxing and waning interest in vocabulary, I have attempted to fashion a vocabulary program that is based on solid research and theory on vocabulary, broad enough to meet the needs of all learners, and particularly attentive to the needs of students who enter school with small vocabularies (Graves, 1984, 1987, 1992, 2000, 2004, 2006; Graves & Fitzgerald, 2006; Graves & Watts, 2002). In the remainder of this chapter, I take a critical look at the research and theory supporting that program. In doing so, I first list the central assumptions underlying the program and then describe the four parts of the program. Next I analyze the extent to which research and theory support each assumption and each part of the program. Finally, I consider how strong an endorsement of the four part program the evidence allows and what kind of research is most needed to strengthen the research base for the four-part program and create an optimal program of vocabulary instruction.

## ASSUMPTIONS UNDERLYING THE FOUR-PART VOCABULARY PROGRAM

Five assumptions underlie the program. They can be briefly listed:

1. Vocabulary is tremendously important—as an index of verbal ability, as a predictor of success in and out of school, as a factor influencing the readability of text, and as a factor that can improve reading comprehension.
2. Written American English contains a huge number of words, something on the order of 150,000 words rather than something on the order of 20,000 words.
3. Students know words to varying degrees. It is not a simple matter of knowing or not knowing a word. One may, for example, have never heard a word, have a vague idea of what it means, recognize some meanings but not others, or know it well.
4. Average and above-average, middle-class, native English speakers know a tremendous number of words. Linguistically advantaged students come to first grade with something like 5,000–10,000 words, most of which are in their oral vocabularies, and graduate from high school with something like 50,000 words, most of which are in both their oral and reading vocabularies.
5. Many children of poverty, English-language learners (ELLs), and poor readers know far fewer words. Giving averages here is extremely

difficult because of individual differences. For example, ELLs who just arrived in the United States may know almost no English words. Still, a figure of 3,000 to 6,000 is a reasonable, if very rough, estimate for linguistically less advantaged first graders. The problem these students face is compounded because after first grade, their vocabularies are likely to grow more slowly than those of their linguistically more advantaged peers, resulting in an ever increasing gap.

## OVERVIEW OF THE FOUR-PART PROGRAM

Here I give a very brief overview of the program, but more details are available in Graves (2000, 2006).

### Part 1: Frequent, Varied, and Extensive Language Experiences

This part of the program includes two subparts. First, from preschool through high school, all students are involved in rich and varied experiences in listening, reading, writing, and discussion. In the early grades, listening and discussion are most prominent, while in the upper grades, reading and writing will become increasingly more prominent. Second, in the primary grades, linguistically less advantaged children engage in shared storybook reading. In shared storybook reading, the teacher typically works with a small group, repeatedly reads a passage aloud, stops periodically to highlight and discuss targeted words, gets children actively involved in working with the words, and gives them opportunities to review the taught words.

### Part 2: Teaching Individual Words

With tens of thousands of words to learn, it is clear that not anything like all of these words can be taught directly, but certainly some words should be taught directly. Teaching important words from selections students are reading can help them avoid stumbling over the words, improve their comprehension of the selections, and remind them of the importance of words. Two particularly important considerations when teaching individual words are that different approaches not only are required for teaching different sorts of words but also will produce varying depths of word knowledge. The program includes over a dozen different techniques ranging from relatively thin approaches to rich and robust ones. One example of a thin approach, appropriate for teaching students new words that do not represent new concepts, is the Context-Dictionary-Discussion Procedure:

1. Give students the word in context.
2. Have them look it up in the dictionary.
3. Discuss the definitions students find and their appropriateness to the context that was given.

Such an approach might require five minutes per word. One example of a rich approach, appropriate for teaching new and difficult concepts, is the Frayer Method (developed by S. A. Frayer):

1. Define the new concept.
2. Distinguish between the new concept and similar concepts with which it might be confused.
3. Give examples of the concept.
4. Give nonexamples of the concept.
5. Have students distinguish between examples and nonexamples.
6. Have students produce examples and nonexamples.

Such a procedure might require 30 minutes, but is necessary to thoroughly teach difficult concepts.

## Part 3: Teaching Word-Learning Strategies

Since it is impossible to teach anything like all of the words students need to learn, it is important to give them strategies for learning words on their own. The most important strategies taught in the program are using context to infer word meanings, using word parts to deduce word meanings, using the dictionary, and (for Spanish-speaking ELLs) taking advantage of Spanish cognates in learning English vocabulary. Instruction in all of these strategies begins with direct explanation:

- Describe the strategy and when and how it should be used.
- Model use of the strategy.
- Collaborate with students in using the strategy.
- Give students guided practice in using the strategy and gradually give them increased responsibility for using the strategy.
- Give students plenty of opportunities to use the strategy independently.

Along with and as a follow-up to direct explanation, the program includes more transactional and constructivist instruction—for example, making sure that students are active participants, making collaborative discussion and critical consideration of the strategies frequent activities, and being sure that students clearly understand the purposes of the strategies.

## Part 4: Fostering Word Consciousness

*Word consciousness* refers to an awareness of and interest in words and their meanings. Word consciousness integrates metacognition about words, motivation to learn words, and deep and lasting interest in words. Although fostering word consciousness differs from grade to grade, it is a vital part of the program at all grade levels. There are many ways for teachers to foster students' word consciousness:

- Model adept diction themselves.
- Recognize and encourage adept diction in students.
- Promote word play and word play books.
- Provide students with rich and robust instruction.
- Involve students in original investigations of words.
- Teach students about words.

## CONCEPTUAL AND EMPIRICAL SUPPORT FOR EACH OF THE FIVE ASSUMPTIONS

Here I consider just how strong the evidence supporting each of the assumptions underlying the program is.

## 1. The Importance of Vocabulary

There is virtually universal agreement that vocabulary is tremendously important in school and out of school—for comprehension, for communicating, and even for thinking. Stahl and Stahl (2004) provide a particularly eloquent statement of this belief:

> Consider the power that a name gives a child. Now this is a *table* and that a *chair*. . . . Having a name for something means that one has some degree of control. . . . As children get more words, they get more control over their environment. . . . Language and reading both act as the tools of thought to bring representation to a new level and to allow the formation of new relationships and organizations. . . . To expand a child's vocabulary is to teach that child to think about the world. (p. 59)

Of course, a testimonial is not empirical evidence, but there is a good deal of that too. There is strong correlational evidence relating vocabulary and IQ, with correlations generally running from .70 to .90 (Miner, 1957); in fact, it has been suggested that a vocabulary test is a good substitute for an IQ test (Anderson & Freebody, 1981). Additionally, an international study of reading comprehension in 15 countries revealed correlations ranging from .50 to .74 between tests of word knowledge and tests of comprehension (R. L. Thorndike, 1973–74).

There is also a good deal of factor analytic evidence on the importance of vocabulary. In his 1944 analysis of comprehension tests and his 1968 replication and extension of that study, Davis concluded that "memory for word meanings" was the most significant component of reading comprehension and recommended that teachers "make students familiar with the meanings of as many words as possible" (1968, p. 543). Further analysis of Davis's data by Spearritt (1972) and R. L. Thorndike (1973–74) produced similar conclusions. In Rosenshine's 1980 review of these and other studies of the component skills of reading, he conducted several analyses that yielded somewhat different results and concluded that "only one skill was consistent across the three analyses: remembering word meanings" (p. 543). And in a recent review of research, Pearson (2005) noted that factor analytic studies in general have shown three factors to be important to comprehension: a gist factor, a reasoning factor, and a word factor.

Analyses of the factors influencing the readability of texts yield similar results. For example, in his 1974–75 and 1984 reviews of readability research, Klare noted that two factors, "a word or semantic variable and . . . a sentence or syntactic variable," are the major predictors of text comprehension and concluded that "the word semantic variable is consistently more highly predictive than the sentence variable" (1974–75, p. 96). These two factors and the greater influence of the word factor can be seen in traditional readability formulas such as those of Spache, Dale and Chall, and Fry, as well as in contemporary formulas such as the Lexile system.

Finally, as already noted, the Report of the National Reading Panel (2000) identified vocabulary as one of the five essential components of reading; the report of the RAND Reading Study Group (2002) identified vocabulary as crucial to reading comprehension; and the No Child Left Behind legislation (NCLB, 2002) identified vocabulary instruction as one of the five required components of Reading First programs.

Nevertheless, as the reports of both the National Reading Panel and the RAND Reading Study Group make clear, and as Baumann (2005) has recently pointed out, the relationship between vocabulary and comprehension—the relationship that more than anything else motivates interest in vocabulary—is far from clearly understood.

As Anderson and Freebody (1981) noted and as Baumann (2005) has emphasized, the repeatedly verified relationships between vocabulary and comprehension can be accounted for by three hypotheses. The first and strongest position, the instrumentalist hypothesis, posits that vocabulary is causally related to comprehension, that teaching vocabulary will increase comprehension. The second position, the knowledge hypothesis, posits that a large vocabulary reflects a large knowledge base and that it is world knowledge rather than word knowledge that accounts for the relationship between vocabulary and comprehension. Based on this hypothesis, teaching vocabulary would not necessarily increase comprehension. The third position, the aptitude hypothesis, posits that a large vocabulary results from having high intelligence or verbal aptitude. Based on this hypothesis, teaching vocabulary would be unlikely to increase comprehension. Although, as Anderson and Freebody note, all three hypotheses contain some truth, the argument for teaching vocabulary would be stronger if there were more evidence supporting the instrumentalist hypothesis.

## 2. The Number of Words in Written American English

There are several, relatively recent and widely cited estimates of the number of words in written American English. Unfortunately, they differ considerably. In the best documented estimate, Nagy and Anderson (1984) began with the corpus of words collected in the *American Heritage Word Frequency Book* (Carroll, Davies, & Richman, 1971), a very well done compilation of the words occurring in books and other material likely to used by students in Grades 3–9. Nagy and Anderson first developed a system for assessing the semantic relation of words and developed the concept of "word families." A word family is "a group of morphologically related words such that if a person knows one member of the family, he or she will probably be able to figure out the meaning of any other members upon encountering it in text" (p. 315). Based on this definition, Nagy and Anderson estimated the number of word families represented in the *Word Frequency Book* and concluded that printed school English contains about 88,000 word families. Subsequent to the original study, Anderson and Nagy (1992) again considered the size of printed school English and concluded that their original estimate was too low. They noted that if proper nouns, multiple meanings of words, and idioms were included, their estimate would increase to about 180,000 word families.

More recently, as part of a line of research investigating the feasibility of directly and systematically teaching young students a specific body of words, Biemiller and Slonim (2001) estimated the number of "root words" that readers need to learn. They took as their corpus the words listed in *The Living Word Vocabulary* (Dale & O'Rourke, 1981). Although this compilation is a very useful tool because it provides information on students' knowledge of specific words, there is no information on how the words listed were selected and therefore no information indicating that it is a valid or complete compilation of English words. Based on this questionable corpus, Biemiller and Slonim estimated that English contains approximately 13,000 root words. More recently still, Biemiller (2004) has revised this estimate to approximately 17,500 root words.

Obviously, having widely cited and widely discrepant estimates of the number of words in written American English reveals a serious lack of agreement.

## 3. Knowing Words to Various Degrees

It is recognized that word knowledge exists on a continuum from not knowing a word at all to knowing it thoroughly (Beck, McKeown, & Kucan, 2002). It is also recognized that knowing a word well includes various abilities:

> [It] involves depth of meaning; precision of meaning; facile access (think of scrabble and crossword puzzle experts); the ability to articulate one's understanding; flexibility in the application of the knowledge of a word; the appreciation of metaphor, analogy, word play; the ability to recognize a synonym, to define, to use a word expressively. (Calfee & Drum, 1986, pp. 825–826).

And it is recognized that we know different words in different ways; for example, that knowledge of an article like *the* is quite different from knowledge of a noun like *tractor* (Nagy & Scott, 2000).

What we do not have is a scale of depth of word knowledge, some agreed upon metric that would allow us to quantify the depth of knowledge that students have about various words.

## 4. The Vocabularies of Average and Above-Average Students

Since there are marked differences in estimates of the number of words that exist, it should come as no surprise that there are marked differences in estimates of the number of words students know. At the low end are Dupuy's (1974) estimate of 7,000 "basic words" for average 12th graders, Biemiller's (2005) estimate of 10,000 "root words" at the end of Grade 6, and Goulden, Nation, & Read's (1990) estimate of 17,000 "base words" for university graduates. At the high end, are Nagy and Herman's (1987) estimate of 40,000 "word families" for high school seniors, a figure recently endorsed by Stahl and Nagy (2006), and Anderson and Nagy's (1992) estimate of 80,000 distinct vocabulary items for high school seniors. Although these discrepancies can be to some extent explained by considering the assumptions and procedures the researchers used in making them, they cannot really be reconciled. The number of words that average and above-average students learn, and therefore the size of the vocabulary learning task students face, remains a matter of debate.

## 5. Vocabulary Deficit Faced by Many Children

While the size of the vocabulary learning task that students face is a matter of considerable debate, the fact that many linguistically less advantaged students have vocabularies far smaller than those of their linguistically more advantaged classmates is not. In an early review of research on learning from listening and reading, Carroll (1971) concluded that "much of the failure of individuals to understand speech or writing beyond an elementary level is due to deficiencies in vocabulary knowledge" (p. 175).

In an influential article published some years later, Becker (1977) considered what we have learned from both the failures and successes of Project Follow Through, the massive federal program designed to test ways of improving first- through third-grade disadvantaged students' basic and cognitive skills. These results indicated that of nine Follow Through projects, only children who participated in the Direct Instruction approach performed above the expectations in reading and that they did so only on a decoding test. The Direct Instruction students did not score above expectations on tests of word meaning and comprehension. Becker attributes this failure to the fact that both Direct Instruction and schools in general "fail to provide instruction in the building blocks crucial to intelligent functioning, namely, words and their referents" (p. 533).

Somewhat more recently, two colleagues and I (White, Graves, & Slater, 1990) investigated the vocabularies of first- through fourth-grade students in three schools—a suburban school enrolling middle-class White students who spoke standard English; an inner-city school enrolling lower SES, dialect-speaking Black students; and a semirural school enrolling lower SES, dialect-speaking Asian/Pacific students. Results showed that fourth graders in the two lower SES schools knew about 13,000 words while those in the middle-class school knew about 19,000 words. Results further showed that in Grades 1 to 3 the rate of vocabulary growth for middle-class students was about one and a half times that for lower SES students.

At this same time, Chall, Jacobs, and Baldwin (1990; see also Chall & Jacobs, 2003) published their study of why and when poor children fall behind in school. What they found is that the low-income children in their study did about as well as the general population in Grades 2 and 3, but began to fall behind in Grade 4 and continued to fall further behind in Grades 5 and 6. The first and strongest factor to show a decline was knowledge of word meaning. By the end of Grade 4, the low-income children had fallen about a year behind, and by the end of Grade 6, they had fallen about 2 years behind. As Chall and Jacobs (2003) note, these children had particular difficulty defining "more abstract, academic, literary, and less common words" (p. 14).

More recently, Hart and Risley (1995; see also 2003) published their longitudinal study of the vocabularies of 1- to 3-year-old children of professional, working-class, and welfare families. Their results indicated that at age 3 the vocabularies of the children of professional parents averaged about 1,100 words, those of the children of working-class families averaged about 700 words, and those of the children of welfare families averaged about 500 words. Their results also showed that by the time they were 3, the children from the welfare families had heard 30 million fewer words than had those from the professional families.

As noted at the beginning of this section, the fact that many children of poverty, English-language learners, and poor readers have small vocabularies is widely recognized and well documented. What we do not know with any precision is the range of deficits that different students face.

## CONCEPTUAL AND EMPIRICAL SUPPORT FOR THE FOUR-PART VOCABULARY PROGRAM

Here I consider just how strong the evidence supporting each of the four parts of the vocabulary program is.

### 1. Rich, Varied, and Extensive Language Experiences

Again, this part of the program includes two subparts. In the first subpart, all students are involved in rich and varied experiences in listening, reading, writing, and discussion at all grade levels. Hart and Risley's (1995, 2003) study of preschool children provides strong evidence for the effects of listening and discussion on children's vocabularies. As noted, by the time they were 3 years old, welfare children had heard 30 million fewer words than children from professional families and as a result knew less than half as many words. More specifically, Hart and Risley found that from birth to age 3 professional families address approximately 40 million words to their children, while welfare families address approximately 10 million words to their children. Listening to stories read aloud has also been shown to produce vocabulary gains in young, school-age children who could not yet read themselves (Robbins & Ehri, 1994; Senechal & Cornell, 1993), as well as in older children who were readers (Elley, 1989; Senechal, Lefevre, Hudson, & Lawson, 1996). Finally, Nagy and his colleagues (Nagy, Anderson, & Herman, 1987; Nagy, Herman, & Anderson, 1985) have demonstrated that students do learn vocabulary from context when reading themselves, and Cunningham and Stanovich (e.g., Cunningham & Stanovich 1991, 2003; Stanovich & Cunningham, 1992, 1993) have found that reading volume is "a very powerful predictor of vocabulary and knowledge differences" (Cunningham, 2005, p. 61). Although I know of no studies investigating the effects of writing or classroom discussion on vocabulary growth, given the effects of these other language experiences, it seems very likely that writing and classroom discussion also produce vocabulary gains.

In the second subpart, linguistically less advantaged primary-grade children engage in a systematic program of shared storybook reading. The effectiveness of shared storybook reading is supported by a number of studies conducted over more than 15 years (e.g., Beals, De Temple, & Dickinson; 1994; Biemiller & Slonim, 2006; Wasic & Bond, 2001; Whitehurst et al., 1988). As a result, we not only know that shared storybook reading works, we know a good deal about the characteristics of effective shared storybook reading. Drawing on both the work of De Temple and Snow (2003) and my own (Graves, 2006) synthesis of the literature, I can state that effective shared storybook reading

- Is interactive; that is, both the reader and the children play active roles.
- Usually involves reading the book several times.
- Directly focuses children's attention on a relatively small number of words.
- Requires adult readers to read fluently, with appropriate intonation, and with expression.
- Requires carefully selected books. The books need to be interesting and enjoyable for children, stretch children's thinking a bit, and of course include some challenging and worthwhile words.
- May involve nonimmediate talk interspersed with the oral reading. As defined by De Temple and Snow (2003), "nonimmediate talk is that talk produced by mother or child which goes beyond the information contained in the text or illustrations to make predictions; to make connections to the child's past experience, other books, or the real world; to draw inferences, analyze information, or discuss the meanings of words and offer explanations" (p. 21).

Despite our very full knowledge about shared storybook reading and its effectiveness, there is one very serious shortcoming in the literature. The existing studies involve students in shared storybook reading over relatively short time periods, weeks or months. In order to markedly lessen the vocabulary deficit that linguistically less advantaged students face—thousands of words—instruction would need to extend over several years.

## 2. Teaching Individual Words

There is a large, robust, easily interpretable, and very consistent body of research on teaching individual words. There are also a number of important summaries of the research on vocabulary instruction. In the remainder of this section, I offer a series of research-based generalizations. In organizing the generalizations, I proceed from considering effects that can be achieved by brief and relatively shallow instruction to effects that can be achieved from more lengthy and more robust instruction.

### Providing at Least Minimal Vocabulary Instruction

Some vocabulary instruction is better than no instruction (Baumann, Edwards, Boland, Olejnik, & Kame'enui, 2003; Petty, Herold, & Stoll, 1967). Although this is a commonsense finding, it is not a trivial one. It means that vocabulary instruction typically works. However, thin instruction—for example, giving students a set of words and asking them to look up the words in the dictionary, or giving them a set of words and their definitions—only serves to teach the basic meanings of the words. That is, simply giving students definitions of words will not result in their learning rich and full meanings, is unlikely to improve their comprehension of the text from which the words were selected, and is unlikely to result in their actively using the words in their speech or writing.

In one study involving thin instruction, Parker (1984) pretaught sixth-, seventh-, and eighth-grade students 10 words out of two short social studies selections over a 2-day period and tested them the day after they received the instruction and 3 weeks later. As part of the study, he compared a dictionary definition treatment in which students simply looked up the words in a dictionary and wrote out their definitions to no instruction. Results indicated that students receiving the dictionary treatment scored about twice as well as the control group immediately after the instruction and about 50% better than the control group 3 weeks later. Although Parker tested students 3 weeks after the instruction, most of the research that employs thin instruction is short-term and tests students knowledge of the words taught within a few days or a week of the instruction. Whether or not students forget many of the words learned from thin instruction over time is a definite question.

## Incorporating Definitional and Contextual Information

Instruction that incorporates both definitional information and contextual information is likely to be stronger than instruction incorporating only one sort of information (Mezynski, 1983; Stahl & Fairbanks, 1986). While simply having students work with definitions of words can improve their word knowledge, giving them both definitional information and contextual information has repeatedly proved a stronger approach. In fact, except in situations where there are far too many unknown words in an upcoming selection to teach and you are forced to do something like giving students a glossary, using a procedure that gives students both definitional and contextual information is the thinnest approach I recommend.

In a study involving several sorts of instruction, Stahl (1983) worked with fifth graders and compared the results of a definition-only treatment, a definition-plus-context treatment, and no instruction. In the definition treatment, students looked up words in the dictionary, wrote definitions of the words, and discussed their meanings. In the definition-plus-context treatment, students also worked with context. And in the no vocabulary treatment, students simply took the pre- and posttests. Results indicated that the definition treatment was superior to no instruction but that the definition plus context treatments was superior to no instruction and to definitions alone.

## Activating Prior Knowledge and Comparing and Contrasting Word Meanings

Instruction that involves activating prior knowledge and comparing and contrasting word meanings is likely to be more powerful than simple combinations of contextual information and definitions (Baumann, Kame'enui, & Ash, 2003; Beck & McKeown, 1991). Not only is instruction that involves activating prior knowledge and comparing and contrasting word meanings a powerful approach to teaching word meanings, but such instruction has also been shown to improve comprehension of selections containing the words taught.

The best known and most widely researched techniques falling in this category are semantic mapping (Heimlich & Pittelman, 1986) and semantic feature analysis (Pittelman, Heimlich, Berglund, & French, 1991). In a study of semantic mapping with third-, fourth-, and fifth-grade students, Johnson, Toms-Bronowski, and Pittelman (1982) found that students receiving semantic-mapping instruction significantly outperformed students in a context group on both immediate and delayed measures. In investigating the effects of semantic feature analysis, Anders, Bos, and Filip (1984) found that high school students with learning disabilities learned more vocabulary and better comprehended a social studies passage containing the taught vocabulary than did students who looked up words in the dictionary and wrote out their definitions.

### Providing Lengthy and Robust Instruction

Instruction that involves active learning, inferences, prior knowledge, and frequent encounters is likely to be more powerful than less time-consuming and less robust instruction (Beck, McKeown, & Kucan, 2002; Nagy, 2005). While semantic mapping and semantic feature analysis are quite robust sorts of instruction, Beck and McKeown and their colleagues have developed, refined, and repeatedly tested several forms of rich vocabulary instruction that involves students in extensive and varied experiences with words (Beck & McKeown, in press; Beck, Perfetti, & McKeown, 1982; McKeown, Beck, Omanson, & Perfetti, 1983; McKeown, Beck, Omanson, & Pople, 1985).

In the initial study in the sequence (Beck et al., 1982), fourth-grade students from an urban school were taught 104 words over a period of 5 months. The words were grouped into semantic sets (for example, the People set included the words *accomplice, virtuoso, rival, miser, philanthropist, novice, hermit,* and *tyrant*), with each set taught over a 5-day cycle that included many varied activities. On day one of a cycle, students were introduced to the words, wrote the words and their definitions in their logbooks, and used the words in one or two ways. On day two, students generated sentences for each word and did a fairly easy activity that involved word meaning. On day three, they generated contexts in which the new words could be used. On day four, they did speeded trials with the words in a gamelike situation. On day five, they took a multiple-choice test on the words. Outside of class, attention to the words was motivated by a gamelike activity in which students received points for bringing in evidence that they had seen, heard, or used the target words outside of class. In all, students received 10–18 encounters with some words and 26–40 encounters with others. Results indicated that as compared to noninstructed students, instructed students learned the words better, were faster and more accurate in timed responses to the words, and demonstrated marginal gains in comprehension. Results also showed that more encounters with the words produced more learning.

A later study, McKeown et al. (1983), showed that instructed students demonstrated substantially better comprehension of passages containing the taught words compared to noninstructed students. And a still later one, McKeown et al. (1985), showed that 12 encounters produced stronger results than 4 encounters and that students who also used the words outside of the classroom learned them more fully that those who did not.

As noted at the beginning of this section, the research on teaching individual words is robust and easily interpretable. Vocabulary can be taught and learned, and if it is taught well, comprehension can be improved. However, there is a limitation to the research in that virtually all of it has been undertaken to answer the question "How can we make vocabulary instruction more effective?" without consideration of the time it takes to provide robust vocabulary instruction—up to 30 minutes per word. Given the number of words that students need to learn, we need more information on less robust instruction, instruction that would only start students on the road to full knowledge of the words taught but that can be delivered in much shorter amounts of time.

## 3. Teaching Word-Learning Strategies

As noted, the most important strategies taught in the program are using context to infer word meanings, using word parts to deduce word meanings, using the dictionary, and (for Spanish-speaking ELLs) taking advantage of Spanish cognates in learning English vocabulary. There is considerable research on using context and word parts, none that I am aware of on using the dictionary, and some on working with cognates.

As Sternberg (1987) has pointed out and as most authorities agree, "most vocabulary is learned from context" (p. 89). No other explanation seems able to account for the huge number of words students learn. There is a substantial body of research showing that students can indeed learn from context (e.g., see Swanborn & de Glopper, 1999), and there are several estimates about the likelihood of learning a word from encountering it in written context.

In one study, Nagy, Anderson, and Herman (1987) found that the probability of students' learning a word well enough to answer a multiple-choice question was .05; and in their meta-analysis, Swanborn and de Glopper (1999) found that the probability of learning a word was .15. It is worth noting, however, that Nagy et al. (1987) also found that "there was simply no learning from context for words at the highest level of conceptual difficulty" (p. 225).

More generally, the research on learning from context has revealed that context can produce learning of word meanings, that the probability of learning a word from a single occurrence is low, and that the probability of learning a word from context increases substantially with additional occurrences of the word. That is how we typically learn from context. We learn a little from the first encounter with a word and then more and more about a word's meaning as we meet it in new and different contexts.

While there is solid evidence that students can and do learn word meanings from context, as Baumann and his colleagues (Bauman, Font, Edwards,

& Boland, 2005) point out, not all instruction in using context clues has been successful. In fact, teaching students to use context clues is a challenging task. There have been a number of studies of successful instruction (e.g., Baumann, Edwards, et al. 2003; Baumann, Edwards, Font, Tereshinski, Kame'enui, & Olejnik, 2002; Buikema & Graves, 1993; Carnine, Kameenui, & Coyle, 1984; Patberg, Graves, & Stibbe, 1984), and Fukkink and de Glopper's 1998 meta-analysis of 21 studies indicated that instruction in context clues does have a positive effect. At the same time, not all studies have indicated successful instruction. For example, a follow-up to the Patberg, Graves, and Stibbe (1984) study designed to strengthen the instruction failed to show positive results (Patberg & Stibbe, 1985). Somewhat similarly, in Baumann and his colleagues' second study (Baumann, Edwards, et al., 2003), context instruction produced positive results on a delayed posttest but not on the immediate posttest. Still needed then are studies of context clue instruction that repeatedly produce solid results.

The evidence for the efficacy of teaching word parts, at least prefixes and suffixes, is stronger. Studies by Graves and Hammond (1980), Nicol, Graves, and Slater (1984), Wysocki and Jenkins (1987), and White, Sowell, and Yanagihara (1989) have clearly demonstrated the efficacy of teaching prefixes and/or suffixes. The recent studies of teaching context clues by Baumann and his colleagues cited above also taught prefixes and suffixes and once again showed that students can learn to use these elements to unlock the meanings of novel words (Baumann et al., 2002; Baumann, Edwards, et al. 2003). I know of no convincing studies of the efficacy of teaching Latin and Greek roots, and one important question that needs to be answered before the efficacy of teaching roots can be fully evaluated is which roots are worthy of instruction.

As noted, I know of no research specifically on teaching students to effectively use the dictionary. Obviously, such research is needed.

Some time ago Garcia and Nagy (1993) and Nagy, Garcia, Durgunoglu, and Hancin-Bhatt (1993) presented results suggesting the efficacy of teaching Spanish-speaking children about the use of cognates in learning English words. Moreover, it has been estimated that up to 20% of English words have Spanish cognates (Bernhardt & Kamil, 1998). However, there has been very little instructional research that actually attempts to teach Spanish-speaking students to use cognates. In a very well designed vocabulary program that included instruction in using cognates, The Vocabulary Improvement Project, Carlo and her colleagues (2004) showed that a multifaceted vocabulary program resulted in students making gains on a number of vocabulary measures and on one measure of comprehension. It is important to recognize that instruction in using cognates was only one facet of this multifaceted program and thus cannot be identified as a causal factor. Additional research on using cognates is clearly needed, and at least one such study is currently underway (Carlo & August, 2005).

## 4. Fostering Word Consciousness

As I have noted, the term *word consciousness* refers to an awareness of and interest in words and their meanings. Approaches to fostering word consciousness can take a variety of forms and can range from brief and informal activities to more time-consuming and formal activities. At the brief end of the continuum are activities such as teachers using adept word choices themselves, complimenting students when they use adept word choices, and encouraging students to read word play books. At the more time-consuming end of the continuum are activities such as involving students in investigations of word usage, for example, comparing the vocabulary used in an article on an upcoming election in a high school newspaper to that used in an article on the same topic in *The New York Times*.

Fostering word consciousness is the most recently developed component of the four-part vocabulary program and a relatively recent construct generally. Nevertheless, it is widely endorsed (see e.g., Anderson & Nagy, 1992; Baumann & Kame'enui, 2004; Beck, McKeown, & Kucan, 2002; Stahl & Nagy, 2006). Several sorts of evidence provide support fostering word consciousness.

One sort of evidence is the importance of motivation to all learning and for all students, from kindergarteners (Pressley et al., 2003) to high school seniors (National Research Council, 2004). Students simply do not learn much unless they are motivated to do so, and if they are going to accomplish the huge task of learning something like 50,000 words by the time they graduate from high school, they absolutely must be motivated to do so.

Another sort of evidence comes from a logical argument for the importance of metalinguistic awareness recently made by Nagy (2007). *Metalinguistic awareness* is the ability to recognize and reflect on various features of language, in this case features of words. It is one part of word consciousness. Students who have metalinguistic awareness of words recognize such features of words as their morphological makeup, their appropriateness in various contexts, and the way definitions function to define words. According to Nagy, a significant part of the relationship between vocabulary and reading comprehension may involve metalinguistic awareness, and some of the more powerful studies of vocabulary instruction may owe a large part of their success to fostering this type of word consciousness.

Still another sort of evidence comes from vocabulary studies. In a series of relatively informal studies undertaken over a 7-year term, Scott and her colleagues (Scott, Butler, & Asselin, 1996; Scott & Nagy, 2004; Scott & Wells,

1998) investigated the effects of a project called The Gift of Words in which they provided students with an enriched focus on words in their reading, writing, and discussion. Results supported the effectiveness of this program on students' use of interesting words in their writing and on students' awareness and interest in words more generally. In another set of related studies—these by different researchers—word consciousness was one part of multifaceted vocabulary programs designed to improve students' reading vocabulary and reading comprehension (Beck, McKeown, & Omanson, 1987; Beck et al., 1982; McKeown et al., 1983), students' use of vocabulary in their writing (Duin & Graves, 1987), and English learners' general proficiency in vocabulary (Carlo et al., 2004). All of these programs produced strong positive results.

In summary, while word consciousness is a recently articulated concept and does not have an extensive research base, experts in the field, the importance of motivation to learning, and several studies support including it as a significant component of the vocabulary curriculum. Unfortunately, the studies are either relatively informal such as those of Scott and her colleagues or confound activities designed to foster word consciousness with many other types of activities as do Beck and McKeown and their colleagues. What is needed are studies that isolate the unique effects of word consciousness activities and clearly show them to produce gains in word knowledge.

## HOW STRONG AN ENDORSEMENT OF THE FOUR-PART PROGRAM DOES THE EVIDENCE ALLOW?

The evidence constitutes strong support for the four-part vocabulary program I have described and for vocabulary instruction more generally. However, this does not mean that the support is as strong as it could be or that we have all of the evidence necessary to create an optimal program of vocabulary instruction. Here I briefly critique the evidence in support of each of the five assumptions behind the program and each of the four parts of the program, noting in each case what sort of research most needs to be done.

- There is strong evidence that vocabulary knowledge is important—as an index of verbal ability, as a predictor of success in school, as a factor influencing readability of text, as a factor that can improve reading comprehension, and to success in and out of school. What is most needed is additional causal evidence showing that teaching vocabulary improves comprehension.
- Some studies estimate the number of words in written American English at less than 20,000 while others estimate it as something like

180,000. Although I believe that the evidence favors the larger estimate, studies that would produce an estimate on which there is broad agreement would be very useful.

- While there is broad agreement that students know words to varying degrees, a measure of depth of word knowledge is much needed.
- Estimates of the number of words known by high school seniors range from 7,000 to 80,000. Although I believe that the evidence favors the larger estimates, studies that would produce an estimate on which there is broad agreement would be extremely useful.
- The evidence that many children of poverty, ELLs, and poor readers have vocabularies markedly smaller than many linguistically more advantaged students is clear, compelling, and widely accepted. What we do not know is the range of vocabulary deficits that different students face.
- There is substantial evidence that listening and reading produce gains in word knowledge and that shared storybook reading is an effective short-term intervention. What has not been documented are the effects of writing, classroom discussion, and long-term shared storybook reading.
- There is substantial evidence on the positive effects of robust vocabulary instruction, instruction that requires a substantial amount of time for each word that is learned. What we need is more research on the effects of less robust and less time-consuming instruction, instruction that is much more feasible given the number of words to be learned.
- There is substantial evidence for the effectiveness of teaching prefixes and suffixes, less consistent evidence on the effects of teaching context clues, only one completed study I am aware of on teaching Spanish-speaking students to use cognates in learning English vocabulary, and no studies I am aware of on teaching students to use the dictionary. What is needed is research on how to teach context so that it consistently produces positive effects, how to teach roots and which roots are worth teaching, how to teach using cognates, and how to teach using the dictionary.
- The efficacy of fostering word consciousness is supported by the substantial literature testifying to the importance of motivation in all learning, by the argument for the importance of metalinguistic awareness, by relatively informal studies, and by formal studies that included word consciousness as one of many instructional components. What is needed are studies that identify and isolate word consciousness instruction and clearly show that it produces vocabulary gains.

## CONCLUDING REMARKS

In summarizing the results of their review of research on vocabulary instruction completed in 1967, Petty and his colleagues were forced to admit that "the teaching profession seems to know little of substance about the teaching of vocabulary" (p. 84). This is clearly no longer the case. There is a wealth of creditable research on vocabulary and vocabulary instruction, and much of it supports the four-part program outlined in this chapter and vocabulary instruction more generally. Still, there is much yet to be learned. One of the most practical questions we need to answer is that of how much time should be devoted to vocabulary instruction. Obviously, vocabulary instruction must compete with many other worthwhile aspects of the literacy curriculum as well as with other important subjects such as social studies, math, and science. Consequently, we must spend only as much time on vocabulary as is necessary.

Toward that end, in an earlier paper (Graves, 2000) I suggested that with the exception of wide reading (which is done for a variety of purposes and which therefore need not be considered as time spent on vocabulary), the four-part program outlined here could be accomplished in about an hour a week. In concluding this chapter, I want to qualify that claim. For linguistically advantaged students, the four-part program outlined here can indeed be accomplished in about an hour a week. However, for many children of poverty, English-language learners, and poor readers—children who know thousands of fewer words than do their more linguistically advantaged peers—vocabulary instruction needs to be a considerably larger part of the curriculum. At a minimum, I suspect, instruction that is likely to markedly assist these students in catching up with their peers is likely to require something like 30 minutes of instruction daily. Moreover, many linguistically less advantaged students will need this amount of instruction over a period of some years.

### Follow-up Activities

1. Identify a grade level and characterize the group of struggling readers you are working with. Rank the four parts of the vocabulary program described in the chapter in terms of the amount of emphasis you would give to each for this group of readers, and justify your rankings.
2. Again identify a grade level and characterize the group of struggling readers you are working with. This can be the group you previously described or another one. Assume that you have 30 minutes a day for vocabulary instruction. Discuss how you will spend those 30 minutes.
3. Identify one of the four parts of the vocabulary program described here that you think is particularly important. Explain why you think

this part is particularly important. Describe the activities you would undertake in providing instruction on this part of the program during a typical week.

*Acknowlegment.* James Baumann's excellent review, "Vocabulary-Comprehension Relationships" (2005), was particularly helpful in framing parts of the argument for the importance of vocabulary.

## REFERENCES

Anders, P. L., Bos, C. S., & Filip, D. (1984). The effect of semantic feature analysis on learning disabled students. In J. A. Niles & L. A. Harris (Eds.), *Yearbook of the National Reading Conference: Vol. 33. Changing perspectives in research on reading/language processing and instruction* (pp. 162–166). Rochester, NY: National Reading Conference.

Anderson, R. C., & Freebody, P. (1981). Vocabulary knowledge. In J. T. Guthrie (Ed.), *Comprehension and teaching: Research reviews* (pp. 77–117). Newark, DE: International Reading Association.

Anderson, R. C., & Nagy, W. E. (1992). The vocabulary conundrum. *American Educator, 16*(4), 14–18, 44–47.

Barr, M., Kamil, P., Mosenthal, P., & Pearson, P. D. (Eds.). (1991). *Handbook of reading research: Vol. 2.* White Plains, NY: Longman.

Baumann, J. F. (2005). Vocabulary-comprehension relationships. In B. Maloch, J. V. Hoffman, D. L. Schallert, C. M. Fairbanks, & J. Worthy (Eds.), *Yearbook of the National Reading Conference: Vol. 54* (pp. 117–131). Oak Creek, WI: National Reading Conference.

Baumann, J. F., Edwards, E. C., Boland E., Olejnik, S., & Kame'enui, E. J. (2003). Vocabulary tricks. Effects of instruction in morphology and context on fifth-grade students' ability to derive and infer word meaning. *American Educational Research Journal, 40,* 447–494.

Baumann, J. F., Edwards, E. C., Font, G., Tereshinski, C. A., Kame'enui, E. J., & Olejnik, S. (2002). Teaching morphemic and contextual analysis to fifth-grade students. *Reading Research Quarterly, 37,* 150–176.

Baumann, J. F., Font, G., Edwards, E. C., & Boland, E. (2005). Strategies for teaching middle-grade students to use word-part and context clues to expand reading vocabulary. In E. Hiebert & M. L. Kamil (Eds.), *Teaching and learning vocabulary: Bringing research to practice* (pp. 179–205). Mahwah, NJ: Erlbaum.

Baumann, J. F., & Kame'enui, E. J. (Eds.). (2004). *Vocabulary instruction: Research to practice.* New York: Guilford Press.

Baumann, J. F., Kame'enui, E. J., & Ash, G. E. (2003). Research on vocabulary instruction: Voltaire redux. In J. Flood, D. Lapp, J. R. Squire, & J. M. Jensen (Eds.), *Handbook on research on teaching the English language arts* (2nd ed., pp. 752–785). Mahwah, NJ: Erlbaum.

Beals, D. E., De Temple, J. M., & Dickinson, D. K. (1994). Talking and listening that support early literacy development of children from low-income families. In D. K. Dickinson (Ed.), *Bridges to literacy: Children, families, and schools* (pp. 19–40). Cambridge, MA: Blackwell.

Beck, I. L., & McKeown, M. G. (1991). Conditions of vocabulary acquisition. In P. D. Pearson (Ed.), *The handbook of reading research, Vol. 2*. New York: Longman.

Beck, I. L., & McKeown, M. G. (in press). Increasing young children's oral vocabulary repertoires through rich and focused instruction. *Elementary School Journal*.

Beck, I. L., McKeown, M. G., & Kucan, L. (2002). *Bringing words to life: Robust vocabulary instruction*. New York: Guilford Press

Beck, I. L, McKeown, M. G., & Omanson, R. C. (1987). The effects and uses of diverse vocabulary instructional techniques. In M. G. McKeown & M. E. Curtis (Eds.), *The nature of vocabulary acquisition* (pp. 147–163). Hillsdale, NJ: Erlbaum.

Beck, I. L., Perfetti, C. A., & McKeown, M. G. (1982). The effects of long-term vocabulary instruction on lexical access and reading comprehension. *Journal of Educational Psychology, 74*, 506–521.

Becker, W. C. (1977). Teaching reading and language to the disadvantaged—What we have learned from field research. *Harvard Educational Review, 47*, 511–543.

Bernhardt, E. B., & Kamil, M. L. (1998). Literacy instruction for non-native speakers of English. In M. F. Graves, C. Juel, & B. B. Graves, *Teaching reading in the 21st century* (pp.432–475). Boston: Allyn & Bacon.

Biemiller, A. (2004). Teaching vocabulary in the primary grades: Vocabulary instruction needed. In J. F. Baumann & E. J. Kame'enui (Eds.), *Vocabulary instruction: Research to practice* (pp. 28–40). New York: Guilford Press.

Biemiller, A. (2005). Size and sequence in vocabulary development: Implications for choosing words for primary grade vocabulary instruction. In E. H. Hiebert & M. L. Kamil (Eds.), *Teaching and learning vocabulary* (pp. 223–242). Mahwah, NJ: Erlbaum.

Biemiller, A., & Slonim, N. (2001). Estimating root word and normative vocabulary growth in normative and advanced populations: Evidence for a common sequence of vocabulary acquisition. *Journal of Educational Psychology, 93*, 498–520.

Biemiller, A., & Slonim, N. (2006). An effective method for building meaning vocabulary in the primary grades. *Journal of Educational Psychology, 98*, 44–62.

Buikema, J. A., & Graves, M. F. (1993). Teaching students to use context cues to infer word meanings. *Journal of Reading, 36*, 450–457.

Calfee, R. C., & Drum, P. A. (1978). Learning to read: Theory, research, and practice. *Curriculum Inquiry, 8*, 183–249.

Calfee, R. C., & Drum, P. A. (1986). Research on teaching reading. In M. D. Wittrock (Ed.), *Handbook of research on teaching* (3rd ed., pp. 804–849). New York: Macmillan.

Carlo, M. S., & August, D. (2005, June). *Building bridges for understanding: Reading success for English language learners*. Paper presented at the University of California, Berkeley Summer Institute on Reading, Berkeley, CA.

Carlo, M. S., August, D., McGlaughlin, B., Snow, C. E., Dressler, C., Lippman, D. N., et al. (2004). Closing the gap: Addressing the vocabulary needs of English-language learners in bilingual and mainstream classes. *Reading Research Quarterly, 39*, 188–215.

Carnine, D., Kameenui, E. J., & Coyle, G. (1984). Utilization of contextual information in determining the meaning of unfamiliar words in context. *Reading Research Quarterly, 19*, 188–202.

Carroll, J. B. (1971). *Learning from verbal discourse in educational media. A review of the literature.* Princeton, NJ: Educational Testing Service.

Carroll, J. B., Davies, P., & Richmann, B. (1971). *The American Heritage word frequency book.* New York: Houghton Mifflin.

Cassidy, J., & Cassidy, D. (2005/06). What's hot, what's not for 2006. *Reading Today, 23*(3), 1.

Chall, J. S., & Jacobs, V. A. (2003). The classic study on poor children's fourth-grade slump. *American Educator, 27*(1), 14–15, 44.

Chall, J. S., Jacobs, V. A., & Baldwin, L. E. (1990). *The reading crisis: Why poor children fall behind.* Cambridge, MA: Harvard University Press.

Clifford, G. J. (1978). Words for schools: The applications in education of the vocabulary researches of Edward L. Thorndike. In P. Suppes (Ed.), *Impact of research on education: Some case studies* (pp. 107–198). Washington, DC: National Academy of Education.

Cunningham, A. E. (2005). Vocabulary growth through independent reading and reading aloud to Children. In E. H. Hiebert & M. Kamil (Eds.), *Teaching and learning vocabulary: Bringing research to practice* (pp. 45–68). Mahwah, NJ: Erlbaum.

Cunningham, A. E., & Stanovich, K. E. (1991). Tracking the unique effects of print exposure in children: Associations with vocabulary, general knowledge, and spelling. *Journal of Educational Psychology, 83*, 264–274.

Cunningham, A. E., & Stanovich, K. E. (2003). Reading matters: How reading English influences cognition. In J. Flood, D. Lapp, J. R. Squire, & J. M. Jensen (Eds.), *Handbook of teaching the English language arts* (2nd ed., pp. 666–675). Mahwah, NJ: Erlbaum.

Dale, E., & O'Rourke, J. (1981). *The living word vocabulary.* Chicago: World Book–Childcraft.

Davis, F. B. (1944). Fundamental factors in reading comprehension. *Psychometrika, 9*, 185–197.

Davis, F. B. (1968). Research in comprehension in reading. *Reading Research Quarterly, 3*, 499–545.

Davis, F. B. (1972). Psychometric research on comprehension in reading. *Reading Research Quarterly, 7*, 628–678.

De Temple, J., & Snow, C. E. (2003). Learning words from books. In A. van Kleeck, S. A. Stahl, & E. B. Bauer (Eds.), *On reading books to children* (pp. 16–36). Mahwah, NJ: Erlbaum.

Duin, A. H., & Graves, M. F. (1987). The effects of intensive vocabulary instruction on expository writing. *Reading Research Quarterly, 22,* 311–330.

Dupuy, H. (1974). *The rationale, development, and standardization of a basic word vocabulary test* (DHEW Publication NO. HRA74-1334). Washington, DC: U.S. Government Printing Office.

Elley, W. B. (1989). Vocabulary acquisition from listening to stories. *Reading Research Quarterly, 24,* 174–187.

Fukkink, R. G., & de Glopper, K. (1998). Effects of instruction in deriving word meanings from context: A meta-analysis. *Review of Educational Research, 68,* 450–469.

Garcia, G. E., & Nagy, W. E. (1993). Latino students' concepts of cognates. In D. J. Leu & C. K. Kinzer (Eds.), *Examining central issues in literacy research, theory, and practice* (pp. 361–373). Chicago: National Reading Conference.

Goulden, R., Nation, P., & Read, J. (1990). How large can a receptive vocabulary be? *Applied Linguistics, 11,* 341–363.

Graves, M. F. (1984). Selecting vocabulary to teach in the intermediate and secondary grades. In J. Flood (Ed.), *Understanding reading comprehension* (pp. 245–260). Newark, DE: International Reading Association.

Graves, M. F. (1987). The role of instruction in vocabulary development. In M. G. McKeown & M. E. Curtis (Eds.), *The nature of vocabulary acquisition* (pp. 165–184). Hillsdale, NJ: Erlbaum.

Graves, M. F. (1992). The elementary vocabulary curriculum: What should it be? In M. J. Dreher & W. H. Slater (Eds.), *Elementary school literacy: Critical issues* (pp. 101–131). Norwood, MA: Christopher-Gordon.

Graves, M. F. (2000). A vocabulary program to complement and bolster a middle-grade comprehension program. In B. M. Taylor, M. F. Graves, & P. van den Broek (Eds.), *Reading for meaning: Fostering comprehension in the middle grades* (pp. 116–135). New York: Teachers College Press.

Graves, M. F. (2004). Teaching prefixes: As good as it gets? In J. F. Baumann & E. B. Kame'enui (Eds.), *Vocabulary instruction: Research to practice* (pp. 81–99). New York: Guilford Press.

Graves, M. F. (2006). *The vocabulary book: Learning and instruction.* New York: Teachers College Press, International Reading Association, National Council of Teachers of English.

Graves, M. F., & Fitzgerald, J. (2006). Effective vocabulary instruction for English language learners. In C. C. Block & J. N. Mangieri (Eds.), *The vocabulary-enriched classroom: Practices for improving the reading performance of all students in grades 3 and up* (pp. 118–137). New York: Scholastic.

Graves, M. F., & Hammond, H. K. (1980). A validated procedure for teaching prefixes and its effect on students' ability to assign meaning to novel words. In M. L. Kamil & A. J. Moe (Eds.), *Perspectives on reading research and instruction* (pp. 184–188). Washington, DC: National Reading Conference.

Graves, M. F., & Watts, S. M. (2002). The place of word consciousness in a research-based vocabulary program. In S. J. Samuels & A. E. Farstrup (Eds.), *What research has to say about reading instruction* (3rd ed., pp. 140–165). Newark, DE: International Reading Association.

Hart, B., & Risley, T. R. (1995). *Meaningful differences in the everyday experience of young American children.* Baltimore: Brookes.

Hart, B., & Risley, T. R. (2003). The early catastrophe: The 30 million word gap. *American Educator, 27*(1), 4–9.

Heimlich, J. E., & Pittelman, S. D. (1986). *Semantic mapping: Classroom applications.* Newark, DE: International Reading Association.

Hiebert, E. H., & Kamil, M. L. (Eds.). (2005). *Teaching and learning vocabulary: Bringing research to practice.* Mahwah, NJ: Erlbaum.

Johnson, D. D., Toms-Bronowski, S., & Pittelman, S. D. (1982). *An investigation of the effectiveness of semantic mapping and semantic feature analysis with intermediate grade level children* (Program Report No. 83–3). Madison, WI: Wisconsin Center for Education Research.

Klare, G. R. (1974–75). Assessing readability. *Reading Research Quarterly, 10,* 62–102.

Klare, G. R. (1984). Readability. In P. D. Pearson, R. Barr, M. L. Kamil, & P. Mosenthal (Eds.), *Handbook of reading research* (pp. 681–794). New York: Longman.

McKeown, M. G., Beck, I. L., Omanson, R. C., & Perfetti, C. A. (1983). The effects of long-term vocabulary instruction on reading comprehension: A replication. *Journal of Reading Behavior, 15,* 3–18.

McKeown, M. G., Beck, I. L., Omanson, R. C., & Pople, M. T. (1985). Some effects of the nature and frequency of vocabulary instruction on the knowledge and use of words. *Reading Research Quarterly, 20,* 522–535.

Mezynski, K. (1983). Issues concerning the acquisition of knowledge: Effects of vocabulary training on reading comprehension. *Review of Educational Research, 53,* 253–279.

Miner, J. B. (1957). *Intelligence in the United States.* New York: Springer.

Nagy, W. E. (2005). Why vocabulary instruction needs to be long-term and comprehensive. In E. H. Hiebert & M. L. Kamil (Eds.), *Teaching and learning vocabulary: Bringing research to practice* (pp. 27–44). Mahwah, NJ: Erlbaum.

Nagy, W. E. (2007). Metalinguistic awareness and the vocabulary-comprehension connection. In R. Wagner, A. E. Muse, & K. R. Tannenbaum (Eds.), *Vocabulary acquisition: Implications for reading comprehension* (pp. 52–77). New York: Guilford Press.

Nagy, W. E., & Anderson, R. C. (1984). How many words are there in printed school English? *Reading Research Quarterly, 19,* 304–330.

Nagy, W. E., Anderson, R. C., & Herman, P. A. (1987). Learning word meanings from context during normal reading. *American Educational Research Journal, 24,* 237–270.

Nagy, W. E., Garcia, G. E., Durgunoglu, A., & Hancin-Bhatt, B. (1993). Spanish-English bilingual children's use and recognition of cognates in English reading. *Journal of Reading Behavior, 25,* 241–259.

Nagy, W. E., & Herman, P. A. (1987). Breadth and depth of vocabulary knowledge: Implications for acquisition and instruction. In M. C. McKeown & M. E. Curtis (Eds.), *The nature of vocabulary acquisition* (pp. 19–35). Hillsdale, NJ: Erlbaum.

Nagy, W. E., Herman, P. A., & Anderson, R. C. (1985). Learning words from context. *Reading Research Quarterly, 20,* 233–253.

Nagy, W. E., & Scott, J. A. (2000). Vocabulary processes. In M. Kamil, P. Mosenthal, P. D. Pearson, & R. Barr (Eds.), *Handbook of reading research: Vol. 3* (pp. 269–284). New York: Longman.

National Reading Panel (NRP). (2000). *Report of the National Reading Panel: Teaching children to read* (NIH Publication No. 00-4769). Washington, DC: National Institute of Child Health and Human Development, National Institutes of Health.

National Research Council. (2004). *Engaging schools: Fostering high school students' motivation to learn.* Washington, DC: National Academies Press.

Nicol, J. A., Graves, M. F., & Slater, W. H. (1984). *Building vocabulary through prefix instruction.* Unpublished manuscript, University of Minnesota, Minneapolis.

No Child Left Behind Act of 2001 (NCLB), Pub. L. No. 107-110 (2002). Available online: http://www.ed.gov/policy/elsec/leg/esea02/index.

Parker, S. L. (1984). *A comparison of four types of initial vocabulary instruction.* Unpublished master's thesis, University of Minnesota, Minneapolis.

Patberg, J. P., Graves, M. F., & Stibbe, M. A. (1984). Effects of active teaching and practice in facilitating students' use of context clues. In J. A. Niles & L. A. Harris (Eds.), *Yearbook of the National Reading Conference: Vol. 33. Changing perspectives in research in reading/language processing and instruction* (pp. 146–151). Rochester, NY: National Reading Conference.

Patberg, J. P., & Stibbe, M. A. (1985, December). *The effects of contextual analysis instruction on vocabulary learning.* Paper presented at the annual meeting of the National Reading Conference, San Diego, CA.

Pearson, P. D. (2005). *Assessing reading comprehension and vocabulary development.* Paper presented at Minnesota Center for Reading Research, St. Paul, MN.

Pearson, P. D., Barr, R., Kamil, M. L., & Mosenthal, P. (Eds.). (1984). *Handbook of reading research.* New York: Longman.

Petty, W., Herold, C., & Stoll, E. (1967). *The state of knowledge about the teaching of vocabulary.* Urbana, IL: National Council of Teachers of English.

Pittelman, S. D., Heimlich, J. E., Berglund, R. L., & French, M. P. (1991). *Semantic feature analysis: Classroom applications.* Newark, DE: International Reading Association.

Pressley, M., Dolezal, S. E., Raphael, L. M., Mohan, L., Roehrig, A. D., & Bogner, K. (2003). *Motivating primary-grade students.* New York: Guilford Press.

RAND Reading Study Group. (2002). *Reading for understanding: Toward an R&D program in reading comprehension.* Santa Monica, CA: RAND Education.

Robbins, C., & Ehri, L. C. (1994). Reading storybooks to kindergarteners helps them learn new vocabulary words. *Journal of Educational Psychology, 86,* 54–64.

Rosenshine, B. V. (1980). Skills hierachies in reading comprehension. In R. J. Spiro, B. C. Bruce, & W. F. Brewer (Eds.), *Theoretical issues in reading comprehension* (pp. 535–554). Hillsdale, NJ: Erlbaum.

Scott, J. A., Butler, C., & Asselin, M. (1996, December). *The effect of mediated assistance in word learning.* Paper presented at the annual meeting of the National Reading Conference, Charleston, SC.

Scott, J. A., & Nagy, W. E. (2004). Developing word consciousness. In J. F. Baumann & E. J. Kame'enui, (Eds.), *Vocabulary instruction: Research to practice* (pp. 201–217). New York: Guilford Press.

Scott, J. A., & Wells, J. (1998). Readers take responsibility: Literature circles and the growth of critical thinking. In K. Beers & B. Samuels (Eds.), *Into focus: Understanding and supporting middle school readers* (pp. 205–215). Norwood, MA: Christopher-Gordon.

Senechal, M., & Cornell, E. H. (1993). Vocabulary acquisition through shared reading experiences. *Reading Research Quarterly, 28*, 361–374.

Senechal, M., LeFevre, J., Hudson, E., & Lawson, E. P. (1996). Knowledge of storybooks as a predictor of young children's vocabulary. *Journal of Educational Psychology, 88*, 520–536.

Spearritt, D. (1972). Identification of subskills of reading comprehension by maximum likelihood factor analysis. *Reading Research Quarterly, 8*, 92–111.

Stahl, S. A. (1983). Differential word knowledge and reading comprehension. *Journal of Reading Behavior, 15* (4), 33–50.

Stahl, S. A., & Fairbanks, M. M. (1986). The effects of vocabulary instruction: A model-based meta-analysis. *Review of Educational Research, 56*, 72–110.

Stahl, S. A., & Nagy, W. E. (2006). *Teaching word meanings.* Mahwah, NJ: Erlbaum.

Stahl, S. A., & Stahl, K. D. (2004). Word wizards all!: Teaching word meanings in preschool and primary education. In J. F. Baumann & E. B. Kame'enui (Eds.), *Vocabulary instruction: Research to practice* (pp. 59–78). New York: Guilford Press.

Stanovich, K. E., & Cunningham, A. E. (1992). Studying the consequences of literacy within a literate society: The cognitive correlates of print exposure. *Memory and Cognition, 20*, 51–68.

Stanovich, K. E., & Cunningham, A. E. (1993). Where does knowledge come from? Associations between print exposure and information acquisition. *Journal of Educational Psychology, 85*, 211–229.

Sternberg, R. J. (1987). Most vocabulary is learned from context. In M. G. McKeown & M. E. Curtis (Eds.), *The nature of vocabulary acquisition* (pp. 89–105). Hillsdale, NJ: Erlbaum.

Swanborn, M. S. W., & de Glopper, K. (1999). Incidental word learning while reading: A meta-analysis. *Review of Educational Research, 69*, 261–285.

Thorndike, E. L. (1921). *The teacher's word book.* New York: Teachers College, Columbia University.

Thorndike, E. L. (1932). *A teacher's word book of the twenty thousand words found most frequently and widely in reading for children and young adults.* New York: Teachers College, Columbia University.

Thorndike, E. L., & Lorge, I. (1944). *The teacher's word book of 30,000 words.* New York: Teachers College Press, Columbia University.

Thorndike, R. L. (1973–74). Reading as reasoning. *Reading Research Quarterly, 9*, 135–147.

Wasic, B. A., & Bond, M. A. (2001). Beyond the pages of a book: Interactive book reading and language development in preschool classrooms. *Journal of Educational Psychology, 93*, 243–250.

White, T. G., Graves, M. F., & Slater, W. H. (1990). Growth of reading vocabulary in diverse elementary schools: Decoding and word meaning. *Journal of Educational Psychology, 82,* 281–290.

White, T. G., Sowell, J., & Yanagihara, A. (1989). Teaching elementary students to use word-part clues. *The Reading Teacher, 42,* 302–308.

Whitehurst, G. J., Falcon, F., Lonigan, C. J., Fischel, J. E., DeBaryshe, D. B., Valdez-Menchaca, M. C., et al. (1988). Accelerating language development through picture book reading. *Developmental Psychology, 24,* 552–559.

Wysocki, K., & Jenkins, J. R. (1987), Deriving word meanings through morphological generalization. *Reading Research Quarterly, 22,* 66–81.

# CHAPTER 5

# Developing Vocabulary in English-Language Learners: A Review of the Experimental Research

Diane August
Catherine Snow

In this chapter, we highlight the critical role that vocabulary plays in comprehension, especially for English-language learners (ELLs). We describe four general methods of building vocabulary in second-language learners and urge school staff to incorporate these methods into their classroom instruction.

### Questions for Reflection and Discussion

- Given that teachers have very little spare time in a day, how can vocabulary instruction be best incorporated into ongoing classroom activities?
- All students will benefit from vocabulary instruction. For teachers with second-language learners in their classrooms, what modifications can be made to high-quality vocabulary instruction so that it is most appropriate for beginning second-language learners? for more advanced second-language learners?

The proportion of language-minority children and youth speaking a language other than English at home has dramatically increased—from 9% in 1979 to 17% in 1999 (National Center for Education Statistics [NCES], 2004, p. 7). In 1979, 6 million children and youth were language minority. By 1999, that number had more than doubled to 14 million. In 1999, one third of 5- to 24-year-old language-minority children and youth reported having difficulty speaking English. We refer to these students as *English-language learners*.

The existence of large and persistent gaps between the reading performance of English-language learners and monolingual English-speaking children represents both an intellectual and a practical challenge. Fourth-grade performance on the National Assessment of Educational Progress (NAEP) reading test shows a 22–29-point scale score advantage for children living in homes where a language other than English was never used compared with children who lived in homes where a language other than English was always used (NCES, 2003). On the practical side, gaining access to the information taught in middle and secondary school content area classes requires that all children exit the elementary grades with good reading comprehension capacity. Without this capacity, access to grade-appropriate content knowledge, entry to challenging courses in secondary school, success on the tests increasingly being required for promotion and graduation, and entry to tertiary education are all unlikely. Thus closing this gap has high priority if U.S. education is to reduce inequities in access to opportunities that are contingent upon successful school achievement.

The intellectual challenge posed by the gap involves isolating its root cause. Research indicates vocabulary is one of the best predictors of reading comprehension outcomes for both English-only readers and for English-language learners (Beech & Keys, 1997; Carlisle, Beeman, Davis, & Spharim, 1999; Carlisle, Beeman, & Shah, 1996; Garcia, 1991; Proctor, Carlo, August, & Snow, 2005; Verhoeven, 1990). Lack of knowledge of the lower frequency academic words encountered in school texts impedes comprehension of those texts, which in turn impedes the natural process of learning new word meanings from exposure during reading—a problem Stanovich (1986) has famously called the "Matthew effect." Thus, while vocabulary relates to reading comprehension scores, the presumption is that the effect is reciprocal—greater vocabulary makes comprehension easier, while wider reading generates larger vocabularies.

Without explicit interventions to build vocabulary, English-language learners will be at risk for reading failure given their poor vocabulary knowledge and slow vocabulary growth. For example, current research (Tabors, Páez, & Lopez, 2003) indicates that the English and Spanish vocabulary skills of English-language learners entering Head Start are extremely limited and furthermore that the children's English skills do not grow fast enough to enable them to catch up with native English speakers. These problems have also been documented by Cobo-Lewis, Pearson, Eilers, and Umbel (2002). The researchers found that high-socioeconomic-status (SES) English-learners outperformed low SES English-language learners in vocabulary knowledge. However, even when controlling for SES, monolingual English speakers outperformed bilinguals in oral language in English. (Oral language was measured by picture vocabulary, verbal analogies, oral vocabulary, and the

Peabody Picture Vocabulary Test [PPVT].) According to the authors, "the differences were large in kindergarten (over 13 points) and second grade (nearly 15 points, approaching a full standard deviation of the test scores), but diminished by fifth grade (to fewer than 7 points or half a standard deviation)" (p. 89).

It should be noted, though, that SES had a large impact on patterns of literacy attainment; "on average, scores for high-SES children were 7.2 points or nearly half a standard deviation higher than for low-SES children" (Cobo-Lewis et al., 2002, p. 87). Because English-language learners in the United States are overwhelmingly from low-SES backgrounds, the gap in vocabulary between English-language learners and monolingual speakers presents a serious problem. In 2000, 68% of English-language learners in pre-kindergarten to fifth grade were low-income, as were 60% of ELLs in Grades 6 to 12. These rates were nearly twice as high as the rates for English proficient students in comparable grades (Capps et al., 2005, p. 25).

The factors that predict vocabulary acquisition for monolingual children are well researched, and constitute a firm basis for extrapolation to second-language learners. For example, it has been demonstrated that frequency of exposure to a word predicts its likelihood of acquisition (Hart, 1991), that cumulative number of words heard predicts total vocabulary size (Hart & Risley, 1995), that exposure to words in rich semantic contexts increases their likelihood of acquisition (Weizman & Snow, 2001), and that exposure to contexts like book reading and focused play increases vocabulary learning (see De Temple & Snow, 2003, for a review).

Vocabulary instruction for English-language learners is more likely to be successful if it builds on first-language research, and is comprehensive and developmentally appropriate. In recent reviews, several researchers (Graves, 2006; Nagy & Stall, 2006) call for a comprehensive approach to vocabulary instruction that integrates four features: the promotion of incidental word learning through rich and varied language experience; direct instruction of individual words; teaching word-learning strategies; and building word consciousness.

In addition, interventions must take into consideration the complex nature of vocabulary knowledge. Knowledge of a word has many components that may be acquired in different contexts and may operate differently to influence reading outcomes. There are many levels and types of word knowledge, and a prerequisite to studying the determinants or the consequences of vocabulary knowledge is specifying and operationalizing the construct "vocabulary" more tightly. What do we mean when we say a child knows a word? That he or she can understand it when it is used in spoken language? That he or she can use it in producing language? That he or she can read it? Spell it? Use it appropriately in writing? Define it? Full knowledge of a word involves having well-structured phonological, orthographic, semantic, and syntactic information, as well as the capacity for metalinguistic analysis (e.g., relating the word to its super- and subordinates, synonyms, and antonyms, and possessing etymological information about it). It is of particular importance to note the difference between the challenges of acquiring reading vocabulary (words that are familiar in oral language may well be difficult to learn to read), acquiring oral vocabulary for use in reading comprehension, and acquiring vocabulary knowledge through reading.

In this chapter, we review the experimental and quasi-experimental research on the development of vocabulary in second-language learners; in reporting on this work we use a framework established by Graves (2006; see also Chapter 4 of this volume) that posits four methods for building vocabulary in children. One way is to expose children to a rich assortment of language experiences. For younger children the experiences will tend to be oral and include such activities as read-alouds and discussion. As children become older, the read-alouds are replaced by students' own reading of text, but discussion remains an important venue for vocabulary development. A second method to help students gain vocabulary is through direct instruction of individual words. First-language research indicates that vocabulary instruction is most effective when learners are given both definitional and contextual information, when learners actively process the new word meanings, and when they experience multiple encounters with the words (Graves, 2006). A third approach is to provide students with strategies they can use to learn words. Strategies include using context to figure out word meanings (Baumann, Kame'enui, & Ash, 2003), using affixes, learning root words, using dictionaries or peers, and in the case of second-language learners whose first languages share cognates with English, using cognate knowledge (Carlo et al., 2004). Finally, a fourth component entails building word consciousness, which involves metacognition about words, motivation to learn words, and interest in words (Graves, 2006).

Given the fundamental importance of vocabulary to reading comprehension and the obvious limitations in the vocabulary knowledge of English-language learners (who have not had the same opportunity as native speakers for oral exposure to English words before learning to read), it is surprising that there are so few experimental studies of English vocabulary learning—seven in total at the elementary level and one at the secondary school level. In contrast, the National Reading Panel (2000) was able to find 45 experimental studies of vocabulary teaching with first-language students.

## PROVIDING RICH AND VARIED
## LANGUAGE EXPERIENCES

One method of building children's vocabulary is to expose them to rich and varied language experiences during which they learn words through listening, reading, discussion, and writing (Alvermann, 2000; Anderson & Nagy, 1992; Stahl, 1998). Two of the intervention programs designed for English-language learners provided these opportunities (Neuman & Koskinen, 1992; Tharp, 1982).

### Using Discussion in Small Groups

In a study of young children, Tharp (1982) examined the impact of a complex instructional approach in which first graders, in a yearlong intervention, received enhanced reading comprehension instruction delivered in small groups. This experiment was carried out in classrooms in which all children spoke Hawaiian Creole. Students were randomly assigned to two experimental and two control classrooms at each of two schools. At one site, research-team teachers instructed the two experimental classrooms and regular classroom teachers instructed the two control classrooms. At the other site, two regular classroom teachers who had been trained in the research-designed program instructed the experimental classrooms and two regular classroom teachers instructed the control classrooms.

During reading time, students in groups of two to five worked in 10–12 centers. While the students were in centers, the teacher directed a reading lesson centered around discussion. The teacher connects the story to students' own experience both at the beginning and end of the lesson. After children read silently for a few pages, the teacher discusses the text using both recall and higher order questions. After 15 minutes of reading and discussion, other aspects of reading are taught (e.g., phonics and drill in sight vocabulary). On the vocabulary subtest of the Gates-MacGinitie Reading Tests, the experimental groups significantly outperformed the control groups.

Six critical elements of the experimental classrooms differentiated them from the control classrooms:

1. More time spent on reading comprehension and relatively less time on decoding
2. More frequent criterion-referenced testing to monitor student progress
3. Classes that relied entirely on small-group discussion for reading lessons characterized by "dominant participation structure [that] was highly informal, continuing overlapping speech, mutual participation by teacher and students, co-narration, volunteered speech, instant

feedback, and lack of penalty for wrong answers" (Tharpe, 1982, p. 519)
4. Child motivation maintained through high rates of praise and other forms of positive interpersonal reinforcement
5. Individualized diagnostic prescriptive instruction
6. A quality control system in which the program characteristics are measured, rated, and used to monitor program implementation

## Using Television with Captions

Neuman and Koskinen (1992) examined the impact of learning words in context on the vocabulary knowledge of 129 second-language learners in 17 seventh- and eighth-grade classrooms. The first-language groups consisted of Cambodian, Laotian, Vietnamese, and Hispanic students who were 2–3 years below grade level; the majority of them were from low-SES backgrounds. Programming from the Children's Television Workshop, *3-2-1 Contact,* was selected for "its motivational presentations of scientific concepts, its special appeal to girls and minorities, and its magazine format, which offered flexibility in selecting scientific content most appropriate to the seventh and eighth grade curricula" (p. 97). Students received 9 weeks of instruction (3 weeks for each of three content units, on survival, protection, and breathing). The experimental groups watched television presentations of content with or without captions, while a control group simply read texts that provided equivalent conceptual information with the same vocabulary. Pretest differences were adjusted statistically. Generally, students in "captioned television" outperformed students in the "just reading" groups in all three units and did better than "television without captions," though not for all units.

The results suggest that the visual representation of words is an important contribution to students' increased word knowledge. Another important finding is that students at the mastery level of linguistic competence and thus relatively fluent in English scored consistently higher than students who were limited English proficient. Students who were most proficient at the outset made more gains than others, confirming the predictions of the "Matthew effect" that the "rich get richer."

## TEACHING INDIVIDUAL WORDS

A second approach to developing vocabulary is to teach individual words. Based on a review of the first-language research, Graves (2006) asserts that "vocabulary instruction is most effective when students are given both definitional and contextual information, when learners actively process the new word meanings, and when they experience multiple encounters with the words" (p. 6). One intervention focused on teaching individual words in the context of rhymes, poems, riddles, and sentences (Perez, 1981), but all others involved teaching words in the context of narrative and expository text that was either read aloud by the teacher or read by the students. In some of the latter interventions, words were pretaught and taught in context; in others they were taught in context only; all interventions used methods to reinforce word knowledge after the reading was completed.

## Using Rhymes, Poems, Sentence Patterns, and Games

Perez (1981) reports on a study of the vocabulary learning of 75 Mexican American third graders; the majority spoke Spanish as their first language, were from low-socioeconomic homes, and had received low scores on reading achievement tests. A control group included 75 students with the same reading achievement levels. For approximately 3 months, the children received 20 minutes of daily oral instruction in word meanings, with a focus on idiomatic expressions, compound words, synonyms, antonyms, and multiple meanings. As previously mentioned, the words were introduced through rhymes, poems, sentence patterns, and competitive games. Although not described by the author, the appendix of instructional materials indicates that pictures were also used to illustrate word meaning. The experimental group showed significant improvement over the control group on the Prescriptive Reading Inventory, a standardized informal reading inventory in which children read text aloud and answer questions. Although the children had studied word meanings, they also improved in their ability to read text orally and to answer questions about what they had read.

## Using Sentences That Form a Narrative

A vocabulary experiment with English-language learners studied two procedures for presenting words to first-grade Spanish-dominant students— one method taught words in sentences that did not form a narrative while the other taught words in sentences that did form a narrative (Vaughn-Shavuo, 1990). The students were randomly assigned to two groups, and both were taught a collection of 31 words for 30 minutes per day for 3 weeks. The first group worked on learning words that were presented in individual sentence contexts that did not form a narrative. More specifically, students looked at a cue card, repeated the sentence related to the card, answered comprehension questions related to the card, and repeated the sentence again.

In the second group, the vocabulary was presented using vocabulary cue cards, and students repeated cue card–related sentences, but in this case the sentences formed a narrative. Oral repetition of vocabulary was supplemented with group writing of language experience stories focused on the target vocabulary. Both groups received supplementary writing activities generated from the target vocabulary for independent reinforcement. The second group, the one that worked on learning vocabulary in the context of narratives, mastered a greater proportion of the vocabulary words that were taught than did the control group (21 words learned versus 9 words).

Most of the interventions that focus on teaching words do so in the context of book reading. In one yearlong study, grade-level children's literature was used to build vocabulary and comprehension in second-grade English-language learners (Calderón et al., 2005). The daily vocabulary intervention was part of a 90-minute Success for All reading lesson (Slavin & Madden, 2001). The project was carried out in 8 experimental and 8 control classrooms in transitional bilingual education programs in two districts in Texas. The control classrooms used a basal reader and instructional approaches called reader's and writer's workshops. Both programs transitioned students at the same grade levels and devoted one year to introducing reading and writing in English. The study employed a nonrandomized, matched control design and employed a series of analyses of covariance (ANCOVA) with condition as the independent variable. The vocabulary subtest of the Woodcock Language Proficiency Test (Woodcock, 1991) was the dependent measure of vocabulary.

For 30 minutes per day in the experimental classrooms, teachers pre-taught vocabulary, developed vocabulary through "text talk," and reinforced vocabulary through oral language activities that occurred after the story had been read. Students listened to and discussed children's literature (50 books during the year) as well as working on daily oral language activities to build word knowledge for key words that appeared in the children's literature.

The selection of words to preteach was based on research by Beck and colleagues (Beck, McKeown, & Kucan, 2002) as well as on the work of the Vocabulary Improvement Project (Carlo et al., 2004) and a study on bilingual cooperative integrated reading (Calderón, Hertz-Lazarowitz, & Slavin, 1998). Words were grouped into three tiers and words in Tier 2 were targeted for instruction. As defined by Beck et al. (2002),

> Tier 2 words include: 1) words that are characteristic of mature language users and appear frequently across a variety of texts; words that can be worked with in a variety of ways so that students can build rich representations of them and their connections to other words and concepts; and words for which students understand the general concept but need precision and specificity in describing the concept. (p. 19)

Tier 1 words are words English-speaking students presumably already know, and Tier 3 words are words students are unlikely to know but are also words that are not frequently used across a variety of domains.

Preteaching vocabulary was a four-step process adapted from Beck and colleagues (2002) integrated with second-language strategies:

1. Teachers said the word in English and in Spanish.
2. They provided a definition of the word based on its use in the story.
3. They provided an example of the word by using it in a sentence whose context clarified the word's meaning.
4. They asked students to repeat the word several times to build a phonological representation of the word.
5. They engaged students in oral language activities to help them apply what they had learned.

This last activity was generally carried out with a partner. For instance, the teacher might say, "Tell your partner about a time you were *mesmerized*," and then ask partners to share their response with the class.

Vocabulary was also developed through ongoing dialogue between the teacher and students about the text during the read-alouds by using different types of questions and stopping at specific intervals in the text to elicit discussion.

The language development activities that follow the story are based in large part on the words the story has provided. Different stories lend themselves to different kinds of activities. But the key focus is on developing conceptual knowledge about the words and reinforcing labels for the word. This is also an opportunity for students to use the word in extended discourse through story retellings or in a different context such as in story mapping or dramatization. The section usually closes with written exercises for reinforcing word meaning and using multiple meanings of words in sentences.

Finally, there were also ongoing activities designed to review words from previous stories. The classroom had "word walls" that contained pictures of the words and labels for words organized by category. The lessons also taught children strategies to learn words and built word consciousness; these activities are described in subsequent sections of the chapter.

After adjusting for the initial pretest difference, the experimental group scored significantly higher than the control group on Passage Comprehension ($F_{1,235} = 3.753$, $p = 0.05$) with an effect size of +0.16. The difference between the experimental and the control group scores was marginally significant on Picture Vocabulary ($F_{1,235} = 3.042$, $p = 0.08$) with an effect size of +0.11.

## Using Stories and Word Explanations

Biemiller and Boote (2006) conducted two studies exploring the use of vocabulary instruction embedded in children's stories. In the first study, subjects were kindergarten, first-, and second-grade children predominately from families that spoke Portuguese at home. Vocabulary was selected from children's books, but a word was omitted if more than 80% of the children at Level 4 of the *Living Word Vocabulary* (Dale & O'Rourke, 1981) knew that word, since prior research indicates these words are known by most second-grade children (Biemiller & Slonim, 2001). In all, 24 words were instructed, and 24 words were not instructed. At each grade, two teachers presented the books and word explanations. During the first reading, the story was read normally with comprehension questions at the end. During the second and third readings on subsequent days, 4–8 words additional words were explained during each reading. As a sentence with a word to be explained was reached, the teacher would reread the sentence and ask if anyone knew what the word meant. If a plausible explanation was given, the teacher agreed and went on. Otherwise the teacher provided an explanation. For a Grade 2 story, the following exemplifies the brief explanations that were provided. "It seemed like a good solution. What does a solution mean? A solution is the answer to a problem" (Bielmiller & Boote 2006, p. 49). The authors examined the magnitude of gains for words that were instructed compared with words that were not. Results indicated the word explanations made a difference in kindergarten and first grade. In all grades, children had higher scores on posttests. Overall, 25% of all words were known at pretest, and 42% were known at posttest. The effect size, Cohen's $d$, was 1.21 (Cohen, 1988). The main effect for pretest-posttest results was highly significant, $F(1,100) = 182.726, p < .001$ (Biemiller & Boote, 2006).

In a second study Biemiller and Boote (2006) attempted to increase the percentage of words learned as well as the absolute number of words learned. The sample for the second study was similar to the first (42–45 children at each of three grade levels, kindergarten through second grade). Over two books, 42 words were taught in kindergarten, 55 words in first grade, and 46 words in second grade. As with the first study, during the first reading, the story was read normally, but unlike the first study, several key words were explained prior to the first reading. As in the first study, for the following 3 days several words (this time 7–10) were instructed during a reading. As each sentence that included a word was reached, the teacher would reread the sentence and provide a brief explanation of the word. Based on feedback from participants, these were teacher-only word explanations rather than both teacher and student explanations. In addition, word reviews were added; each day the words were reviewed by reading the context sentences and providing explanations. After 3 days the words were reviewed a second time, and on the 5th day all words that had been studied were reviewed again using context sentences not based on the book. The completed cycle took 5 days, with about 30 minutes per day. ANOVAs comparing pretest to immediate posttest showed gains that were highly significant. In addition, there were further gains in vocabulary over the 4 weeks after instruction even though no further instruction occurred.

## Using the Vocabulary Improvement Program

Another study examined the effects of enhanced vocabulary teaching with fifth-grade English-language learners (Carlo et al., 2004; August, Carlo, Lively, McLaughlin, & Snow, 2006). Although the study included both English-language learners and native speakers of English, the data were analyzed separately, making it possible to determine the effects of the intervention on the population of interest. There were 94 students in the experimental group and 48 students in the control group. Students in the treatment group received 15 weeks of instruction, and learned about 10 to 12 words per week. Vocabulary instruction lasted for 30 to 45 minutes a day for 4 days per week, with 1 additional day per week devoted to review. The vocabulary was presented thematically and included homework assignments and a weekly test. Prior to each week's instruction, the words and texts containing them were available in Spanish for students who needed native language support. The lessons then involved teaching specific words as well as teaching strategies for word learning and also aimed to develop word consciousness; these latter activities will be described in subsequent sections of the chapter. Although there were no treatment gains on the Peabody Picture Vocabulary Test, the English-language learners improved on several other measures of vocabulary and comprehension. Students improved in their ability to generate sentences that conveyed different meanings of multimeaning words, in tests of knowledge of word meanings, and on measures of word association and morphological knowledge. Students showed significant improvement on a cloze test used to evaluate comprehension, but the impact on comprehension was much lower than that on word learning. It is clear from these results that this training led to improved knowledge of the words studied.

Although the intervention focused on only a few words each week, its goal was to provide students with opportunities to process new words at a deep level; that is, to make semantic links to other words and concepts and thus attain a deeper and richer understanding of a word's meaning as well as learn many other words connected to the target word. Beck and colleagues have suggested that one way to have students make these connections and process words more deeply is to have them answer questions about target words that indicate they have a clear understanding of their meaning and then write sentences that use the word in a related way (Beck, McKeown, & Omanson, 1987; Beck, Perfetti, & McKeown, 1982). We modified this strategy by selecting the target words from our own text, teaching students the word meanings prior to the activity, and engaging students in activities to use the words in novel ways. In the examples below, the target words are italicized.

For example, in one activity a pair of students were told to pretend that one was famous and one was a magazine reporter. The reporter's job was to ask questions of the famous person and write down the answers on a worksheet. After a few moments, they exchanged places. All the questions included target words. Examples of questions include: Name three situations that might make you feel some *anxiety*? What are three words that describe your *heritage*? Name four of your family's *values*? What is an experience that could *transform* your life? What are three things that you would like to *obtain* this year? Name two things that you do *periodically*?

Well-known games were also used to build depth of word meaning. For example, in Charades students had to act out a target word's meaning for his or her team; in Word Bee, team members worked together to define a target word they had been given and then present the definition to classmates for approval; in Word Substitution, team members had to replace a target word with another word or phrase that meant the same thing; and in Word Guess, the team that needed the fewest clues to guess a target word won.

## TEACHING WORD-LEARNING STRATEGIES

A third approach to help students acquire vocabulary is to teach word-learning strategies. Strategies that have been successful in the first-language literature include using context (Baumann, Kame'enui, & Ash, 2003; Kuhn & Stahl, 1998), teaching word parts (Anglin, 1993; Baumann, Font, Edwards, & Boland, 2005; White, Power, & White, 1989), and using cognates (Blachowicz & Fisher, 2004; Graves, Juel, & Graves, 2004).

### Using Context

To stimulate learning from context, interventions used in the Vocabulary Improvement Project (August et al., 2006; Carlo et al., 2004) began each unit with an exercise in which students inferred the meaning of specific words from the text for that week. Words were deliberately selected where there were enough cues for students to determine the meaning. However, because many words cannot be defined by the context in which they appear, teachers also helped children figure out what to do if that were the case. Teachers taught students to

1. Note context clues (if any)
2. Determine if there are enough context clues to figure out a target word's meaning, and if so provide a plausible meaning and an explanation for why the meaning was plausible
3. Ask a friend or use a dictionary if the context does not support the word's meaning

On the 2nd day of the unit, students further developed their inferencing skills by working in small heterogeneous groups on contexting activities. Each group was charged with figuring out the correct target words for sentences that supported the words' meaning and, when called on, explaining why the answer made sense. Note that students had already learned the definitions of the target words. Two examples follow: (1) "I think my teacher *symbolizes* Columbia. She represents the country, language, and the country's traditions." (2) "When the new boy was asked a question in English, he felt foolish and *embarrassed*. The teacher *humiliated* the boy accidentally because he didn't know the boy had recently come from the Dominican Republic."

## Using Structural Analysis

Some reading researchers (Dale & O'Rourke, 1981; Nagy & Anderson, 1984; Stahl, 1999) have argued that one of the best ways to expand a child's vocabulary is through "structural analysis" or helping children figure out the parts of words and what these parts mean. For example, the word *unfruitful* has the prefix *un-*, the root *fruit*, and the suffix *-ful*. Other words, such as *snowman*, are compounds of two words.

In the Vocabulary Improvement Project (August et al., 2006; Carlo et al., 2004) because children enjoy word play and games with words, the authors developed a number of games to teach roots and affixes. For example, in Roots Rummy teams created words by combining roots and affixes (e.g., *demo-graph-er*; *phono-graph*; *tele-graph*; *photo-graph*; *bio-graph-er*). In Roots Sort teams sorted words with the same root (e.g., *television*, *telephone*, *telegraph*, *telescope*) and then tried to figure out what the root meant. In Suffixes teams added either "*-er*" or "*-ment*" or both to word roots and then developed sentences using their new words.

In teaching structural analysis the authors kept several issues in mind. They avoided "phantom" prefixes, such as "*re*" in *reality*. They helped students so they didn't look for "little words in big words" (leading to such mistakes as finding *moth* in *mother* and *fat* in *father*). In developing the exercises they recognized that some suffixes, such as *-ness* and *-ity*, are relatively easy to teach. Others, such as *-tion*, have meanings that are more abstract and are difficult to convey. Finally, where possible, they began with words that were already familiar to the students.

## Using Cognates

Cognates are a rich source of information for many English-language learners, especially those whose first language is Spanish. Research has found that when students' English vocabulary knowledge was controlled, their Spanish vocabulary knowledge and post hoc ability to recognize cognates significantly predicted their English reading comprehension, indicating they were making use of cognate relationships in English reading (Nagy, Garcia, Durgunoglu, & Hancin-Bhatt, 1993).

To help students learn more about cognates, students involved in the Vocabulary Improvement Project (Carlo et al., 2004; August et al., 2006) were divided into heterogeneous groups. In each group, the Spanish-speaking students would help the English-speaking students. Each group would read a passage in Spanish and try to define the underlined words (those that had English cognates). Based on the cognates, each group would try to explain what the story was about. In another activity, heterogeneous groups of students would read a passage in English and circle all the English words they thought had Spanish cognates and, based on knowledge of Spanish, define the English word.

## FOSTERING WORD CONSCIOUSNESS

According to Graves (2006), "the term *word consciousness* refers to an awareness of and interest in words and their meanings" (p. 7).

Although all programs that focus children on learning vocabulary may indirectly build word consciousness, several interventions worked on this explicitly by using an activity called Word Wizard (August et al., 2006; Calderón et al., 2005; Carlo et al., 2004). In Word Wizard students are instructed to listen for words they don't know, jot down the words and the sentences in which they appear, and look up the words' definition. At the end of the week, students share these words with the class. In the case of the Vocabulary Improvement Project, students posted the words on a project Web site so they could be shared with fellow students across the country.

In addition, in the Vocabulary Improvement project, teachers were trained to focus students' attention on words across the content areas. For example, if teachers encountered the word *degree* in science, they might ask for the definition of the word in its scientific context as well as what the word might mean in other contexts (math, literature, geography, for example). They might then ask students to think up new sentences on the spot using various definitions of the target word.

# CONCLUSION

## Summary

The few experimental studies that focus on developing vocabulary in English–language learners build on the same strategies as those used to develop vocabulary in monolingual English speakers; they provide rich and varied language experiences, teach individual words and word-learning strategies, and build word consciousness. The method most often cited in the studies was teaching individual words and doing so in the context of the reading of narrative text; one study found that this was more effective than teaching words in isolated sentences (Vaughn-Shavuo, 1990). Almost all the studies took place with students in the elementary grades; only one focused on older learners (Neuman & Koskinen, 1992). Review of the vocabulary is an important element of vocabulary interventions with first-language learners, but may be particularly important for second-language learners; it appeared as an element of many of the studies cited above (Biemiller & Boote, 2006; Calderón et al., 2005; Carlo et al., 2004; Vaughn-Shavuo, 1990).

Even though effective interventions for second-language learners share many attributes of effective instruction for monolingual learners, there are modifications for these second-language learners consistent with best practices for this group of students (August & Hakuta, 1997). For example, although many of the interventions target the same kind of words that would be targeted for monolingual speakers (Tier 2 words like *bolster*), they also include words that most monolingual speakers already know (Tier 1 words like *outside* and *learn*). Many of the interventions use pictures and demonstrations to get across word meaning (August et al., 2006; Calderón et al., 1998; Carlo et al., 2004; Neuman & Koskinen, 1992; Perez, 1981; Vaughn-Shavuo, 1990). Some interventions used cognate knowledge to help students figure out word meaning in the second language (August et al., 2006; Calderón et al., 2005; Carlo et al., 2004). Some interventions made use of students' first language in defining second-language words (August et al., 2006; Calderón et al., 2005; Carlo et al., 2004). Finally, many of the interventions focused on building other aspects of oral language, not only vocabulary, through discussion around text (August et al., 2006; Calderón et al., 2005; Carlo et al.,

2004; Tharp, 1982; Vaughn-Shavuo, 1990). For example, to build oral language, the initial questions in work by Calderón and colleagues (2005) prompted students to talk about ideas rather than provide one-word responses and used follow-up questions to help students develop their likely sparse first responses. They also used questions that helped students move from using just pictures and background knowledge to more elaborated responses tied to the text. Finally, one study took advantage of more proficient English speakers by creating lots of opportunities for second-language learners to interact with native English speakers (August et al., 2006; Carlo et al., 2004).

## Recommendations for Future Research

There is clearly a need for more research in the area of vocabulary. We located only seven experimental or quasi-experimental studies of vocabulary development in English-language learners; many of these were extremely limited in duration and reported no long-term outcomes.

Several areas of research warrant attention. First, because it is impossible to teach students all the words they need to know it is imperative to figure out which words students are likely to acquire on their own without intervention. This requires studies that track students' vocabulary development over time and assessments that are carefully constructed to allow inferences about the kinds of words that will be difficult for second-language learners to acquire.

Second, as teaching time is limited, it is critical to determine what kinds of incidental learning benefits second-language learners. For example, work by Neuman and Koskinen (1992) is encouraging; students exposed to high-quality captioned television where the images were aligned with the oral and written language helped students acquire vocabulary. However, it is important to align interventions that use incidental methods with students' level of second-language proficiency. The work by Neuman and Koskinen indicate this method worked only for students with a certain threshold of oral English proficiency.

Third, it is important to find the most efficient methods of teaching individual words. There are only so many words that can be pretaught; it takes a lot of time to preteach individual words, and young students can take only so much of this kind of instruction before getting restless. It may be that other methods such as defining words in context (Biemiller & Boote, 2006) are more efficient. It is important to determine what kinds of words lend themselves to which methods. For example, in the work by Calderón and colleagues, different methods were used depending on the nature of the word (e.g., Can exemplars of the word be pointed to? Can its meaning be acted out?), its cognate status, depth of word meaning, and utility. Concrete words were demonstrated; for cognates, teachers would tell students the cognate in Spanish or ask students for the cognate in English; Tier 2 words that were pretaught were reinforced through questions that required students to use and understand the words. For Tier 3 words, teachers provided a definition in Spanish if the word could not be demonstrated or explained simply in English. However, the authors did not construct the research study in a manner that allowed us to determine how these particular approaches worked with different kinds of words.

Future research is desperately needed to address the gap in knowledge about the transfer of skills from the first language to the second. Transfer is a central concept in bilingualism research but one that has often been either presupposed or prematurely dismissed, and which has itself too rarely been a focus of study. The possibility of transferring skills from a first to a second language has been widely invoked as an argument in support of bilingual education, but there has been remarkably little focus on the transfer of vocabulary skills. What second-language vocabulary skills show an effect of transfer? Do some skills transfer more easily than others? What conditions promote the likelihood or efficiency of transfer? For example, do children need to be instructed in first-language literacy to take advantage of cognate knowledge, or is it sufficient for them to speak a first language that shares cognates with English? How does age of the learner and level of first-language and second-language proficiency influence the relationship between first- and second-language vocabulary?

Our research indicates that the Spanish and English noncognate vocabularies of young children from Spanish-speaking homes typically correlate negatively—a finding suggesting that transfer in the domain of vocabulary breadth is either absent or not automatic (Tabors et al., 2003). However, our research shows that cognate vocabulary is positively correlated across languages, but only for children who have received formal instruction in Spanish reading—an important result indicating limitations on the conditions under which transfer occurs (August, Calderón, & Caro, 2002). Metalinguistic aspects of word knowledge (use of superordinates, analyticity of definitions) also transfer from Spanish to English, even when breadth of vocabulary is unrelated (Ordóñez, Carlo, Snow, & McLaughlin, 2002).

There is clearly a need for more research with older second-language learners and research that focuses on the acquisition of vocabulary germane to particular subject areas. Only one study investigated older learners learning outside of language arts (Neuman & Koskinen, 1992).

In the conduct of future research we urge that certain methodological commitments be made to ensure the strongest basis for evaluating effectiveness: longitudinal studies employing individual and multilevel growth modeling; and experimental designs with random assignment at the classroom level. An advantage of randomization at the classroom level is that it offers us opportunities to spend time in schools and to develop and fine-tune robust procedures for professional development with teachers focused on the content of the intervention. Procedures for evaluating fidelity of interventions, general classroom quality, and teacher background and professional development experiences should be put in place. Further, we urge that studies examine the development of English and Spanish in a variety of instructional situations that provide differing levels of support and status for the two languages. Finally, the measures used to assess word knowledge should be linguistically sophisticated; in analyzing word knowledge they should attend to phonological, morphological, syntactic, and semantic aspects of lexical representation and to cross-linguistic influences, and should measure oral connected discourse and comprehension, not only word knowledge.

## Follow-up Activities

1. Discuss the two framing questions presented at the beginning of the chapter in the context of your own classroom. How will you incorporate vocabulary instruction in your ongoing classroom activities? Keep in mind there are four components of effective vocabulary instruction and that instruction should be developmentally appropriate.
2. Not all students have the same level of English proficiency. What kind of vocabulary instruction might be especially beneficial for monolingual English-speaking students? for second-language learners who are newcomers? for second-language learners who are moderately proficient in English?
3. Think of a vocabulary strategy you are already using or one that you have developed as a result of reading this chapter and working on activities 1 and 2. How would you set up a study of this strategy in your classroom to determine whether or not it is effective?

## REFERENCES

Alvermann, D. E. (2000). Classroom talk about text: Is it dear, cheap, or a bargain at any price? In B. M. Taylor, M. F. Graves, & P. van den Broek (Eds.), *Reading for meaning: Fostering comprehension in the middle grades* (pp. 136–151). New York: Teachers College Press.

Anderson, R. C., & Nagy, W. E. (1992). The vocabulary conundrum. *American Educator, 16*(4), 14–18, 44–47.

Anglin, J. M. (1993). Vocabulary development: A Morphological analysis. *Monographs of the Society for Research in Child Development, 58*(10, Serial No. 238).

August, D., Calderón, M., & Caro, M. (2002). *Transfer of skills from Spanish to English: A study of young learners. Final researchers' report.* Washington, DC: Center for Applied Linguistics.

August, D., Carlo, M., Lively, T., McLaughlin, B., & Snow, C. (2006). Promoting the vocabulary growth of English learners. In T. Young & N. Hadaway (Eds.), *Supporting the literacy development of English learners.* Newark, DE: International Reading Association.

August, D., & Hakuta, K. (1997). *Educating English Language Learners.* Washington, DC: National Academy Press.

Baumann, J. F., Font, G., Edwards, E. C., & Boland, E. (2005). Strategies for teaching middle-grade students to use word part and context clues to expand reading vocabulary. In E. Hiebert & M. L. Kamil (Eds.), *Teaching and learning vocabulary: Bringing research to practice* (pp. 179–205). Mahwah, NJ: Erlbaum.

Baumann, J. F., Kame'enui, E. J., & Ash, G. E. (2003). Research on vocabulary instruction: Voltaire redux. In J. Flood, D. Lapp, J. R. Squire, & J. M. Jensen (Eds.), *Handbook on research on teaching the English language arts* (2nd ed., pp. 752–785). Mahwah, NJ: Erlbaum.

Beck, I. L., McKeown, M. G., & Kucan. L. (2002). *Bringing words to life: Robust vocabulary instruction.* New York: Guilford Press.

Beck, I. L., McKeown, M. G., & Omanson, R. C. (1987). The effects and uses of diverse vocabulary instructional techniques. In M. G. McKeown & M. E. Curtis (Eds.), *The nature of vocabulary acquisition* (pp. 147–163). Hillsdale, NJ: Erlbaum.

Beck, I. L., Perfetti, C. A., & McKeown, M. G. (1982). The effects of long-term vocabulary instruction on lexical access and reading comprehension. *Journal of Educational Psychology, 74,* 506–521.

Beech, J. R., & Keys, A. (1997). Reading, vocabulary, and language preference in 7- to 8-year-old bilingual Asian children. *British Journal of Educational Psychology, 67*(4), 405–414.

Biemiller, A., & Boote, C. (2006). An effective method for building vocabulary in primary grades. *Journal of Educational Psychology 98*(1), 44–62.

Biemiller, A., & Slonim, M. (2001). Estimating root word and normative vocabulary growth in normative and advanced populations: Evidence for a common sequence of vocabulary acquisition. *Journal of Educational Psychology, 93,* 498–520.

Blachowicz, C., & Fisher, P. (2004). Keep the "fun" in fundamental: Encouraging word awareness and incidental word learning in the classroom through word play. In J. F. Baumann & E. J. Kame'enui (Eds.), *Vocabulary instruction: Research to practice* (pp. 218–237). New York: Guilford Press.

Calderón, M., August, D., Slavin, R., Durán, D., Madden, N., & Cheung, A. (2005). Bringing words to life in classrooms with English language learners. In E. H. Hiebert & M. L. Kamil (Eds.), *Teaching and learning vocabulary: Bringing research to practice* (pp. 115–136). Mahwah, NJ: Lawrence Erlbaum.

Calderón, M., Hertz-Lazarowitz, R., & Slavin, R. E. (1998). Effects of bilingual cooperative integrated reading and composition on students making the transition from Spanish to English reading. *Elementary School Journal, 99*(2), 153–165.

Capps, R., Fix, M., Murray, J., Ost, J., Passel, J., & Herwantoro, S. (2005). *The new demography of America's schools: Immigration and the No Child Left Behind Act*. Washington, DC: Urban Institute

Carlisle, J. F., Beeman, M. M., Davis, L. H., & Spharim, G. (1999). Relationship of metalinguistic capabilities and reading achievement for children who are becoming bilingual. *Applied Psycholinguistics, 20*(4), 459–478.

Carlisle, J. F., Beeman, M. M., & Shah, P. P. (1996). The metalinguistic capability and English literacy of Hispanic high school students: An exploratory study. In D. J. Lev, C. K. Kinser, & K. A. Hinchman (Eds.), *Yearbook of the National Reading Conference: Vol. 45. Literacies for the 21st century: Research and practice* (pp. 306–316). Chicago: National Reading Conference.

Carlo, M. S., August, D., McLaughlin, B., Snow, C. E., Dressler, C., Lippman, D., et al. (2004). Closing the gap: Addressing the vocabulary needs of English language learners in bilingual and mainstream classrooms. *Reading Research Quarterly, 39*(2), 188–215.

Cobo-Lewis, A. B., Pearson, B. Z., Eilers, R. E., & Umbel, V. C. (2002). Effects of bilingualism and bilingual education on oral and written English skills: A multifactor study of standardized test outcomes. In K. Oller & R. E. Eilers (Eds.), *Language and literacy in bilingual children* (pp. 64–97). New York: Multilingual Matters.

Cohen, J. (1988). *Statistical power analysis for the behavioral sciences* (2nd ed.). Hillsdale, NJ: Erlbaum.

Dale, E., & O'Rourke J. (1981). *The living word vocabulary*. Chicago: World Book/Childcraft International.

De Temple, J., & Snow, C. E. (2003). Learning words from books. In A. van Kleeck, S. A. Stahl, & E. B. Bauer (Eds.), *On reading books to children: Parents and teachers* (pp. 16–36). Mahwah, NJ: Erlbaum.

Garcia, G. E. (1991). Factors influencing the English reading test performance of Spanish-speaking Hispanic children. *Reading Research Quarterly, 26*(4), 371–392.

Graves, M. F. (2006). *The vocabulary book: Learning and instruction*. New York: Teachers College Press.

Graves, M. F., Juel, C., & Graves, B. B. (Eds.). (2004). *Teaching reading in the 21st century* (3rd ed.). Boston: Allyn & Bacon.

Hart, B. (1991). Input frequency and children's first words. *First Language, 11*, 289–300.

Hart, B., & Risley, T. R. (1995). *Meaningful differences in the everyday experience of young American children*. Baltimore: Brookes.

Kuhn, M. R., & Stahl, S. A. (1998). Teaching children to learn word meanings from context: A synthesis and some questions. *Journal of Literacy Research, 30*, 119–138.

Nagy, W. E., & Anderson, R. C. (1984). How many words are there in printed English? *Reading Research Quarterly, 19*, 304–330.

Nagy, W. E., Garcia, G. E., Durgunoglu, A., & Hancin-Bhatt, B. (1993). Spanish-English bilingual students' use and recognition of cognates in English reading. *Journal of Reading Behavior, 25*, 241–259.

Nagy, W. E., & Stahl, S. A. (2006). *Teaching word meanings*. Mahwah, NJ: Erlbaum.

National Center for Education Statistics (NCES). (2003). *National Assessment of Educational Progress reading assessments*. Retrieved from http://neces.ed.gov/nationsreportcard/reading

National Center for Education Statistics (NCES). (2004). *Language minority learners and their labor market indicators—Recent trends*. Retrieved September 21, 2004, from http://nces.ed.gov/pubs2004/2004009.pdf

National Reading Panel (NRP). (2000). *Report of the National Reading Panel: Teaching children to read* (NIH Publication No. 00-4769). Washington, DC: National Institute of Child Health and Human Development, National Institutes of Health.

Neuman, S. B., & Koskinen, P. (1992). Captioned television as comprehensible input: Effects of incidental word learning from context for language minority students. *Reading Research Quarterly, 27*(1), 94–106.

Ordóñez, C., Carlo, M., Snow, C. E., & McLaughlin, B. (2002). Depth and breadth of vocabulary in two languages: Which vocabulary skills transfer? *Journal of Educational Psychology, 94*(4), 719–728.

Perez, E. (1981). Oral language competence improves reading skills of Mexican-American third graders. *The Reading Teacher, 35*, 24–27

Proctor, P. C., Carlo, M., August, D., & Snow, C. (2005). Native Spanish-speaking children reading in English: Toward a model of comprehension. *Journal of Educational Psychology, 97*(2), 246–256.

Slavin, R. E., & Madden, N. (2001). Effects of bilingual and English-as-a-second-language adaptations of Success for All on the reading achievement of students acquiring English. In R. E. Slavin & M. Calderón (Eds.), *Effective programs for Latino students* (pp. 207–230). Mahwah, NJ: Lawrence Erlbaum Associates.

Stahl, S. A. (1998). Four questions about vocabulary. In C. R. Hynd (Ed.), *Learning from text across conceptual domains* (pp. 73–94). Mahwah, NJ: Erlbaum.

Stahl, S. A. (1999). *Vocabulary development*. Cambridge, MA: Brookline Books.

Stanovich, K. E. (1986). Matthew effects in reading: Some consequences of individual differences in the acquisition of literacy. *Reading Research Quarterly, 21*, 360–407.

Tabors, P., Páez, M., & Lopez, L. (2003). Dual language abilities of bilingual four-year olds: Initial findings from the Early Childhood Study of Language and Literacy Development of Spanish-Speaking Children. *NABE Journal of Research and Practice, 1*(1), 70–91.

Tharp, R. G. (1982). The effective instruction of comprehension: Results and descriptions of the Kamehameha Early Education Program. *Reading Research Quarterly, 17*(4), 503–527.

Vaughn-Shavuo, F. (1990). *Using story grammar and language experience for improving recall and comprehension in the teaching of ESL to Spanish-dominant first-graders*. Unpublished doctoral dissertation, Hofstra University, Hempstead, NY.

Verhoeven, L. T. (1990). Acquisition of reading in a second language. *Reading Research Quarterly, 25*(2), 90–114.

Weizman, Z. O., & Snow, C. E. (2001). Lexical imput as related to children's vocabulary acquisition: Effects of sophisticated exposure and support for meaning. *Developmental Psychology, 37,* 399–424.

White, T. G., Power, M. A., & White, S. (1989). Morphological analysis: Implications for teaching and understanding vocabulary growth. *Reading Research Quarterly, 24,* 283–304.

Woodcock, R. W. (1991). *Woodcock Language Proficiency Battery—Revised: English and Spanish Forms.* Itasca, IL: Riverside Publishing.

# PART III

# Effective Instruction to Develop Students' Comprehension

# CHAPTER 6

# The Comprehension Conversation: Using Purposeful Discussion During Read-Alouds to Promote Student Comprehension and Vocabulary

Lana Edwards Santoro

Scott K. Baker

David J. Chard

Lisa Howard

We have found that read-alouds can be used in the early elementary grades to promote comprehension before students can read text independently. In this chapter we provide framework for thinking about comprehension as an active conversation between the reader and text. Critical research-based aspects of the "comprehension conversation," such as the use of text-based discourse, text structure, interactive vocabulary learning, and metacognitive self-monitoring, are discussed. A description of our research study evaluating the use of the framework with first-grade students during read-aloud time is also presented.

Questions for Reflection and Discussion:

- How should read-aloud books be selected to help students learn comprehension skills and strategies?
- How can instruction be embedded into traditional read-alouds without compromising children's interests in listening to books?

- What would a good teaching plan include for an effective read-aloud?
- If read-alouds are connected to other content and the state's curriculum standards in content areas, how would you create a cohesive set of lessons?

Recent state and federal investments in research and classroom implementation have focused largely on improving reading outcomes in K–3 education. These efforts have been designed to ensure that all children are reading independently and on grade level by the end of third grade. In addition to overwhelming evidence suggesting the need to improve students' foundational skills like phonological awareness and phonological recoding, the Rand report *Reading for Understanding* urges educators to increase emphasis on comprehension instruction in the earliest grades (Snow, 2002). Often some assume that comprehension instruction must wait until students in the early grades develop beginning reading skills and start to read basic text independently. Recent research, however, reveals that comprehension instruction can be beneficial if it begins in the context of oral language activities *before* students read independently.

Decontextualized oral language expands children's exposure to topics and events beyond their everyday experiences (Heath, 1983; Snow, 1993; Snow & Dickinson, 1991). Beck and McKeown (2001) assert that one reasonable approach to providing decontextualized language and building vocabulary is through "read-alouds" that challenge young children's comprehension. Though some preliminary efforts to develop an effective approach for reading aloud to children for the purpose of comprehension development have been explored, there is limited evidence supporting the current classroom practice of simply reading a text aloud to students (Whitehurst et al., 1994). The following classroom scenarios describe the typical classroom practice of using read-alouds as text-exposure opportunities and read-alouds where integrated teacher and student discourse is used to intentionally model comprehension strategies and promote text understanding.

If you were to observe a first-grade teacher, Ms. Woods, doing a read-aloud for the book *Albert's Impossible Toothache* by B. Williams (2003), you might see her introduce the book by showing the book's cover. Students are asked to make predictions about what the book is going to be about. As Ms. Woods reads the book aloud to her class, you see her pause to clarify a vocabulary word or ask students a comprehension question or two. Ms. Woods focuses on reading and doesn't stop the flow of the story to discuss whether or not student predictions are confirmed. Overall, Ms. Woods likes to let her students enjoy listening to the book. She keeps discussion about what happens in the text to a minimum to avoid extensive interruptions of the read-aloud. After reading, Ms. Woods might ask the class a literal comprehension question about what happened to confirm student understanding. Ms. Woods views the purpose of her read-aloud as an opportunity for students to learn about literature and how text works.

Unlike Ms. Woods, who keeps discussion during the read-aloud relatively minimal, Mrs. Vollner integrates her comprehension instruction into read-aloud time. Like most teachers, Mrs. Vollner has many things to accomplish during the school day. To optimize her instructional time, Mrs. Vollner finds ways to incorporate comprehension instruction into read aloud time while attempting to maintain the integrity and overall experience of a read-aloud.

Mrs. Vollner begins the read-aloud by helping her students prepare to read. She says, "Because this is a new book, what is the first thing we want to know before reading? What question can we ask to help us know our purpose for reading?" After one or two student responses, Mrs. Vollner confirms,

> Right, and the reason we ask "Is this a storybook or an information book?" is because we read information and story books for different reasons. Knowing whether a book is a storybook or information book helps us know what our purpose is and what we should be doing before, during, and after reading.

Mrs. Vollner continues to prepare students for the read-aloud. She shows students the cover of *Albert's Impossible Toothache*, and she guides students in making "text to self" connections about *toothaches*. Mrs. Vollner says, "Everyone, point to the part of your body where you would have a toothache. Have any of you ever had a toothache? How did if feel?" Also before reading, Mrs. Vollner previews and explicitly defines one or two critical vocabulary words, has students make predictions about whom they think the story will be about, and reminds students to listen for story elements during the read-aloud.

While reading, Mrs. Vollner pauses to review and clarify vocabulary. She also reminds students that one way to make sure they are paying attention to the story is to predict what will happen next. During the story, Mrs. Vollner asks students to share and discuss their predictions with a Book Club partner. She says,

> I want you and your Book Club partner to discuss what you think Albert's mother is going to do next and what words you think the author is going to use to describe what she does. This is a discussion so you both have to talk. You'll have to make sure you both get a chance to talk, and you'll want to think about and respond to what your partner says. I want you both to agree, as Book Club partners,

on what you think is going to happen next. I will be asking for volunteers to share what they and their partner think.

Throughout the read-aloud, Mrs. Vollner pauses at intentional moments to ask questions and clarify story elements. Her use of conversation is planned and purposeful. She tries to incorporate brief teacher-to-student and student-to-student discussions at critical points in the story. She always tries to focus discussion on the main story elements because she knows these story features can be used as a framework when students do their postreading retells of part of the story or the whole story.

Rather than ending the read-aloud with one or two comprehension questions, Mrs. Vollner wants students to demonstrate their understanding of the story by retelling. She uses a large chart with graphic representations of the main parts of a story. As she points to the graphic organizer, Mrs. Vollner describes the parts of a story retell. For example, "The first thing we say in a retell is the book type and title. Next we tell who the story is about." She passes out student copies of the retell chart and asks students to practice retelling the story with their Book Club partner. During the student retells, Mrs. Vollner circulates among students to make sure that each student gets a chance to talk, discuss, and retell the story.

As the above scenarios indicate, Ms. Woods and Mrs. Vollner have very different approaches for their classroom read-alouds. While there isn't anything inherently "wrong" with Ms. Woods' read-aloud, Mrs. Vollner's read-aloud includes much more strategically integrated instruction. If the purpose of read-alouds is to optimize instructional time by finding opportunities to boost student comprehension, Mrs. Vollner's approach to read-alouds may have some advantages. At first glance, the major difference between Ms. Woods and Mrs. Vollner is the extent to which analytic conversation is used during the read-aloud. Can conversation and planned talk during a read-aloud really have an impact on comprehension? The following discussion of the critical aspects of comprehension suggests that the nature of text-based discourse may have instructional impact.

## THE COMPREHENSION CONVERSATION

*Comprehension* is a highly complex cognitive process involving the *intentional interaction between the reader and text* to extract or construct meaning (National Reading Panel, 2000). By definition, comprehension is not an automatic or passive process. Rather, comprehension is highly purposeful and interactive (Honig, Diamond, & Gutlohn, 2000). Whether reading text to extract and construct meaning or listening to text read aloud, comprehension can be seen as an active conversation between the reader or listener and the text. An active comprehension conversation includes the use of previewing before reading: "Am I going to read a storybook or information book?" It includes question asking during reading: "Who is the main character in this story? What will happen next? What does that word mean?" This conversation is about actively and continuously monitoring understanding through an exchange of questions (Wong, 1992). Overall, the comprehension conversation involves asking why you are reading or listening to the text, finding the main idea, searching for answers, thinking of questions about the content and searching for more answers, and looking back on both the questions and answers to decide how each provided additional information about the content.

Most important, the comprehension conversation is intentional, purposeful, and interactive. When thinking about the use of classroom read-alouds to promote comprehension, there must be more than passive listening. If teachers simply read a text aloud to a classroom of students and incorporate a comprehension question or two during and after the reading, there isn't intentional interaction or an active discourse between teacher, text, and students.

In this chapter, we discuss how we designed a read aloud curriculum based on the theoretical and research-based understanding of comprehension as an intentional interaction between the reader and the text. Our goal was to find ways to integrate more intentional and purposeful comprehension instruction within classroom read-alouds. We tried to structure a classroom text-focused dialogue between teachers and students during read-aloud time. These "dialogic interactions" were central to demonstrating how comprehension is an interactive process between the listener and the read-aloud text. Because reading comprehension is an active and continuous internal dialogue about text, we wanted to make this conversation overt through the use of teacher-facilitated "think-alouds" with planned and purposeful text-focused discourse. By using read-alouds, we hoped that the critical aspects of a reading-comprehension conversation could be demonstrated through listening comprehension. Therefore, comprehension instruction could begin in the early grades before students read independently with listening-comprehension instruction integrated in the context of read-alouds. A research-based rationale for how we designed our read-aloud curriculum is presented followed by an overview of our study, the results, and a discussion about outcomes.

## TEXT-FOCUSED DISCOURSE

Existing research on storybook reading with preschool children has examined the effects of different teacher-child interaction styles during book reading (Dickinson & Smith, 1994; Teale & Martinez, 1996). Dickinson and

Smith (1994) found that the use of analytic talk requiring children to reflect on story content or language was most beneficial to comprehension. The most effective analytic talk includes discussion that features major story elements, deals with ideas as they are encountered, and involves children in the discussions with opportunities to be reflective.

More recently, Beck and McKeown (2001) explored the use of "text talk" in lessons for children in first-grade classrooms. Their preliminary findings suggest that dialogue focused on read-alouds may promote increased vocabulary acquisition and comprehension. "Text talk," or structured text-focused discourse, requires a child to become part of the dialogue by contributing to the discussion or engaging more actively with the text. For example, questions such as "What is the author trying to say?" or "What is the author talking about?" are used to initiate discussion. Questions like "Does that make sense?" or "Is that said in a clear way?" or "Did the author explain that clearly?" are used to identify difficulties with the way the author presents information or ideas. Overall, the strategic use of discourse leads to deeper comprehension processing, repetition, and additional connections (Beck, McKeown, Hamilton, & Kucan, 1997; Whitehurst et al., 1994). Discourse appears to help students understand text at more sophisticated levels (Wilkinson & Silliman, 2000).

Despite a limited number of specific research studies on read-aloud practices with the intentional use of text-based discourse, there is considerable interest in this topic. In recent years the interest in read-alouds has been represented in articles that focus on practices that teachers could employ to help enhance traditional methods of reading aloud to children, for example, Hickman, Pollard-Durodola and Vaughn, 2004, and Fisher, Flood, Lapp, and Frey, 2004. In both of these empirical reviews, the authors point out that effective read-alouds can contribute to students' comprehension development. Beck, McKeown, & Kucan (2002) also describe related activities that can help children develop discursive book-related skills by building background knowledge and language.

In an early study of read-alouds and their influence on children's achievement, Mason (1989) asked kindergarten teachers to read narrative, information, and easy-to-read picture books. She found that teachers across all reading situations spontaneously shifted the focus and nature of the accompanying discussion and surrounding activities, resulting in both student and teacher changes in language complexity. More recently, Fisher, Flood, Lapp, and Frey (2004) found that although most of the 120 teachers they observed read aloud to their students regularly, they did not consistently prepare by practicing reading the texts, did not read the text fluently, and did not adequately establish a purpose for the read-alouds by introducing and connecting their read-alouds to subsequent extensions of the text. For these 120 teachers, read-alouds were simply opportunities to read text aloud to students without the use of intentional and specific dialogic interactions.

Based on the research on text-focused discourse, we wanted to incorporate structured, interactive teacher-student dialogue in read-alouds. Rather than just simply reading a text aloud to a classroom of students without conspicuous pauses for discussion, we hoped to create intentional opportunities in our read-alouds where children could step back and reflect on the story line or the language in the text, for the purpose of promoting comprehension. For example, when reading a story, a teacher might pause to ask students to identify the main character and then expand the discussion about the main character by asking students about specific character clues. Dialogue could also be focused around predictions. Instead of just asking students to make predictions, a teacher could ask why students made a particular prediction. After reading the part in the story when the prediction is confirmed, teachers could ask students to use the text to prove whether or not their prediction was correct. Most important, the purpose of text-focused discourse is to have students become true partners in the comprehension conversation by attending to the text and actively contributing to discussions. Central to teacher-student dialogue in the comprehension conversation is the use of text structure, interactive vocabulary learning, and active metacognitive thinking.

## Text Structure

Text-focused discourse requires that text be a central part of the conversation (Snow, Burns & Griffin, 1998). One of our goals in the development of our read-aloud intervention was to extend the "text talk" work of Beck and McKeown (2001) by anchoring teachers' questions on text structure within and between related stories and informational texts. *Text structures* can be described as abstract features that serve as a frame to identify important information and connections between ideas (Dickson, Simmons, & Kame'enui, 1998; Englert & Thomas, 1987; Goldman & Rakestraw, 2000; Pearson & Fielding, 1991). Strong empirical evidence links readers' awareness of text structure to reading comprehension and their ability to retell stories and comprehend text (Baker, Gersten, & Grossen, 2002; Hansen, 1978; Weaver & Dickinson, 1982; Williams, 1993). Focusing discourse on text structure provides an anchor for student understanding and a framework of "sameness" that can be applied across multiple texts (Carnine & Kinder, 1985).

Despite students' early familiarity with narrative text structures, their actual understanding of those structures varies greatly (Adams, 1990). The early elementary grades are an ideal time to teach text structure because of children's interest in and informal understanding of stories. Identifying narrative text structure, for example, during a story read aloud would provide students a framework for discussing and retelling stories. As a story is read, the teacher can help students discuss who the story is about, what happened first, what happened next, and what happened at the end. If these same target story elements are always used to identify critical features of a story during read-alouds, students have repeated opportunities to discuss story elements and make text-to-text connections related to main characters and story sequence. In other words, not only could students identify story elements in Jan Brett's *The Mitten*, but they could also compare characters and story sequence using the same set of story elements for Jan Brett's *The Hat* or Karma Wilson's *Bear Snores On*. A consistent read-aloud format would help students understand increasingly complex narrative structures, which may be beneficial as students develop independent reading skills and read increasingly complex stories.

Young children get very little exposure to or training in reading informational texts (Caswell & Duke, 1998; Duke, 1999). However, as reading development progresses, children are eventually expected to read expository or information books. Reading informational text requires a different set of comprehension skills and an understanding about how informational text structure differs from narrative text structure. Often skills for understanding informational text are not taught until fourth grade, if at all. Because informational texts use a variety of organizational patterns (e.g., compare and contrast, cause and effect) that are different from traditional narrative texts, understanding them is more difficult for nearly all students (Williams, 2000). Reading informational texts often involves reading to locate (and possibly record) particular information (Dreher, 1993; Guthrie & Kirsch, 1987), rather than reading to learn something in a linear, sequential fashion. Several recent studies suggest that young children can benefit from exposure to informational text (Donovan, 1996; Hicks, 1995). For example, Duke and Kays (1998) studied what young children know and can learn about expository text. These researchers found that "inattention to expository texts in early childhood settings cannot be justified on the basis that children are unable to interact productively with these texts" (p. 314). Despite the difficulties of using expository text, it seems that exposure can result in knowledge of expository text structure and book language. Kletzien and Szabo (1998) documented that some young children even prefer informational text.

## Interactive Vocabulary Learning

The correlation of vocabulary knowledge with school success and reading comprehension is widely documented (Anderson & Freebody, 1981; Anderson & Nagy, 1991; Baker, Simmons, & Kame'enui, 1998). Because vocabulary is critical to comprehension, a discussion of word knowledge and meanings must be part of the comprehension conversation. Words are typically learned gradually (Baumann et al., 2002). The more actively, purposefully, and deeply students process words, the better they learn them (Fisher & Blachowicz, 2005; Stahl & Fairbanks, 1986). Simply stated, vocabulary gains are greatest if the meanings of words are explicitly discussed (Dickinson & Smith, 1994; see also Chapters 4 and 5 of this volume).

Reading stories to children provides context for vocabulary discussions and opportunities to learn word meanings before children can read on their own (Biemiller, 2001a). Text-focused instruction supports vocabulary development, in part because speech is "lexically impoverished" compared to written language. Though this may seem counterintuitive in the context of what often appears to be the simplistic nature of children's literature, Cunningham and Stanovich (1998) point out that "the relative rarity of the words in children's books is, in fact, greater than that in all of the adult conversation, except for courtroom testimony" (p. 9). In other words, children's stories are valuable sources both of rare words and diverse vocabulary.

Recognizing the richness of vocabulary is important for two primary reasons. First, the use of text to facilitate comprehension and word learning has the added benefit of exposing children to varied vocabulary. Vocabulary differences between children are often attributed to disparate exposure to print and the corresponding differences in quality of vocabulary between text and speech (Cunningham & Stanovich, 1998; McKeown & Curtis, 1987).

Second, vocabulary and comprehension appear to be more highly correlated when a child's exposure to rich and varied vocabulary words is complemented with direct and sequential vocabulary instruction requiring accuracy of word knowledge, fluency of accessing the word's meaning, and rich, decontextualized examples of a word's application (Beck, McKeown, & Omanson, 1987; Biemiller, 2001b). In other words, although story reading provides a rich context for word learning (e.g., Dickinson & Smith, 1994; Elley, 1989), neither dramatic vocabulary improvement nor sufficient vocabulary learning for students with limited vocabulary knowledge will result from simply reading aloud to children (Meyer, Stahl, Linn, & Wadrop, 1994).

In addition to providing a context for learning unfamiliar words, vocabulary must be taught directly and sequentially (Biemiller, 2001a). For example, before reading Eric Carle's *The Grouchy Ladybug*, the word *grouchy* could be explicitly defined and discussed in the read-aloud context. The teacher might say:

The title of this book is *The Grouchy Ladybug*. *Grouchy* means grumpy or mad. Someone who is grouchy is not happy. What does *grouchy* mean? Show me, with your face, what "grouchy" looks like.

Look at the book cover again. How would you describe the ladybug on the cover?

Later, when discussing story elements like main character, *grouchy* would be used to describe the ladybug. "The grouchy ladybug is grouchy, mean, and not polite." Finally, to promote additional discussion and interactions with words, questions such as "Who can tell me a time when you would feel grouchy?" or "When you're grouchy you're really unhappy; how does that feel?" or "If someone is grouchy, how are they acting, what do they do?" can extend student word knowledge (Beck, McKeown, Kucan, 2002).

## Metacognition: The Action of Thinking and Knowing

Effective readers remember more if they ask themselves questions during reading and actively monitor their understanding (Wong, 1992). The active monitoring of understanding, or "thinking about thinking," is the metacognitive awareness that initiates and maintains the comprehension conversation throughout the reading process. Metacognition is an interactive internal dialogue that focuses on what a reader is thinking and what a reader knows during reading.

Despite the cognitive complexity of monitoring understanding during reading, metacognition is viewed as an instructional priority in Grades K–3. For example, the National Research Council (1998) included the ability to "distinguish whether simple sentences are incomplete and fail to make sense" and the ability to "notice when texts fail to make sense" as first-grade goals. At first thought it might seem to be an enormous instructional challenge to teach elementary students self-monitoring strategies especially if students are not reading independently. While research on metacognition in the early grades is relatively limited, using text-based dialogic interactions appears to be an ideal way to teach students to self-monitor. For example, teacher "think-alouds" during text-based discourse can be used to model the internal self-monitoring dialogue. During the book, *Bear Snores On*, a teacher might pause and say, "We just read that the bear was slumbering. I'm not sure what *slumbering* means. Let's reread this page to see if we can figure out what *slumbering* means." Another example of using text-based discourse for the purpose of promoting self-monitoring is a teacher's modeled retelling of the story. "I'm going to retell the story *Bear Snores On*. [Teacher models the retell.] Did I include all the story information in my retell?" Finally, students can even be taught to listen to a partner retell a story and see whether or not their partner included all of the critical text information in their retell. A teacher might say:

Listeners, think about whether your partners said everything they were supposed to say during their retell. If they included the book type, topic, and information about what makes an animal a mammal and what types of animals are mammals, tell your partners that they did a good job. If your partners didn't say one or more of those things, you need to tell them that they should do so the next time.

As discussed previously, regular participation in text-based discussions that involve reflection and analysis appear to help children distance themselves from the story and become more aware of their own thinking. Prior research has speculated that children may be more adept at noticing words whose meanings they do not know, more likely to search for their meanings, and more able to use available information to figure out the text's meaning (Dickinson & Smith, 1994).

## OVERVIEW OF THE STUDY

In our study we sought to investigate the efficacy of a read-aloud intervention delivered during whole-class instruction with students in first-grade general education classrooms. The framework used in developing the intervention focused on helping children understand complex text by processing common structural elements of narrative and information text and making connections across related texts. Instructional procedures highlighted (1) dialogic interactions among students and teachers aimed at extending discussions using decontextualized language, (2) visual representations of narrative and informational text elements that facilitate intertextual connections, and (3) strategic and interactive vocabulary instruction.

Intervention effects were investigated for students in general education classrooms who were most at risk for overall reading and comprehension problems, as well as for students who were on track for successful reading development, including comprehension.

Three school districts were recruited to participate in the study. One district was located in the Pacific Northwest, the other two districts were located in Pennsylvania. In these 3 districts, 13 schools participated. Across the 13 schools, there were 42 classrooms involving one participating teacher from each classroom.

Prior to randomly assigning schools to condition, all students in the 42 first-grade classrooms were administered a series of brief measures to screen for reading problems. Our objective in screening for reading problems was to make sure these students were included in the sample of students used to determine intervention impact. Screening measures were individual tests selected from the *Dynamic Indicators of Basic Early Literacy Skills* (DIBELS; Good & Kaminski, 2002). At the same time, the 42 general education teachers independently rated all students in their classrooms on degree of risk they believed each student possessed related specifically to reading comprehension difficulties.

## LESSON DESIGN AND COMPONENTS

The intervention was implemented during a 15-week period from February to May, 2004. Instruction was scaffolded across the 15 weeks so in the early units teachers were more active in directing the read-aloud lessons. In later units, more emphasis was placed on independent student responses. In units 1 through 5, the lessons emphasized teacher demonstration of comprehension tasks using think-alouds, explicit models, and concise explanations. In units 6 through 10, greater emphasis was placed on guiding student responses to match the types of responses teachers demonstrated regularly in units 1 through 5. Teachers asked questions and elicited answers with prompts and support as necessary. In units 11 through 15, the degree of teacher guidance continued to be reduced systematically, but the intervention design included sufficient flexibility so that teachers could increase explicit support and instruction if they felt students needed greater direction.

In terms of lesson structure, there were four lessons in each unit. Two lessons focused on narrative text, and two lessons focused on information text. Each lesson lasted approximately 30 minutes. Teachers were not given specific instructional plans for the 5th day of the week, but were asked to use the read-aloud for related activities based on the week's thematic unit. For example, teachers could reread one of the read-aloud texts again, do writing-based retell activities with students, or review texts used previously.

### Before-During-After Reading Framework

When planning a read-aloud lesson for narrative and information texts, we included before, during, and after reading lesson components. The purpose of the discrete components was to structure interactive dialogue about the text, demonstrate how the "comprehension conversation" would work throughout the reading process, and explicitly and intentionally apply multiple comprehension strategies (NAP, 2000). The before, during, and after reading lesson structure would also allow teachers to model interactive comprehension strategies in a listening comprehension context. While not the focus of our research, the hope would be that this reading framework would transfer to reading comprehension when students would begin to read independently.

### Before Text Reading

Before reading, the purpose for reading was established by identifying the book type (narrative or information), and preparing for reading based on book type. Learning that we read story and information books differently is essential to comprehension because the reader (or listener) will know what framework or text structure to use to anchor comprehension. For narrative books, this involved making predictions regarding what the story might be about. For informational books, students were asked to identify "what they thought they knew" and "what they wanted to know" about the topic using a K-W-L chart (What I Know, What I Want to know, What I Learned). Vocabulary necessary to understand the book (narrative or informational) was taught before text reading.

### During Text Reading

During reading, lessons centered on story grammar for narrative texts and K-W-L components for informational texts. Questioning strategies were used to prompt discussions, and these strategies emphasized techniques to produce higher level thinking skills such as making predictions and drawing inferences. To promote text-based dialogue, questions elicited more than simple "yes" or "no" responses. Students were often asked to elaborate on what they where thinking or feeling about an event, topic, or character in the story. It was important that different levels of questions, from literal to more implicit and complex, were used to facilitate discussion. Finally, regular, structured opportunities were also provided for students to talk about aspects of the text with one another. These "Book Club" activities occurred in groups of two or four students and always included a focus question. Vocabulary words were taught or reviewed as they occurred in the text.

### After Text Reading

After reading, teachers modeled retelling the story or information book. A common retell format was used for all story books. Teachers used a visual prompt sheet that included icons representing whom the story was about, what happened first, what happened next, and what happened at the end. They linked their verbal retellings to the prompt sheet. When students practiced retells with each other, they used their own story retell sheets to prompt their retells. The K-W-L chart provided the format for informational book retells. As with the narrative retells, students practiced retelling as a group or in pairs. Vocabulary words were also reviewed after reading.

### Making Connections

Another important component of the lesson structure was teacher attempts to help students make text-to-text and text-to-life connections. These connections were emphasized before, during, and after reading. Connection opportunities were built into the lessons. Text-to-text connections helped students see linkages between books within and across units. Text-to-life connections helped students see linkages between aspects of their own lives and the content they studying in the read aloud lessons.

## Content of the Texts

Within each unit, whether a narrative or informational text was used in the first two lessons depended on the unit focus. For units featuring general animal categories (i.e., mammals, reptiles, and insects), the narrative book was used in the first two lessons followed by the informational book for the last two lessons. The narrative book was used first with general animal categories to capture student interest with a story featuring an animal character. For units focusing on specific animals, like bats and elephants, we thought it would be more effective to introduce content and build background knowledge with the informational book prior to reading narrative text.

### Narrative Lessons

The first narrative lesson in a unit included a 5-minute introduction to the book, discussion of whether the text was a story or information book, and story predictions. During a 10- to 15-minute read-aloud of the story, teachers paused to confirm predictions and used think-alouds to clarify story events or vocabulary and to make connections to other texts. The first read-aloud lesson centered on story structure and the content students would need for the retelling, although this shifted somewhat as the intervention progressed over the course of the study. After the read-aloud, the teacher used a story retell chart to model story retelling. Vocabulary was also discussed and reviewed. The modeled retell and vocabulary activities took approximately 10 minutes.

The second narrative lesson began with a brief review of the title, author, and illustrator. Teachers also asked students to identify whether the book was a story or information book and describe the text features that helped them decide. The story retell chart was reviewed with students before the text was read a second time. During the second reading, the teacher paused much more often for discussions, and an increased emphasis was placed on inferential understanding as opposed to literal understanding. There were also more opportunities for students to discuss focus questions in Book Clubs during pauses in the read aloud. The increase in discussions during the second lesson lengthened the time it took to read the text to approximately 15 to 20 minutes. After reading, the teacher guided student retells using a large retell chart. The lesson ended by having students work with a partner from their Book Club to practice story retellings using the retell prompt sheets. The teacher-guided retell and student retell practice took approximately 10 minutes.

### Information Lessons

The first information lesson in a unit began with a 5- to 10-minute introduction of the topic, identification of the book title and author, and a discussion of whether the text was a story or informational book. A K-W-L chart was used to help students prepare for the read-aloud. Teachers guided students through a brief brainstorm of what they thought they knew about the text's topic and wrote student responses in a "What I think I know" section on a large K-W-L chart. Next, teachers asked students to think about what they wanted to learn about the topic. In the interest of time and instructional focus, we asked teachers to use predetermined "What do you want to know?" questions in addition to soliciting one or two student generated questions. For example, when reading texts on specific animal types, like crocodiles, teachers would always use the questions "What does a crocodile look like?" and "What does a crocodile eat?"

Reading of the informational text on the first day's lesson took approximately 10 to 15 minutes. Because of informational texts' density, we selected book excerpts for the read-aloud. These excerpts focused on content that addressed the questions generated in the "What do you want to learn?" component of the K-W-L chart and would also be of high interest to students. The read-aloud focused on student predictions, drawing conclusions, making connections, and vocabulary. Teachers read only the first part of the informational book during the first lesson. Unlike the repeated reading format used for narrative book lessons, the informational book was read in two parts across the two lesson days. At the end of the read-aloud in the first lesson, teachers guided students through a retell and summary of the text excerpts read during that lesson. The classroom K-W-L chart was used to facilitate a teacher-directed retell by focusing on the "What we learned" component of the chart. Teachers spent approximately 5 to 10 minutes concluding the lesson with the retell and text summary.

The second information lesson began with a 5- to 10-minute review of the topic and purpose for reading. Teachers reviewed information completed on the K-W-L chart from the previous lesson. Before teachers read the text, students were prompted to listen for new information that they could add to the "What we learned" component of the chart. As with the 1st day, the 2nd day's read-aloud focused on making predictions, drawing conclusions about content, and making connections to personal experiences and other texts. Emphasis was also placed on helping students learn content details that addressed the focus questions asked for the K-W-L chart's "What do you want to learn?" component. Because these content details and focus questions were used to structure student retellings, emphasis was placed on recalling details during the read-aloud. In the second lesson teachers spent approximately 10 to 15 minutes on the read-aloud. The lesson concluded with a teacher-directed review of the completed K-W-L chart. Students then met in Book Clubs to talk about the things they learned from the information text. After this, students practiced retells with a partner. Students used a fact sheet highlighting the content details that answered the focus questions used in the K-W-L chart's "What do you want to learn?" component. The teacher-directed summary of the K-W-L chart and the student retell practice took approximately 5 to 10 minutes to complete.

## Comparison Condition

Teachers in the comparison condition were asked to engage in read-aloud activities an average of 4 days per week during the 15-week study. Comparison teachers had a scheduled read-aloud time and were asked to use their normal read-aloud procedures with their students during that time. For the purposes of the study, we made three specific requests regarding daily read-aloud time. First, we asked teachers to select a target text of their choice, either narrative or informational, that would serve as the focus for their classroom read-alouds. Second, we asked teachers to engage in read-aloud activities for approximately 30 minutes per day. Teachers could use whatever procedures they thought would promote student comprehension. Third, at three times during the intervention, at weeks 3, 8, and 14, we asked comparison teachers to read a specific book to their students on 2 consecutive days. As a result, both experimental and comparison teachers read the same book during weeks 3, 8, and 14. We observed full read-aloud lessons of comparison and experimental teachers during weeks 3, 8, and 14 for the purpose of documenting implementation fidelity.

## CONCLUSION

Our study examined the impact of a 15-week read-aloud intervention on the comprehension and vocabulary performance of at-risk and average-achieving first-grade students.

### Outcomes of Our Study

In terms of comprehension overall, as measured by a composite of all the comprehension measures used in the study, the significant impact favored intervention students. (For details about measures used in evaluation and the results of the testing, see the Appendix at the end of this chapter.) In terms of narrative text impact specifically, students in the intervention group provided significantly more retell statements than students in the comparison condition. Students in intervention classrooms demonstrated retells that reflected a depth of text comprehension. For example, instead of retelling a story or information text in basic sequence, students who received the Read-Aloud Curriculum told retells with more text-based examples and elaborative utterances. Not only were retells longer, but quality and depth were documented when retells were scored. Components of the Read-Aloud Curriculum that may have contributed to this outcome include the strategic emphasis on text structure throughout lessons, the use of visual prompt sheets to facilitate student retellings, daily practice for student retellings, and the teacher's use of decontextualized language.

Significant differences on retell measures were enhanced, of course, by the fact the intervention focused explicitly on improving the content and quality of student retells. The intervention included frequent models of retells by teachers and numerous opportunities for students to practice retells of narrative and information text. Teachers were trained to provide specific feedback to students on their retells, and retell expectations were scaffolded over the course of the curriculum so that students built systematically to a complete retell by learning to provide sections of quality retells in manageable chunks.

While performance on retell assessments are encouraging, results also indicated that the read-aloud intervention had an impact on reading comprehension as measured by the standardized measure used in this study. This finding is particularly noteworthy because the intervention focused on dialogic interactions and verbal expressions of comprehension. Because students were expected to demonstrate their understanding through a variety of assessment modes, we intentionally structured the text-based discourse used in the curriculum to promote deep processing. The significant results observed for quality and content of retellings, and metacognitive understanding of the purpose for reading, reflect the Read-Aloud Curriculum's emphasis on active and intentional dialogic interactions and use of decontextualized language about text before, during, and after the reading process.

## Lack of Impact

We were surprised that the impact on vocabulary was not significant, in part because students in the intervention condition had a distinct advantage. Test words were sampled from narrative and informational books that students in the intervention condition were taught. However, given the challenges associated with explicit vocabulary instruction (Baker, Simmons, & Kame'enui, 1998), as well as the minimal exposure students were likely to have had for the words on the vocabulary test, perhaps it is not surprising that impact approached but did not reach statistical significance.

The read-aloud intervention did not have significant impact on a standardized measure of listening comprehension (the Gates-MacGinitie) or on the TOLD vocabulary subtest. Although the listening comprehension measure was more closely aligned with the intervention than reading comprehension (where there was a significant impact), it is not entirely unsurprising that we did not obtain a significant impact on this measure. The nature of the questions asked on the Gates-MacGinitie listening comprehension measure provide some insight into potential alignment problems. A typical question on the listening comprehension subtest was to have students listen to the examiner describe an action, such as a boy walking a dog along a river. Students chose a picture out of four that best described the statement read by the examiner. Although this is a listening comprehension activity, it is far removed from the challenge of listening to a story or a story part, or a section of information text, and constructing a representation of that text based on the application of strategies taught. The lack of a significant finding on the TOLD vocabulary subtest measure also was not surprising given that on the more closely aligned vocabulary measures sampled from the Read-Aloud Curriculum there also was no significant vocabulary effect.

## Limitations

Limitations must also be considered when discussing the findings of this study. There was limited control over the amount of instructional time spent on read-alouds in comparison classrooms. Instructional time in read-aloud classrooms, however, was controlled by prescribed lessons and the content of the curriculum. Even though teachers in the comparison classroom were asked to use read-alouds for 30 minutes each day, there was variability in instructional time. While we documented an average time spent on read-alouds in comparison classrooms, it was difficult to determine which activities or what specific components of instruction were considered as a read-aloud. Many comparison teachers did not integrate comprehension within the actual context of a classroom read-aloud. Rather, they included add-on instruction or a separate book related activity before or after a read-aloud. Certainly instructional time, specifically the intensity of instructional time, makes an impact on student performance.

The assessment battery used in the study should also be considered when examining results. Due to the somewhat limited availability of instruments with documented technical adequacy to measure comprehension and vocabulary in young children, we created an assessment battery to address direct and indirect skill outcomes. As described earlier, we also adapted some assessment protocols and scoring procedures to align more directly with skills taught in the Read-Aloud Curriculum. Given the role of researcher-developed measures and scoring analysis procedures, as well as a set of measures within the battery directly aligned with the curriculum, it is important to consider what specific skills are actually being assessed. Broader questions related to the generalization of language and comprehension, and how transfer and generalization are measured, can also be raised as future studies are designed to document instructional impact on student comprehension.

Another issue related to assessment concerns the selection criteria used in this study to identify both at-risk and average-achieving students in comprehension. We used a combination of teacher referrals and performance scores on beginning reading measures to select students for the study. A valid criticism of the selection criteria is how poor readers with comprehension difficulties and good readers without comprehension difficulties are identified. In other words, what screening battery is best to identify a student with poor comprehension, and how do you know if a particular student has difficulties with comprehension or struggles with more language-based deficits? We have unanswered questions about whether we truly identified students with specific reading skill difficulties, comprehension difficulties, language deficits, or a combination of skills. Establishing a more accurate and practical screening battery should be considered in future research.

## Directions for Future Research

Our results reveal that we can positively impact comprehension through a read-aloud approach with text-based discourse. When considering possible directions for future research it is important to consider the challenge of reading intervention research articulated by Lyon and Moats (1997). They suggest that intervention research should attempt to determine:

Which instructional reading approach or method, or combination of approaches or methods, provided in which setting or combination of settings, under which student-teacher ratio conditions and teacher-student interactions, provided for what period of time and by which type of teacher, have the greatest impact on well-defined elements of reading behavior and reading-related behaviors, for which children, for how long, and for what reasons? (p. 579)

Our efforts to incorporate intentional and purposeful text-based discourse in classroom read-alouds optimized read-aloud time by explicitly focusing on text structure, establishing a clear purpose for reading narrative or informational text, and using visual prompts to practice daily retellings. Unfortunately, the nature of the intervention package precludes conclusions regarding which components contributed to the significant effects. As we continue to expand our research, we hope to learn about the impact of specific instructional and comprehension conversation components on comprehension and vocabulary outcomes.

## Follow-up Activities

1. Discuss how you will enhance classroom read alouds to further promote comprehension. Will you focus more on vocabulary? Will you incorporate additional teacher-to-student and student-to-student talk?
2. Implement a classroom read-aloud by including some of the instructional components discussed in this chapter. What worked well? What didn't work well? What aspects of your read aloud and instruction will you modify to impact student comprehension?
3. It's essential to make the most of instructional time. What are some ways to extend the content of read-alouds into other academic areas? For example, how could you use the structure for student retells discussed in this chapter (e.g., use of retell prompt sheets) for writing instruction?
4. The chapter discusses the importance of "intentional" and "strategic" talk during read-alouds. How does the intentional aspect of analytic talk impact planning and preparing for read-alouds? Will you need to plan for read-alouds differently? If so, how?

## APPENDIX: MEASURES AND RESULTS

### Measures of Early Literacy

All students in the 42 participating classrooms were individually administered three DIBELS measures prior to the intervention to help identify student risk status for reading problems and to use as possible covariates to explain intervention impact. Measures selected were Letter Naming Fluency, Phonemic Segmentation Fluency, and Nonsense Word Fluency. These measures are part of the DIBELS assessment system (http://dibels.uoregon.edu) and are routinely used to screen students for problems in early reading. Technical information on the measures, including information about their reliability and validity, can be found in Good and Kaminski (2002).

## Measures of Comprehension

The following comprehension measures were administered to determine the impact of the intervention. All of the measures, except the Reading Comprehension measure, were administered at pretest and posttest to the target students (3 at-risk and 2 average-achieving) in each classroom. The Reading Comprehension measure was administered at posttest only.

### Strong Narrative Assessment Procedure (SNAP)

Our primary measure of comprehension impact was the SNAP (Strong, 1998), an oral retell measure administered individually to all target students. The SNAP assesses comprehension of narrative texts through story retell. At pretest and posttest, students listened to a tape-recorded story while following along in a wordless picture book. Two stories were administered to each child, one at pretest and one at posttest. Story administration was counterbalanced. An auditory signal (i.e., a beep) indicated when to turn the page and an examiner was present to ensure that students followed along properly. At the end of the story, the examiner removed the book and, using standardized prompts, asked the student to retell the story in his or her own words. The student's retelling was audiotaped for scoring and analysis.

### Information Texts

We adapted SNAP procedures to assess student comprehension of information text at pretest and posttest. At pretest and posttest, an expository passage was shown to each target student, and the topic of the text was identified. Students were asked to tell what they knew about the topic and what they wanted to learn about the topic, and then listened to an audiotape of the text being read. The reading included key information from the text. At the conclusion of the audiotaped passage, students completed a retell. Students were asked to tell everything they could about the information they just heard. So, for example, at the end of a text about community spiders, students were asked to retell everything they had just learned about community spiders. Trained project staff listened to the students' retellings and rated them on a 4-point scale (0–3) in terms of overall quality (Englert & Mariage, 1991). Approximately 40% of the retellings were scored by two raters. Reliability of ratings within one point of each other was .98.

After their retelling, students were asked 10 specific comprehension questions following the same procedures used with the narrative texts. For informational texts, the comprehension questions probed factual recall and vocabulary knowledge.

### Vocabulary Assessments

At pretest and posttest, students were tested on 10 words randomly sampled from the Read-Aloud Curriculum's target vocabulary. Students were asked to tell the meaning of each word presented orally by the examiner. Responses were audiotaped for analysis. Target words were sampled from a total of 33 target words taught in the curriculum's narrative lessons and 41 target words taught in the information lessons. Target words were of two types. Words essential for understanding the meaning and content of the text represented the most frequent type. A smaller number of words were selected as enrichment words or bonus words. These were words that, although not essential for understanding the meaning of the text, offered considerable benefit to children in a variety of other contexts. Two alternate forms of the vocabulary assessment were generated from the 74 total words taught. Alternate-form administration was counter-balanced so that the same number of students in the experimental and comparison conditions were assessed on the same forms at pretest and posttest. The number of words the students correctly identified was determined. Scores were verified by a second, expert examiner.

### Test of Oral Language Development—Primary, Third Edition

The Test of Oral Language Development (Newcomer & Hammill, 1997) is an individually administered measure of language proficiency, assessing skills in the areas of semantics, syntax, and phonology. To assess expressive vocabulary, we administered the Oral Vocabulary subtest to all target students at pretest and posttest. On this subtest, the examiner orally presents words one at a time to students, who tell what each word means. Examiners use standard prompts to help solicit student responses. We scored this measure according to standardized procedures in the manual.

### Gates-MacGinitie Listening Comprehension Subtest

The Gates-MacGinitie (MacGinitie, MacGinitie, Maria, & Dreyer, 2000) is a standardized, group-administered test of listening comprehension, which was administered to all target students at pretest and posttest. Students listened to short story scenarios read aloud by an examiner and selected one of three picture choices about the story. This measure provides a general indicator of overall listening comprehension skills.

### Gates-MacGinitie Reading Comprehension Subtest

This standardized, group-administered test is similar to the listening comprehension subtest, but instead of listening to the story segments, students read story segments before choosing which of three pictures most closely matches the story (MacGinitie, MacGinitie, Maria & Dreyer, 2000). The subtest was administered to all target students at posttest only.

## Implementation Fidelity

Fidelity observations were conducted during the intervention in all intervention classrooms. During the first two weeks of the implementation, a project staff member with strong knowledge of the curriculum and instrument observed each intervention classroom for the purpose of providing information about implementation fidelity. Observers answered teacher questions about implementation and emphasized what teachers should do to make sure they followed all lesson components. In some cases, suggestions were offered about how to improve implementation through general instructional principles (e.g., providing all students with opportunities to respond) rather than specific features of the intervention (e.g., providing models of retells).

In addition to these early observations, which constituted the final component of read-aloud training, and ongoing informal observations for the purpose of monitoring major implementation variables, two formal fidelity observations were also conducted toward the middle and end of the study. Observations were conducted in both intervention and comparison classrooms. One observation focused on teachers' reading of information text and the other on their reading of the narrative text. All teachers read the same information and narrative text to their students. Fidelity was coded by tallying teacher behaviors aligned with the intervention, such as providing retell models prior to text reading for the day. Other quantitative indices were general procedures that could characterize any read-aloud time in which teachers engaged in interactive reading with students, such as asking questions and explaining vocabulary.

All of the intervention teachers used the Read-Aloud Curriculum during the informal and formal observations and they engaged in all of the major components. In addition, there were notable differences in how teachers conducted their read-alouds based on condition. Intervention teachers involved students in more activities before and after reading. Of 14 activities coded before and after reading, intervention teachers engaged in more of these activities than comparison teachers in 13 of them. The lone activity engaged in more frequently in the comparison condition occurred after reading, where comparison teachers made more connections from the target text and other texts and life experiences.

During reading however, intervention and comparison teachers engaged in similar amounts of modeling, asking questions, and using the text to make explicit connections to other texts and life experiences beyond what was stated directly in the text. The difference between conditions was that the intervention teachers used the curriculum framework to engage in these activities and comparison teachers did not.

## Results

Table 6.1 presents means and standard deviations for the measures administered at the preintervention and postintervention phases. Our results indicated that enhancing read-alouds with the strategic integration of comprehension strategies and dialogic discussions made a positive difference in student performance. Students from classrooms where teachers used our Read-Aloud Curriculum demonstrated higher levels of comprehension when compared to students from classrooms that did not use the curriculum. Students who participated in the Read-Aloud Curriculum were able to include more accurate information in retells and provide higher quality retells than students from classrooms that did not use the curriculum. Participating students also demonstrated more metacognitive awareness about comprehension. For example, they could articulate why it would help you understand better if you identified the type of book (i.e., expository or narrative) that you would be reading. Most positively, we didn't find differences in comprehension and vocabulary by the end of the 15-week study for the at-risk students and average-achieving students in classrooms that used the Read-Aloud Curriculum. (For more information about the research study, analysis, and results, see Baker, Chard, Edwards-Santoro, Otterstedt, & Gau, 2006; Baker, Chard, & Edwards-Santoro, 2005).

**Table 6.1.** Descriptive statistics by intervention condition

| Outcome measure | Intervention condition (N = 112) | | | | Comparison condition (N= 91) | | | |
| --- | --- | --- | --- | --- | --- | --- | --- | --- |
| | Pretest | | Posttest | | Pretest | | Posttest | |
| | Mean | SD | Mean | SD | Mean | SD | Mean | SD |
| Gates-MacGinitie Listening Comprehension subtest | 11.8 | 4.3 | 15.3 | 4.2 | 13.4 | 3.2 | 16.1 | 3.1 |
| Test of Oral Language Development—Primary, Oral Vocabulary subtest | 10.2 | 5.9 | 12.8 | 5.9 | 12.8 | 4.8 | 13.8 | 5.1 |
| Number of target vocabulary words correctly identified | 1.6 | 1.4 | 3.0 | 2.0 | 2.1 | 1.2 | 2.9 | 1.6 |
| Narrative retell: statements | 2.8 | 3.6 | 7.9 | 6.0 | 4.8 | 4.2 | 6.7 | 5.4 |
| Expository retell: rating | 0.8 | 0.7 | 1.0 | 0.8 | 1.1 | 0.6 | 1.0 | 0.6 |
| Narrative comprehension total score | 17.6 | 5.9 | 19.9 | 5.6 | 18.1 | 4.9 | 21.3 | 5.3 |
| Expository comprehension total score | 9.9 | 4.4 | 11.6 | 5.3 | 11.1 | 4.6 | 12.6 | 5.3 |

*Note. SD* = standard deviation.

# REFERENCES

Adams, M. J. (1990). *Beginning to read: Thinking and learning about print.* Cambridge, MA: MIT Press.

Anderson, R. C., & Freebody, P. (1981). Vocabulary knowledge. In J. T. Guthrie (Ed.), *Comprehension and teaching: Research reviews* (pp. 77–117). Newark, DE: International Reading Association.

Anderson, R. C., & Nagy, W. E. (1991). Word meanings. In R. Barr, M. L. Kamil, P. B. Mosenthal, & P. D. Pearson (Eds.), *Handbook of reading research: Vol. 2* (pp. 690–724). New York: Longman.

Baker, S., Chard, D., & Edwards-Santoro, L. (2005, October). *Story read aloud: Teaching students vocabulary and comprehension strategies in the context of teacher read-alouds in first-grade classrooms.* Paper presented at the Guy Bond Memorial Conference on Reading, Minneapolis/St. Paul, MN.

Baker, S., Chard, D., Edwards-Santoro, L., Otterstedt, J., & Gau, J. (2006). *Reading aloud to students: The development of an intervention to improve comprehension and vocabulary of first graders.* Unpublished manuscript, Eugene, OR.

Baker, S., Gersten, R., & Grossen, B. (2002). Remedial interventions for students with reading comprehension problems. In M. R. Shinn, G. Stoner, & H. M. Walker (Eds.), *Interventions for academic and behavior problems: Vol. 2. Preventive and remedial approaches* (pp. 731–754). Bethesda, MD: National Association of School Psychologists.

Baker, S., Simmons, D. C., & Kame'enui, E. J. (1998). Vocabulary acquisition: Research bases. In D. C. Simmons & E. J. Kame'enui (Eds.), *What reading research tells us about children with diverse learning needs* (pp. 183–218). Mahwah, NJ: Erlbaum.

Baumann, J. F., Edwards, E. C., Font, G., Tereshinski, C. A., Kame'enui, E. J., & Olejnik, S. F. (2002). Teaching morphemic and contextual analysis to fifth-grade students. *Reading Research Quarterly, 37*(2), 150–176.

Beck, I. L., & McKeown, M. G. (2001). Text talk: Capturing the benefits of read-aloud experiences for young children. *The Reading Teacher, 55,* 10–20.

Beck, I. L., McKeown, M. G., Hamilton, R. L., & Kucan, L. (1997). *Questioning the author: An approach for enhancing student engagement with text.* Newark: DE: International Reading Association.

Beck, I. L., McKeown, M. G., & Kucan, L. (2002). *Bringing words to life: Robust vocabulary instruction.* New York: Guilford Press.

Beck, I. L., McKeown, M. G., & Omanson, R. C. (1987). The effects and uses of diverse vocabulary instructional techniques. In M. McKeown & M. Curtis (Eds.), *The nature of vocabulary acquisition* (pp. 147–164). Hillsdale, NJ: Erlbaum.

Biemiller, A. (2001a). Estimating root word vocabulary growth in normative and advantaged populations: Evidence for a common sequence of vocabulary acquisition. *Journal of Educational Psychology, 93,* 498–520.

Biemiller, A. (2001b). Teaching vocabulary: Early, direct, and sequential. *American Educator, 25*(1), 24–28.

Carle, E. (1996). *The grouchy ladybug.* New York: HarperCollins Children's Books.

Carnine, D., & Kinder, B. D. (1985). Teaching low-performing students to apply generative and schema strategies to narrative and expository material. *Remedial and Special Education, 6*(1), 20–30.

Caswell, L. J., & Duke, N. K. (1998). Non-narrative as a catalyst for literacy development. *Language Arts, 75,* 108–117.

Cunningham, A. E., & Stanovich, K. E. (1998). What reading does for the mind. *American Educator, 22*(1 & 2), 8–15.

Dickinson, D. K., & Smith, M. W. (1994). Long-term effects of preschool teachers' book readings on low-income children's vocabulary and story comprehension. *Reading Research Quarterly, 29*(2), 104–122.

Dickson, S. V., Simmons, D. C., & Kame'enui, E. J. (1998). Text organization: Research bases. In D. C. Simmons & E. J. Kame'enui (Eds.), *What reading research tells us about children with diverse learning needs: Basis and basics* (pp. 239–278). Mahwah, NJ: Erlbaum.

Donovan, C. A. (1996). First grader's impressions of genre-specific elements in writing narrative and expository texts. In D. J. Leu, C. K. Kinzer, & K. A.

Hinchman (Eds.), *Yearbook of the National Reading Conference: Vol. 33. Literacies for the 21st century: Research and practices* (pp. 183–194). Chicago, IL: National Reading Conference.

Dreher, M. J. (1993). Reading to locate information: Societal and educational perspectives. *Contemporary Educational Psychology, 18*, 129–138.

Duke, N. K. (1999). The scarcity of informational texts in first grade (Report No. 1–007). Ann Arbor, MI: University of Michigan, School of Education, Center for the Improvement of Early Reading Achievement.

Duke, N. K., & Kays, J. (1998). "Can I say 'Once upon a time'?": Kindergarten children developing knowledge of information book language. *Early Childhood Research Quarterly, 13*(2), 295–318.

Elley, W. B. (1989). Vocabulary acquisition from listening to stories. *Reading Research Quarterly, 24*, 174–186.

Englert, C. S., & Mariage, T. V. (1991). Shared understandings: Structuring the writing experience through dialogue. *Journal of Learning Disabilities, 24*, 330–342.

Englert, C. S., & Thomas, C. C. (1987). Sensitivity to text structure in reading and writing: A comparison between learning disabled and non-learning disabled students. *Learning Disability Quarterly, 10*, 93–105.

Fisher, D., Flood, J., Lapp, D., & Frey, N. (2004). Interactive read-alouds: Is there a common set of implementation practices? *The Reading Teacher, 58*(1), 8–17.

Fisher, P. J., & Blachowicz, C. L. A. (2005). Vocabulary instruction in a remedial setting. *Reading & Writing Quarterly, 21*(3), 281–300.

Goldman, S. R., & Rakestraw, J. A. (2000). Structural aspects of constructing meaning from text. In M. L. Kamil, P. B. Mosenthal, P. D. Pearson, & R. Barr (Eds.), *Handbook of reading research: Vol. 3* (pp. 311–336). Mahwah, NJ: Erlbaum.

Good, R. H., & Kaminski, R. (2002). *Dynamic indicators of basic early literacy skills* (6th Ed.). Eugene, OR: Institute for the Development of Education Achievement.

Guthrie, J. T., & Kirsch, I. S. (1987). Distinctions between reading comprehension and locating information in text. *Journal of Educational Psychology, 79*(3), 220–227.

Hansen, C. L. (1978). Story retelling used with average and learning disabled readers as a measure of reading comprehension. *Learning Disability Quarterly, 1*, 62–69.

Heath, S. B. (1983). *Ways with words.* New York: Cambridge University Press.

Hickman, P., Pollard-Durodola, S., & Vaughn, S. (2004). Storybook reading: Improving vocabulary and comprehension for English-language Learners. *The Reading Teacher, 57*(8), 720–732.

Hicks, D. (1995). Discourse, learning and teaching. *Review of Research in Education, 21*, 49–95

Honig, B., Diamond, L., & Gutlohn, L. (2000). *Teaching reading: Sourcebook for kindergarten through eighth grade.* Novato, CA: Arena Press.

Kletzien, S. B., & Szabo, R. J. (1998, December). *Information text or narrative text? Children's preferences revised.* Paper presented at the National Reading Conference, Austin, TX.

Lyon, G. R., & Moats, L. C. (1997). Critical conceptual and methodological considerations in reading intervention research. *Journal of Learning Disabilities, 30*(6), 578–588.

MacGinitie, W., MacGinitie, R., Maria, K., & Dreyer, L. (2000). *Gates-MacGinitie Reading Tests.* Itasca, IL: Riverside.

Mason, J. M. (1989). *Reading and writing connections.* Boston: Allyn & Bacon.

McKeown, M., & Curtis, M. (Eds.). (1987). *The nature of vocabulary acquisition.* Hillsdale, NJ: Erlbaum.

Meyer, L. A., Stahl, S. A., Linn, R. L., & Wadrop, J. L. (1994). Effects of reading storybooks aloud to children. *Journal of Educational Research, 88*(2), 69–85.

National Reading Panel (NRP). (2000). *Report of the National Reading Panel: Teaching children to read* (NIH Publication No. 00-4769). Washington, DC: National Institute of Child Health and Human Development, National Institutes of Health. Available at http://www.nichd.nih.gov/publications/nrp/smallbook.cfm

National Research Council. (1998). *Preventing reading difficulties in young children.* Washington, DC: National Academy Press.

Newcomer, P. L., & Hammill, D. D. (1997). *Test of language development: Primary* (3rd ed.) Austin, TX: Pro-Ed.

Pearson, P. D., & Fielding, L. (1991). Comprehension instruction. In R. Barr, M. L. Kamil, P. B. Mosenthal, & P. D. Pearson (Eds.), *Handbook of reading research: Vol. 2* (pp. 815–860). New York: Longman.

Snow, C. E. (1993). Families as social contexts for literacy development. In C. Daiute (Ed.), *The development of literacy through social interaction* (pp. 11–24). San Francisco: Jossey-Bass.

Snow, C. E. (2002). *Reading for understanding: Toward an R&D program in reading comprehension.* Santa Monica, CA: RAND.

Snow, C. S., Burns, S. M., & Griffin, P. (1998). *Preventing reading difficulties in young children.* Washington, DC: National Academy Press.

Snow, C. E., & Dickinson, D. K. (1991). Some skills that aren't basic in a new conception of literacy. In A. Purves & T. Jennings (Eds.), *Literate systems and individual lives: Perspectives on literacy and schooling* (pp. 175–213). Albany: State University of New York Press.

Stahl, S. A., & Fairbanks, M. M. (1986). The effects of vocabulary instruction: A model-biased meta-analysis. *Review of Educational Research, 56*(1), 72–110.

Strong, C. (1998). *The Strong Narrative Assessment Procedure.* Eau Claire, WI: Thinking Publications.

Teale, W. H., & Martinez, M. G. (1996). Reading aloud to young children: Teachers' reading styles and kindergartners' text comprehension. In C. Pontecorvo, M. Orsolini, B. Burge, & L. B. Resnick (Eds.), *Children's Early Text Construction* (pp. 321–344). Mahwah, NJ: Erlbaum.

Weaver, P. A., & Dickinson, D. K. (1982). Scratching below the surface structure: Exploring the usefulness of story grammar. *Discourse Processes, 5,* 225–243.

Whitehurst, G. J., Arnold, D. S., Epstein, J. N., Angell, A. L., Smith, M., & Fischel, J. E. (1994). A picture book reading intervention in day care and homes for children from low-income families. *Developmental Psychology, 30,* 679–689.

Wilkinson, L. C., & Sillman, E. R. (2000). Classroom language and literacy learning. In M. L. Kamil, P. B. Mosenthal, P. D. Pearson & R. Barr (Eds.) *Handbook of reading research: Vol. 3* (pp. 337–360). Mahwah, NJ: Erlbaum.

Williams, B. (2003). *Albert's impossible toothache.* Cambridge, Mass.: Candlewick Press.

Williams, J. P. (1993). Comprehension of students with and without learning disabilities: Identification of narrative themes and idiosyncratic text representations. *Journal of Educational Psychology, 85,* 631–641.

Williams, J. P. (2000). *Strategic processing of text: Improving reading comprehension for students with learning disabilities* (ERIC/OSEP Digest No. E599). Arlington, VA: ERIC Clearinghouse on Disabilities and Gifted Education.

Wong, B. Y. L. (1992). On cognitive process-based instruction: An introduction. *Journal of Learning Disabilities ,* 25(3), 150–152.

# CHAPTER 7

# Accelerating Expository Literacy in the Middle Grades: The ACCEL Project

Carol Sue Englert
Troy V. Mariage
Cynthia M. Okolo
Carrie Anna Courtad
Rebecca K. Shankland
Kathleen D. Moxley
Alison K. Billman
Nathan D. Jones

In this chapter, we discuss strategies to improve how students deal with informational complexity, as well as to help them to access, develop, and organize expository information around particular literacy goals, content, and genres. We recommend that content area teachers focus on teaching and support literacy strategies in the context of the disciplinary content of the expository curriculum.

### Questions for Reflection and Discussion

- How can you promote and support the development of expository reading and writing skills in the context of the content area curriculum?
- What conversations do you need to have within the content area classroom, in order to improve the expository reading and writing abilities of all students, especially those who are struggling to read? How often should those conversations be held?
- What outcomes and processes can you measure in order to evaluate whether your students are developing the capacity to effectively read and write expository texts?

The demand for competent reading, writing, and quantitative performance has steadily increased over the past few decades. Recent federal education policies have mirrored the public's concern about the achievement of American students. The *No Child Left Behind Act*, signed into law in 2002, requires that annual assessments of students' mastery of state standards in reading and mathematics be conducted by 2005, with science achievement to be measured by 2007. Each school district is expected to make adequate yearly progress toward meeting state standards, and adequate progress must be documented for specific subgroups of students, including those with disabilities.

Nevertheless, schools have a long way to go before no child is left behind. At the present time, the portion of children who fail to master academic standards remains significant. Nationwide, nearly 38% of fourth-grade students read below the Basic level of proficiency on the 2005 National Assessment of Educational Progress (NAEP); and only 30% of fourth graders read at Proficient or Advanced levels (Perie, Grigg, & Donahue, 2005). Performance is similar among eighth graders, with 29% of eighth-grade students reading below Basic level, and only 29% reading at Proficient or Advanced levels. Although the expectation that students will be able to extract, synthesize multiple sources, and summarize expository material increases as they matriculate into middle school (Gersten, Fuchs, Williams, & Baker, 2001), the number of students who reach Proficient level remains disappointingly low. In fact, beginning at the fourth-grade level, researchers have noted a persistent and measurable decrease in reading that is known as the "fourth-grade slump" (Chall, Jacobs, & Baldwin, 1990), which coincides with the increased prominence of expository materials in the curriculum.

Furthermore, among students with learning disabilities (LD), more than 90% of students have reading problems (Deshler, Ellis & Lenz, 1996), and the vast majority of students with LD experience significant difficulties when required to take notes and write reports or themes (Ellis & Colvert, 1996). They make insufficient use of cognitive strategies (e.g., activating background knowledge, predicting, self-questioning, clarifying, rehearsing, summarizing) and fail to self-regulate or monitor their performance (Gersten et al., 2001; Graham, 2006; Mastropieri & Scruggs, 1997; Pressley, Brown, El-Dinary, & Afflerbach, 1995; Wong, Wong, & Blenkinsop, 1989). They struggle with determining the purposes and identifying the organization of different kinds of expository texts (Englert & Hiebert, 1984; Englert, Raphael, Anderson, Gregg, & Anthony, 1989; Wong et al., 1989). In fact, Deshler et al. (2001) reported that the academic growth of students with LD plateaus in middle school and high school, resulting in a widening "performance gap" between students with LD and their grade-level peers as they matriculate through school.

The need for instructional models that can guide teachers in responding to the literacy difficulties of students in reading and writing expository texts is urgent. Although research demonstrates that intervention programs can ameliorate students' cognitive and strategic abilities (Ellis, 1993; Gersten, 1998), teachers lack adequate models for teaching expository strategies in the upper-elementary and middle school grades. Conventional instruction at these levels rarely provides guidance in how to extract relevant information from expository texts (Gersten et al., 2001), much less how to employ an array of skills and strategies associated with effective reading and writing. A number of textual factors negatively impact reading performance in the middle and secondary grades. Expository texts contain a denser and more technical vocabulary than that found in narrative texts (Ogle & Blachowicz, 2002). This makes it more difficult for students to visualize concepts, to infer meanings, or to relate content to their background knowledge.

Organizationally, expository texts also are less familiar to students and the organization shifts among a number of text structures within a section. This imposes greater cognitive demands on the young readers and writers to fill in the gaps, to make inferences, or to employ sense-making strategies (Kim, Vaughn, Wanzek, & Wei, 2004). At the same time, few teachers have received preparation that equips them to provide cognitive and text structure strategy instruction (Trabasso & Bouchard, 2002), and teachers feel less prepared to teach literacy strategies in the context of informational texts. Consistently, students do less well in reading and comprehending informational texts than they do narrative texts (Ogle & Blachowicz, 2002).

## WHAT IS NEEDED?
## ACCEL INSTRUCTIONAL RESPONSE

Project ACCEL (Accelerating Expository Literacy) was designed to improve how middle school students deal with the complexity of expository content by teaching them to access, develop, and organize information around particular literacy and disciplinary goals, content, genres and dilemmas. ACCEL is a serviceable instructional model that can be implemented by teachers across literacy and content area curricula to address the literacy needs of middle school students in general and in special education. Project ACCEL was engineered to reflect the research literature on effective performance in literacy and the disciplinary domains of the expository curriculum, as well as to use pedagogical practices associated with the effective presentation and acquisition of strategy and content knowledge. We sought an integration of literacy and content-area goals, so that literacy was an integral part of the teaching and learning of expository material, whether the core content was derived from English, science, or social studies classes. Although we will explain how these goals were achieved in the following sections, a basic assumption was that all middle school teachers support literacy through their emphases on the employment of evidence-based reading and writing strategies within an inquiry process of knowledge acquisition and production. Three research and design–based features are threaded through the development and implementation of the ACCEL model:

1. Pedagogical practices that emphasize a cognitive apprenticeship approach to teaching and learning
2. Literacy strategies
3. Inquiry-driven content investigations

Each feature will be discussed in the following sections.

## PEDAGOGICAL PRACTICES

### Apprenticeship Model

Pedagogically, ACCEL was designed on several critical teaching assumptions, including a strong belief that effective teachers apprentice their students in the largely invisible mental processes underlying reading and writing. Given the fact that many students do not activate or transfer their knowledge from one setting to the next (Baker, Gersten & Scanlon, 2003; Gersten & Baker, 1998), ACCEL literacy and content area teachers sought to think aloud and model the thoughts, actions, and meaning-making practices used by readers and writers in the situated context of the content curriculum (Baker, 2002; Duffy, 2002). Rather than teach strategies out of context or in literacy pull-out settings, teachers used the expository texts of the school curriculum as the real-world terrain for modeling how good readers and writers think, talk, read, write, and engage in literacy practices in an authentic meaning-making activity. Literacy was taught hand in hand with the teaching of expository comprehension and composition across the disciplinary content of the school curriculum.

### Common Language

A second objective of ACCEL was to provide a common language for all teachers and students to use to talk about the literacy strategies and expository content of the curriculum. Teachers met in professional development activities to discuss and construct the mutually agreed on language to reference the literacy strategies. In addition, recognizing that expository text lends itself to the acquisition of a specialized language, ACCEL teachers also considered the discipline-specific habits of mind that could be fostered in their particular curricular domain. For example, social studies teachers agreed that some of the pedagogical tools and conceptual lenses that students should acquire for historical interpretation were multiple perspectives and points of view, analyzing primary sources and evidentiary data, engaging in argumentation and supporting arguments with evidence, and examining evidence for bias. For science teachers, emphases on investigations, interpretation of data, visual literacy, and argumentation were habits of mind that they wished to cultivate. Across all curricular domains, we adopted the position of Cervetti, Pearson, Bravo, and Barber (2005) that literacy lay at the heart of expository inquiry, involving common emphases in predicting, generating questions and hypotheses, gathering information, summarizing, synthesizing multiple sources, and reporting.

## Instructional Discourse

Third, we recognized that a strategic and specialized language needed to be acquired and rehearsed in the practical context of texts and classrooms. Hence teachers sought to create an interactive and instructional discourse in which they modeled strategy and tool use in the flow of problem solving and constructive literacy activity (Englert & Dunsmore, 2004; Englert & Raphael, 1989; Palincsar & Brown, 1984; Roth & McRobbie, 1999). As part of this discourse, teachers modeled and involved students in discussions about what readers/writers do, and how they think, read, write, and talk when they are interacting with expository material (Cervetti et al., 2005). The introduction of each literacy strategy was accompanied by teacher demonstrations in which they modeled and thought aloud about their ideas, self-talk, inner questions, interpretations, corrective actions, insights, and meaning-making efforts in the context of the content area curriculum. Teachers explained why a particular strategy was selected, how it was performed, and when or in what conditions it was to be used (Duffy, 2002).

Bearing in mind that proficiency in a school-based language develops when students use the discourse in conversation and tool-based activity with others, teachers provided frequent occasions for students to engage in strategic talk by asking them to explain, think aloud, and justify their thinking to their peers, as well as to share their thoughts and ideas in small groups, and then make their thinking public to the entire class. Writing was at the heart of the process of promoting metacognitive knowledge about how one directs and monitors one's cognitive performance. Since writing is a tool and mirror into the mind

(Cervetti et al., 2005; Scribner, 1997), ACCEL students wrote and recorded their ideas frequently in order to develop their metacognitive awareness of the literacy process, and their consciousness of the content-bearing tools associated with the deployment of literacy strategies. Simultaneously, the sharing of the written artifacts engendered greater knowledge of the declarative and procedural conditions associated with tool use, and made possible the dissemination of the agreed-upon tools among the members of the class. Ultimately, teachers wanted students to be able to explain what effective readers and writers do, including the mental or physical tools that they use before, during, or after they read or write a section of expository text (Block & Israel, 2004). To further these conversations, teachers involved students in collaborative arrangements with their peers and engaged students in jointly designing and engineering written texts in a manner that prompted problem solving and communication about tool use (Roth, 1998).

## Procedural Facilitators

Fourth, ACCEL teachers used procedural facilitators to support students' reasoning and strategic abilities (Baker et al., 2003; Gersten, 1998). Procedural facilitators are tools, prompts, and cues that support and mediate literacy performance (Vygotsky, 1978). Facilitators include language symbols, instruments, written symbols, organizers, procedures, rules of thumb, and any tools that are used in the transformation and construction process (Wertsch, 1995, 1998, 2002; Vygotsky, 1978). With an eye to the role of tools in supporting thinking, we wanted students to employ their pens and pencils as tools that were used hand in hand with their cognition, just as many mature readers and writers coordinate their mental thoughts with the simultaneous recording of their ideas in the form of notes, highlighting, and questions.

The literacy strategies were also designed with several procedural facilitators to support students' development of self-regulatory talk and procedures that we associated with proficient literacy performance. We used "think-sheets," cue cards, and rubrics that presented a series of self-statements that prompted students to take various cognitive actions. These tools mediated performance by reminding students of the language and procedures associated with strategic performance. Raphael, Pardo, Highfield, and McMahon (1997) also contend that think-sheets help students develop their skills in "using writing as a tool for thinking and as a means for personal expression" (p. 31). We used think-sheets at several points in the reading and writing process, particularly when strategies were newly introduced to facilitate strategy performance and to further students' participation in the literacy discourse as part of a process of text interpretation.

## LITERACY STRATEGIES

In designing the ACCEL curriculum, we drew upon a solid body of literature indicating that strategy instruction can positively influence the reading and writing performance of students with disabilities (Deshler et al., 2001; Gersten et al., 2001; Graham, 2006; Palincsar & Brown, 1984; Scanlon, Deshler, & Schumaker, 1996; Swanson, 1999; Vaughn, Gersten & Chard, 2000; Williams, 2003). For middle-grade students, we recognized that it was critical that cognitive strategy instruction target the essential learning-to-learn strategies, such as accessing background knowledge, generating hypotheses, organizing information, inferencing, summarizing, self-questioning, and monitoring performance (Block & Pressley, 2002; Englert et al., 1989; Gersten, 1998; Goldman et al., 1996; Kolligan & Sternberg, 1987; Palincsar, 1986; Palincsar & Brown, 1989; Pearson & Duke, 2002; Presley et al., 1995; Scanlon et al., 1996; Wong, 2000). However, a unique feature of the ACCEL project was that teams of teachers used the same language to present and rehearse the strategies. This minimized the possibility that the strategy knowledge might lie inert, or nongeneralizable from one setting (e.g., literacy classroom) to another context (content area classroom) (Baker et al., 2003; Gersten & Baker, 1998).

A heuristic that we used to make the project strategies visible is shown in Figure 7.1 Premised on the notion of a strategy toolbox (Mehigan, 2005), this figure lists a portfolio of strategies with their associated tools that might be applied to achieve different purposes and goals. Thus ACCEL was envisioned as a strategy toolbox, containing the research-based strategies that improve students' abilities to comprehend and compose expository text. Teachers and students could select the strategies most appropriate for a given purpose and situation.

The ACCEL toolbox contained strategies that assisted students before, during, and after reading and writing. Many of these strategies were mental and representational tools that served an important role in making the writing process and ideas clear. For example, in preparing to read, students used the *Plan-It* strategy log, which asked them to establish a purpose, preview the content, activate background knowledge, ask questions, and make predictions.

While they read, students used the Read-It log to identify the topic and main idea, summarize the information, ask questions, clarify vocabulary, connect to knowledge, and make predictions. They also had the option of using the Mark-It and Highlight-It logs, which included steps for highlighting or marking the key ideas of the text, questioning, interacting, and connecting to prior knowledge. To help students gather, organize, rehearse, and synthesize the information, they could use the following representational

**Figure 7.1.** ACCEL strategies and self-talk

| Reading Stage | Strategy | Component Strategies and Self Talk | Procedural Facilitator |
|---|---|---|---|
| Before Reading | Plan-It | *Purpose* by asking "Why Am I reading/writing this?" List Topics and *Preview* (skim and scan). "What's it about?" *Activate knowledge.* Connect to self, text, and world. "What do I know?" *Note your questions.* "What do I want to know?" *Structure.* "What are the categories & Details? Structure?" | Plan-It Log |
| During Reading | Read-It | *Summarize* by asking "What is this mostly about?" Include the main idea and 3–4 related details in your summary. *Question.* Ask a question about the main idea. Ask a text structure question. *Clarify.* Clarify unfamiliar ideas or words. "I'm confused about . . ." "I don't understand . . ." *Connect.* "What do I want to know?" *Structure.* "What are the categories and details? Structure?" | Read-It Log |
| During Reading | Highlight-It | *Highlight* the main ideas and related details. *Reread* the highlighted text. Ask, "Does it make sense?" *Pair-share-compare.* | Highlight-It cue card |
| During Reading | Mark-It | *PK: Prior knowledge:* What do I already know? *Q?: Question:* Confusing parts, unclear words, or sections that need clarifying. *CL: Clarify* (idea or word). *P: Predict:* What will the author talk about next? *S: Summarize:* Put the main ideas, details, or concepts in your own words. *C: Connect:* Connect to self, text, world. | Watch teacher model. Use highlighter, marker, pen, or pencil Mark own passage Use markings Make text messy Record questions and thoughts |
| During Reading | Note-It | 3-column notes Outline 2-column notes Map or web (see below) | 3-column notes 2-column notes |

145

| After Reading | Maps-It | Categories/detail<br>Story structure<br>Timeline<br>Compare/contrast<br>Classification/list<br>Problem/solutions<br>Persuasion/argumentation<br>Sequence/explanation<br>Cause/effect | Categories/details map<br>Compare/contrast map<br>Problem/solution map<br>Sequence map |
|---|---|---|---|
| After Reading | Respond-To-It | I can *Interpret* this section with . . . [text structure]<br>This *Reminded* me of . . . .<br>I want to *Respond* to . . . .<br>This made me *Wonder* about . . . .<br>The *Perspectives* this represented was . . . .<br>My *Opinion* is . . . .<br>A *Question* I have . . . .<br>One *Critique* I have is . . . . | Critical literacy Respond-<br>To-It Log<br>Text structure Respond-<br>To-It cue card |
| After Reading | Report-It | *Preparing* for the discussion/report (Plan-It)<br>*Beginning* the discussion/report (Plan-It, Read-It, Note-It, Report-It)<br>*Maintaining* the discussion/report<br>*Wrapping-up* and *reporting out* the discussion/report | Supporting discussions<br>Supporting understanding<br>Writing cue card |

*Note.* Reprinted with permission. Englert, C. S., Mariage, T., & Okolo, C. (2006). The Project ACCEL Curriculum Materials: Teacher Handbook. East Lansing: Michigan State University, Literacy Achievement Research Center.

tools: Note-It (make notes of the key events, vocabulary, questions, or ideas); Map-It (represent the information using one or more graphic organizers).

Finally, students could reflect on the text using the strategies Respond-to-It (go more deeply by making intertextual links, query the text, or critique the information) and Report-It (write a written report that is published, shared, and commented upon). Each of these strategies incorporated a suite of strategies and tools that prompted students to activate and self-regulate their performance. These strategies are described in more depth in the following sections.

## Before Reading

Plan-It involved a preparatory stage for reading and writing during which students considered the topic, made plans, and brainstormed ideas. Since goal setting and activating background knowledge are areas in which struggling readers are often lacking (Graham, MacArthur & Schwartz, 1995), this phase was designed to address deficiencies in strategy production that affected students' ability to anticipate and predict central information, as well as to apply their prior knowledge to support comprehension and inferential reasoning. ACCEL teachers understood that preparing students for content area topics was an important aspect of reading comprehension, especially for struggling readers and writers who often fail to relate new information to what is known. Thus teachers sought to help students think consciously about what they would be reading and how that information might be organized, and prepped students to read by relating the information to their prior knowledge and by generating prereading questions (Neufield, 2005).

Teachers modeled planning strategies using the Plan-It log. The Plan-It log scaffolded talk related to reading as teachers and students discussed and thought aloud about the Purpose, Listed the topics after previewing the text, Activated their prior knowledge, Noted their questions, and anticipated the Structure. Within the Plan-It preparatory literacy stage, teachers modeled how to survey text headings, examine illustrations and tables, and preview bolded topics or vocabulary as part of a process of gathering information. Students tried out these strategies with partners and independently, and the information that they assembled was recorded in a class Plan-It log.

To alert students to the potential organization of the textual ideas, teachers guided students to identify the possible ways the text might be organized, and then to predict the organization of the central content by listing the possible categories and subtopics in a text structure map that corresponded to the predicted structure. The selection of possible organizational structures was guided by an array of text structure choices (e.g., classification, compare/contrast, sequence, position, and problem/solution or cause/effect), which were located near the bottom of the Plan-It log. Since students with reading problems tend to be less aware of text structure and have poorer recall of textual ideas (Jitendra, Hoppes, & Xin, 2000), we sought to prompt their attention to the possible arrangement of the ideas in text by providing symbolic icons for each of the text structures. Based on their selection of the text structure, students could choose a compatible graphic organizer upon which they could quickly plot the vocabulary and concepts from the text and their background knowledge to help them become more active readers in anticipating, identifying, and comprehending the main ideas and details of the textual material. As students read, new elements then could be incorporated into these existing structures, which made it easier for readers to use their expectations and experiences as a filter through which text ideas could be constructed, perceived, and transformed.

Throughout the modeling and guided preparatory stages, teachers promoted metacognitive awareness by emphasizing that the Plan-It log represented some of the critical literacy strategies of good readers and writers that could be employed to improve performance as part of preparing to read and write expository texts. Teachers encouraged students to use the Plan-It log to prepare to read, and they reviewed the log when new chapters were introduced. Each chapter unit began with a preparatory planning stage signified by the Plan-It strategies. The Plan-It log was placed in a learning log that contained the big ideas, themes, and interpretative responses of students related to the content of the informational texts.

## During Reading

We recognized that many students tended to be passive readers, and we wanted to foster an active stance during reading that would engage them to "get the information" and unpack the text meaning. They were encouraged to utilize strategies related to identifying main ideas and details, asking questions, clarifying ideas, monitoring text understanding, clarifying vocabulary and ideas, and making predictions about the text (Palincsar & Brown, 1984; Pressley et al., 1995). Many of the strategies incorporated into ACCEL were based on the successful multistrategy frameworks that formed the foundation of other effective programs, including reciprocal teaching (Palincsar & Brown, 1984, 1989), transactional strategies (Brown, Pressley, Van Meter, & Schuder, 1996; Pressley et al., 1995), and collaborative strategic reading (Klingner & Vaughn, 1996, 1998; Vaughn, Klingner & Bryant, 2001). These programs have been successful in providing struggling readers with active reading strategies that underlie effective reading.

During Read-It, for example, students used four strategies that appeared on the Read-It log: *summarize, question, clarify, connect,* and *predict* (see Figure 7.2). Each of the strategies was modeled by teachers in think-alouds.

**Figure 7.2.** Read-It log

## Read-It!   During Reading Log

Good readers and writers use a number of strategies while they read to get meaning and monitor their understanding. Five strategies are important to use while reading informational text: (1) Summarize the category topic and related details. (2) Ask questions (about the topic & text structure). (3) Clarify the words and ideas; (4) Connect to self, text, world, & topics. (5) Predict. Use this think-sheet to record the information that you have acquired through applying these strategies.

| Page | 1. Summarize<br>Topic + 3–4 details | | 2. Question<br>Big Idea | 3. Clarify | 4. Connect/Predict<br>• Topics<br>• Texts, Self, World |
|---|---|---|---|---|---|
| | *My summary is . . .*<br>*(include category and 3–4 details)* | | *My question about this topic is . . .*<br>*Ask Text structure question* | *I'm confused about . . .*<br><br>*A term that I don't know is . . .* | *This reminds me of . . .*<br>*I wonder . . .* |
| | *Category/topic* | *Details* | | | |
| | | | | | |
| | | | | | |
| | | | | | |

Ask a text structure question/Question starters:
*Who? What? When? Where? How? Why?*

Note: Reprinted with permission. Englert, C. S., Mariage, T., & Okolo, C. (2006). Project *ACCEL Curriculum Materials: Teacher Handbook*. East Lansing: Michigan State University, Literacy Achievement Research Center.

## Summarize

Teachers taught summarization by emphasizing how students could identify the main idea topic and construct the summary by reading each paragraph and asking oneself, "What is this mostly about?" As Williams (2003) states, the process of main idea identification is similar to the task of summarizing through a classification process. Students first identify the general topic based on its recurrence in a section of the text, and then identify the specific topic by inferring the more precise intent or purpose of the statements that are proximal to that topic. For example, in a passage about a wild animal (e.g., "Cheetah"), students would identify the general topic based on the author's frequent mention of this topic, and then students would construct the specific topic by inferring what the remaining ideas have in common based upon their collective intent, meaning or purpose (e.g., "How cheetahs hunt"). In this manner, teachers helped students identify the symbolic meanings that were represented in the content material (Kozulin, 2003).

An analogy was used to communicate the importance of this strategy in the reading process. Teachers talked about the importance of organization in filing, storing, and locating information in a file cabinet or desk drawer. If a person simply throws everything into the cabinet without planning, matching, or organizing, it is impossible to find the information when it is needed. However, if the person takes the time to organize the information by placing related items into a folder or stack and labeling the contents with a title that indicates what the items have in common, it is easy to locate and retrieve the necessary information. In the same way, good readers are always trying to identify what a set of ideas have in common and how they can be labeled. Once the ideas are classified and labeled, it is easier for the reader to gather the relevant ideas in response to a question or an association. Thus readers who search for relationships and create labels to describe the relationships are improving their reading comprehension and are more likely to perform at advanced reading levels.

Teachers then modeled how to summarize while reading a content area text. Teachers explained how they decided upon the specific topic or main idea, as well as thought aloud about how to infer the main idea topic from the collection of related ideas. Once the main idea was identified, they also showed how to construct the gist of the section by restating the main idea or category ("This section is about how the cheetah hunts its food") and the related details in that section ("Cheetahs use their sight to hunt; they hunt in the daylight; they chase their prey at high speeds"). The teacher explained that producing the gist of the section involved reduction, inasmuch as readers summarize by applying rules in which they eliminate redundancy and duplication, combine ideas related to the same topic, restate ideas in fewer words, and delete trivial details that are not important (Block, Schaller, Joy, & Gaine, 2002; Trabasso & Bouchard, 2002). Students practiced with partners the process of constructing the main idea that conveyed the general and specific topic of the paragraph, and shared their findings with their partner and the class. In this manner, teachers sought to prompt students to become more active readers, and to guide students in distinguishing between the important and less important ideas in a passage. Summaries were constructed that reflected the meaning and purpose of the subsections of the passage and that incorporated the main ideas and related details. Finally, teachers listed the agreed-upon main idea topics and related details on an overhead of the text so that students would have a visual representation that reflected their categorization and summarization decisions. Likewise, students could record their decisions about the category topic and details under the "Summarize" heading of the Read-It log (see Figure 7.2).

### Question

The second Read-It strategy was question generation. Two types of question asking were fostered. First, teachers encouraged students to ask a question about the main idea or topic as part of a rehearsal strategy to review the material and the text's key points. Students simply learned to take the category or main idea label and turn it into a question using one of the question words (who, what, when, where, how, why). By asking questions about the main idea, the gist of the passage was retrieved in the form of relevant details that answered the question. Teachers likened this strategy to recovering the key details that have been filed in the information folder. Students were told that this was an effective rehearsal strategy that many adults employ in order to learn the important information and to improve their comprehension recall. For example, in the passage that described the cheetah's hunting process, students might ask the question: "How does the cheetah hunt?"

However, we also wanted students to ask questions that required drawing inferences across the sections of the text and even larger units, such as text chapters. This was the second type of questioning. We found that text structures offered excellent interpretative tools. Realizing that text structures seldom existed in a single paragraph, ACCEL teachers and students employed text structures to understand the ideas across larger sections of the text. For example, students might compare and contrast the Romans with the Greeks, or they might see causes and effects in describing the factors associated with the fall of the Roman Empire. A set of text structure questions and keywords was supplied to help students learn to interrogate the text in flexible ways. During reading and at the conclusion of each unit, teachers and students talked about the text structure genres, and the different questions that the information in the text might answer.

### Clarify

The third during-reading strategy to be introduced was clarifying. We also borrowed the language of "clunks" from Collaborative Strategic Reading (Klingner & Vaughn, 1998; Vaughn et al., 2001) to help students recognize when they had encountered a comprehension breakdown. Clunks could be unknown words, vocabulary, or ideas that interrupted the flow of reading. When a clunk occurred, students were taught to clarify the meaning by rereading the preceding and succeeding text and using context clues. Based on Raphael et al.'s (1997) work, we also provided a Vocabulary Log for students to record new vocabulary and concepts as they employed the clarifying strategies. Students could record the new vocabulary on the Read-It log or on the Vocabulary log to keep a record of the new concepts and terms associated with a particular unit of study.

### Connect and Predict

As the fourth strategy, students learned to connect topics to other texts, themselves, and the world, just as teachers had emphasized connecting to prior knowledge in the preparatory stage of reading. Again, students were encouraged to discuss ideas in terms of their funds of knowledge, and to share their prior knowledge with peers to connect to the text or to answer their own or others' questions. Students followed the connection process by predicting what they might read next in the text.

### Applying the Strategies

Once students learned the Read-It strategies, teachers asked students to apply the strategies to chunks of text as they worked with partners or a small group of students. Two procedural facilitation tools were provided to support the Read-It strategies. One tool was a discussion cue card. The cue card contained the essential language to support the conversation between pairs of students or small groups by reminding students of the strategy steps and the self-talk that would promote interaction to understand and interpret the text. We offered several versions of the cue card that provided more or less scaffolding based on teachers' perceptions of students' reading needs. A more elaborated cue card with more detailed language was available to more skilled readers, but we also offered a less elaborated cue card with the same strategies but less detailed language for low-achieving readers or special education students. The purpose of the cue cards was to support the use of the comprehension strategies as a springboard for talk and understanding (Palincsar, 1986).

We patterned group discussions about text upon the interactions of reciprocal teaching (Palincsar, 1986; Palincsar & Brown, 1989). As was the case with reciprocal teaching, students were expected to take turns guiding the discussion of sections of the text using the four strategies. The leader could ask the group for a summary, as well as guide the group in asking questions, clarifying, connecting the ideas to other resources and experience, and predicting. When students became confused about what they might say or do in support of the reading discussion, students could refer to the cue cards to see what strategies they might employ, or what observations, insights, or comments they might share. The cue card also prompted students to

- Attend to text structures by asking questions about relationships among ideas within and across sections of the text
- Remain sensitive to summarizing the main ideas and related details, and the important information in the passage
- Develop an inner dialogue about texts and the meaning of ideas
- Share their knowledge of the text and the strategies
- Monitor their comprehension.

In this way, we sought to help readers converse about their text comprehension and understanding.

Finally, teachers could assign a reading log to students to complete and bring to their discussion groups, or to use as they worked with their partner or during independent reading time (Raphael et al., 1997). Material objects such as learning logs become tools for social thinking (Bracewell & Witte, 1997), and we wanted the talk surrounding the artifact's construction to be internalized as part of an inner dialogue that might support the meaning-making process. In essence, the artifact became an object to think with, to talk with, to read with, to write with, and to learn with (Wertsch, 1998). Students recorded their questions, thoughts, ideas, summaries, and their connections in the reading log. Even if the teacher merely asked students to record the group's decisions in a single paragraph, it was considered valuable to involve students in writing to support their participation in collaborative talk that focused on joint problem solving and decision making. Thus writing in the log served several purposes, including

- Archival of reading decisions
- A record of collaborative conversations and inner talk about texts and the meaning-making process

- Dissemination of shared knowledge about literacy practice
- A summary of the metacognitive strategies applied to content area texts

Employing the log with a partner or a small group supported a type of "shop talk" about the text. When sections of the reading log were completed, students placed it with the Plan-It log in their learning notebook to represent their ever-developing knowledge related to the larger unit of study.

## Extending the Read-It Strategies in Learning-to-Learn Tasks

To complement the Read-It strategies, ACCEL teachers introduced several additional tools that students might use in order to extend strategy implementation across the curriculum and within an inquiry or learning-to-learn process. As Kozulin (2003) has proposed, cognitive tools serve as mediational devices that influence the mind and behavior of oneself and others (Daniels, 2001). By using tools to interact with the written word and to record their own inner thoughts and responses, students were taught to employ the discursive strategies more broadly in a generative, interactive, and problem-solving fashion. In an active way, we hoped to cultivate a dialogic stance in which students used literacy tools to interact with and to respond to textual ideas as part of an ongoing discourse in which they overlaid and interpreted the words of authors with their own answering voices (Bakhtin, 1981).

Tools included readily available writing implements, such as pens, pencils, highlighters, and markers. Many adults read technical information with a pencil in hand, and we wanted our students to learn to read and think with pencils in their hands (Harvey, 1998; Harvey & Goudvis, 2000). However, this required explicit instruction since writing as a tool for thinking and communicating is not a spontaneous process, but represents a new mode of literacy thinking that must be acquired by young students (Wells, 1999). Thus, ACCEL teachers sought to link the literacy tools, textual medium, and metacognitive process and to bring them into the conscious awareness of students. The specific strategies that were taught for this purpose included the Highlight-It, Mark-It, and Note-It strategies.

### Highlight-It and Mark-It

A set of during-reading strategies that had been modeled and shared with students were Highlight-It and Mark-It. For Highlight-It, students were given highlighters, and they were told that they could use the markers to highlight copies of the text as they identified essential main ideas and details. Highlighting was like a pointer system that referenced and directed attention to the important concepts and ideas in the text. Highlighted text included technical vocabulary, main ideas, and other important ideas. For main ideas, teachers reminded students that they could mark through ideas that answered the question "What is this mostly about?" Teachers stressed the importance that good readers place in understanding the main points of a text (Williams, 2003), which is a fundamental ability in comprehending expository texts. Furthermore, the functionality of the highlighting process was emphasized by telling students that the highlighted text could help them quickly locate the important information as they reread or reviewed the text. Highlighting important ideas relieved the reader from the task of holding ideas in memory, and it lessened the demand on the readers to reread the passage in its entirety to locate the key ideas. Teachers related the practicality and value of this strategy by pointing out its frequent employment by college students as a means to study and rehearse text.

To the extent that the ACCEL strategies could be brought forward from one cognitive process to the next, it was possible to produce a faster result in terms of the acquisition and transfer of reading strategies related to tool use. Teachers instructed students to generalize the Read-It strategies to help them highlight the important ideas. Teachers emphasized the similarities in the mental processes between summarizing in reading and summarizing in highlighting. Simultaneously, the act of highlighting ideas helped students to become more conscious of the reading strategies.

Starting with the identification and the highlighting of the text's main ideas and related details, teachers provided explanations of the concepts that they highlighted. Using an overhead of the passage, the teachers modeled and thought out loud as they guided students in highlighting the main ideas and details for a given section of the text. They focused attention on how they made decisions about the important information; how they used passage information to identify the important details, facts, or evidence related to those main ideas; and how they highlighted only necessary words and phrases. When the main idea was not explicitly stated in the text, the teacher modeled how to infer the main idea from the textual ideas in the passage section.

Recognizing that readers use a wide array of strategies beyond highlighting, teachers introduced the companion strategies for reading, the Mark-It strategies. As part of the Mark-It process, students applied symbolic codes to mark the places in the text where they experienced specific thoughts, strategies, or questions. Some of the notations that students used included

- *PK* for prior knowledge
- *Q* for questions
- *C* for connections to self, text, or world
- *Cl* for clarifications

- *P* for predictions
- *S* for summarize
- *V* for vocabulary
- Stars for major ideas.

Students were encouraged to invent their own shorthand codes to represent their mental actions and thoughts (Harvey & Goudvis, 2000; Wells, 1999). Using these symbols, any thought, response, question, note, or connection could be recorded in the margins or on Post-it notes as part of the Mark-It process. Mark-It strategies deepened strategy use by engaging students in a conversation with the written text, as student talk moved back and forth between the author's textual ideas and the readers' internal responses. Simultaneously, students directly marked up the places in the text where they had questions, insights, comments, interpretations, and notes. Some teachers used Post-it notes for this purpose when they did not have the benefit of consumable texts for demonstration or practice purposes. Together with Highlight-It, the Mark-It strategies encompassed the entire set of the Read-It strategies, including summarizing, questioning, clarifying, connecting, and predicting.

The physical imposition of recording a particular symbol on a written page influenced reading activity in an active way that altered the entire flow and structure of intellectual functions (Wells, 1999). By recording symbols that corresponded to specific thoughts, the conceptual and physical worlds of reading and writing were unified in an integrated web of literacy activity, as the marriage of the hand and the mind created an avenue into cognition and thought (Rose, 1999). At the same time, the artifact of the marked-up page became an object of further conversation and reflection (Roth, 1998) which allowed students to communicate their understandings, to share their practices, to participate in decision making, and to engage in knowledge building (Roth, 1998; Wells, 1999). Students' participation in transcriptional activities was not just what they learned, it was how they learned (Kozulin, 2003).

At the end of a section, students turned to their partners and shared their thoughts, strategies, and decisions as a mechanism for promoting deeper awareness of the literacy strategies and outcomes. Also important, the dialogue between partners helped students understand the different meanings that might result from text, as well as the fact that text interpretations varied across readers based upon their own experiences, thought processes, strategies, and prior knowledge.

For example, in a passage about Soviet culture, a student responded to text information with a number of thoughtful reflections. When the passage stated that "the Soviet space program of the 1950s and 1960s brought international attention to that country," the student asked, "What kind of attention? Good or bad?" When the passage stated that "Most people were poor and had little, if any, say in their government," the student asked "Why was life so difficult?" and "What was daily life like?" Later the student responded to the statement that "The Soviet government was fearful that some ethnic groups might want to break away from the Soviet Union" with the question "Why was the Soviet government fearful?" These questions are examples of the ways in which the students were becoming more active in responding to text with authentic and meaningful questions. The ambiguities in the text triggered internal responses that led students to question the author and the text (Beck, McKeown, Hamilton & Kucan, 1997). This was an important aspect of evaluating the message "and the author's point of view and purpose" (Ogle & Blachowicz, 2002, p. 262).

*Debriefing* was another important part of the process of making the cognitive strategies available to everyone. During the debriefing phase, teachers asked students to share their ideas and to reread their highlighted phrases to see if the recorded ideas captured the important ideas, formed an outline of the passage, and made sense to the reader. A discussion was held in which students shared the ideas that they had highlighted, provided justifications for their highlighted ideas, shared their questions, and discussed what strategies were used, when and how they might use the strategies, and why they were important. Sharing both the textual ideas and cognitive strategies was an important facet underlying strategy acquisition and implementation throughout ACCEL. Hence written notations served as records of mental operations that had its impetus in the interactions between the student and the textual object (Cole & Engestrom, 1993). Simultaneously, by using writing tools for social thinking, students learned the talk and actions associated with the construction of meaning in the comprehension process.

## Note It

Finally, a during-reading strategy that evolved from highlighting and marking was Note-It. Note-It supported students as they took notes on the main ideas and details. This crucial step bridged the gap between students who knew how to take notes and students who did not know how to take effective notes. Given the prior groundwork laid by teachers as they modeled reading and highlighting strategies, the progression into note taking was relatively straightforward.

There were three avenues into modeling the note-taking process, depending on teachers' appraisal of their students' abilities. One avenue into Note-It was based on the aforementioned highlighting process. Teachers simply modeled how to take the highlighted sections of the text and to record the information into a Note-It log consisting of a two-column, note-taking table corresponding to the main ideas and details. Thus the highlighted ideas represented a virtual outline of the text, which was transformed into an actual outline of main ideas and details. A third column could also be added in which students listed their interpretations, questions, or personal responses. This process helped students become aware of how the highlighting and note-taking processes were related.

A second type of note taking was recording ideas and notes into a graphic organizer. We provided students with several types of graphic organizers, including two-column and three-column tables, webs of categories and details, Venn diagrams, compare/contrast tables, time lines, and problem/solution organizers. At first, these organizers were introduced and modeled by teachers. However, the purpose of offering an array of organizers was to help students become strategic about text structure and organization. Often, students were asked to choose a particular type of graphic organizer for note taking depending on their purpose and the structure of the text material. After students applied the graphic organizer to take notes on the material, ACCEL teachers invited students to share their choice of the graphic organizer and the type of information afforded students by the use of each organizer. As a result, students become more strategic about the different ways of organizing expository information, and they were encouraged to explore alternative formats for their utility in representing and organizing the central meanings of the text.

## After Reading

Whereas the Plan-It and Read-It strategies focused on meaning-making strategies, we also wanted students to respond more deeply and personally to the content material following reading.

Using Respond-to-It, students learned to express and support their opinions in a persuasive and evidentiary format that is similar to the standards-based assessments conducted in the state of Michigan and on the National Assessment of Educational Progress (Donahue, Voekl, Campbell, & Mazzeo, 1999; Morocco, Hindin, Mata-Aguilar & Clark-Chiarelli, 2001). They were prompted to go beyond the facts (identifying author's purpose and bias, examining the credibility of information, recognizing points of view) and then share their ideas with others (offering claims and warrants) (Raphael et al., 1997). Further, since research suggests that many struggling readers and students with disabilities have difficulty explaining their ideas to peers and self-directing project work (Okolo & Ferretti, 1996), we wanted to encourage critical literacy by emphasizing a discursive framework and a response rubric designed by Okolo and Ferretti (1996) to assist students in constructing strong arguments. Students were encouraged to (1) state their opinion or provide evidence, (2) give a reason for that opinion, (3) explain why theirs is a good reason, and (4) give examples that illustrate their position. Students were given access to the rubric and a set of prompts on ACCEL that were designed to help them evaluate the credibility of opinions, and to guide them in how to create opinion statements that are well formed and well substantiated with arguments and statements.

There were two types of Respond-To-It strategies. One type of strategies was based on the structure underlying expository texts including

- Compare/contrast in history and literature (e.g., comparing/contrasting people or events)
- Sequence or explanation in science (e.g., experiments and procedures)
- Enumeration or taxonomies (in science and geography)
- Description in science and literature (e.g., descriptions of traits of animate or inanimate objects, people or animals, settings)
- Cause/effect and problem/solution in history and literature

Students were reminded that each text structure provided answers to different types of questions and the topically relevant answers were signaled by different types of keywords.

However, we also emphasized that text structure was not an entity that existed in single paragraphs, but instead knowledge of text structures served as an inferencing and representational tool that could be applied in order to understand and interpret texts across multiple sections of the text. Project ACCEL emphasized text structures in a flexible manner as part of preparing students to read or write, synthesizing multiple sources, or guiding students to identify the text structure during or after reading. For example, within a chapter unit on Europe, students might survey the text to identify the potential organization of the text, as well as to reflect on the chapter by asking text structure questions as part of an interpretative process (e.g., constructing a sequence or time line of events, comparing and contrasting the social classes, identifying the causes and effects of a specific event). Multiple and iterative applications of text structures could be used to understand and interpret the same text in different ways. As noted above, each text structure is situated in different types of disciplinary texts for different purposes. To teach students to use expository text structure was to endow them with the metaknowledge related to how texts are organized, interpreted, and transformed in different ways to produce effects for different purposes (Cope & Kalantzis, 1993). The flexible use of these interpretative strategies was also generative in interpreting literature when students read fictional stories.

A cue card to support students in using six text structures is shown in Figure 7.3. Similar to the text structure questions that were applied during

**Figure 7.3.** Respond-to-It text structure cue card

**Timeline**

I can interpret this section with a timeline of events.
My evidence for thinking I can use a timeline is . . .
Some of the key events or people are . . .
The sequence or dates of the events are . . .
Do others think this is a timeline?
I think this timeline is important because . . .
Other discussion or structures for this section?

**Sequence/Steps**

I can interpret this section with sequence.
My evidence for thinking it is a sequence is . . .
Some of the steps in the sequence are . . .
(first, second, third, then, next, last)
Other discussion or structures for this section?

**Cause(s)/Effect(s)**

I can interpret this section with cause and effect.
My reason for thinking I can use cause and effect is . . .
I think the causes are . . .
I think the effects are . . .
Other discussion about causes and effects?

**Problem/Solution**

I can interpret this section with problem/solution.
My reason for thinking it is problem/solution is . . .
I think the main problem(s) are . . .
I think the main solution(s) are . . .
Other discussion or structures for this section?

**Categories and Details**

I can interpret this section with main ideas and details.
The main ideas are . . .
The details that support the main idea(s) are . . .
Does anyone have a different main idea?
Are there other details we should consider?
Other discussion or structures for this section?

**Compare/Contrast**

I can interpret this section with compare and contrast . . .
My reason for thinking it is compare/contrast is . . .
How the two concepts are alike or different is . . .
Does anyone have a different idea about what is
being compared and contrasted? likenesses or differences?
Other discussion or structures for this section?

**Respond-to-It**
**Text Structure Cue Card**

160

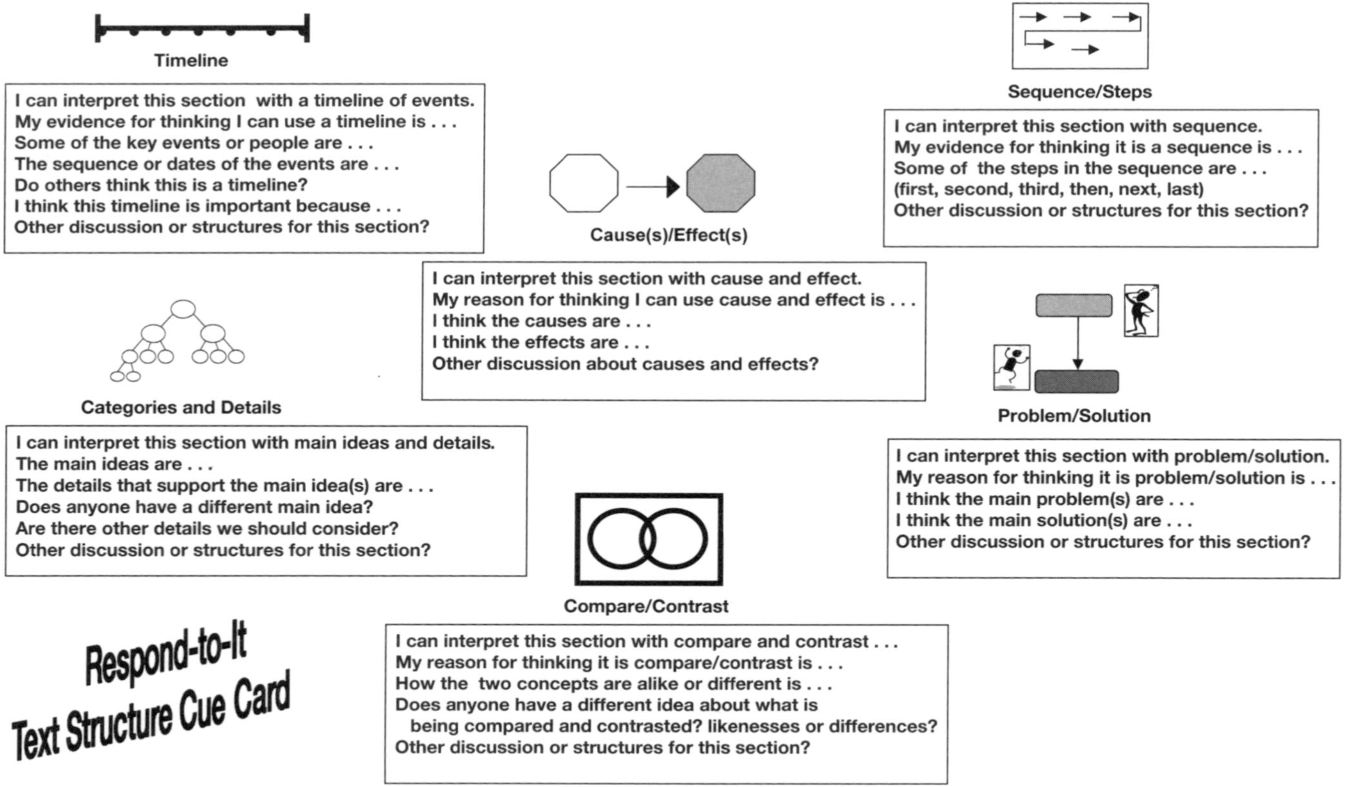

Reprinted with permission. Englert, C. S., Mariage, T., & Okolo, C. (2006). *Project ACCEL Curriculum Materials: Teacher Handbook*. East Lansing: Michigan State University, Literacy Achievement Research Center.

reading, students were asked to interpret larger sections of the text using one or more of six text structures, including (1) time line, (2) sequence/steps, (3) cause/effect, (4) categories and details, (5) problem/solution, and (6) compare/contrast. By having students choose a text structure to understand and arrange the text information, we hoped to promote greater awareness of how conscious knowledge of the text purpose and organization could be used to support interpretation and understanding.

Drawing upon a model for the use of interpretative strategies in a literature-based program known as Book Club (Raphael, 2000), we encouraged teachers and students to think flexibly about how these organizational patterns might be employed to interpret and reinterpret the information. Instead of accepting text as information to be received, encoded, and stored, we wanted students to take an active stance toward text by selecting and using text structure in order to respond to, question, and extend the text (Wertsch & Toma, 1995). Based on their selection of a particular interpretative purpose (e.g., compare/contrast, problem/solution, sequence/steps, cause/effect), students could reconstitute and represent the chapter meanings in new, more abstract modes of response (Wells, 1999). By reframing the ideas in different relationships and arrangements, students might be able to more consciously inspect ideas or to think more deeply in order to construct text meanings. In this manner text structures might lead to greater control of conscious thought as a tool for expressing and transforming ideas (Wells, 1999). Ultimately, readers might come to understand that text structure provides a medium for a progressive discourse that would allow readers to engineer a constructive interpretation, reinterpretation, and representation of the text.

A second set of Respond-to-It interpretative strategies was based on the application of critical literacy skills. Students were taught to apply critical literacy skills that related to interpreting, evaluating, and challenging the expository information based on multiple perspectives ("I am wondering if there is another point of view"; "Another position on this issue is . . ."), personal response ("This made me feel . . ."; "I like/dislike"), critique of the text ("I think the author failed to discuss . . ."; "The author could have improved the text by . . ."), and evaluation of the credibility of the ideas and information ("What evidence has been presented to support this idea?" "Do I think the evidence or explanation is sufficient?"). ACCEL teachers encouraged students to employ the critical literacy skills when they were reading expository text and resources. The ability to criticize one's own and others' opinions and actions, and the propensity to look for diverse points of view are vital to the development of reflective abilities in students (Raphael et al., 1997).

Many of the Respond-to-It interpretative responses were regularly applied in literature-based discussions of narrative text (Raphael, 2000). By extending these interpretative responses to the expository curriculum, students' literacy knowledge might be deepened and expanded, leading to greater automaticity in responding to text or searching for personal evidence based upon its effect, purpose, perspective, or impact. This is especially important with informational materials where students often assign authority to another author or speaker other than to themselves. The Respond-to-It strategies positioned students to assume greater authority and responsibility for thinking about the purposes, effects, and evidence that supported or limited the text information. In the end, we hoped that students' involvement in a critical literacy process might help them think more deeply and constructively about their own thoughts about the various topics, as well as examine the positions and evidence provided by other people. The Respond-to-It log was kept in the learning log.

## INQUIRY-DRIVEN
## CONTENT INVESTIGATIONS

Although there were additional strategies that constituted ACCEL, including the Map-It and Write-It strategies, one of the goals of the project was the Report-It strategy because its all-inclusive character that rooted students in the intersection of reading and writing. During Report-It, students were expected to develop competence in expressing their opinions (oral and written), offering reasons and evidence, and writing well-structured expository reports based on their research. The publication and dissemination emphases were designed to

- Provide teacher and student participants with authentic purposes for gathering and integrating information from multiple sources
- Expand the classroom walls and curriculum to include distant audiences
- Engage teachers and students in an inquiry-driven knowledge construction and dissemination process
- Encourage curricular interactions and a shared discourse among teachers and students (Dwyer, 1994)

Ultimately, in ACCEL, teachers engaged students in investigating a question or problem in a cycle of inquiry that culminated in the construction and publication of reports and artifacts. The strategies and learning logs guided students through the process, and the artifacts produced by students in the various phases of the inquiry process were annotated and entered into a cumulative learning log that was tied to a specific thematic topic, chapter, or unit. Students engaged in a complete cycle of inquiry in which they used all the strategies as they planned (Plan-It), read (Read-It), highlighted (Highlight-It and Mark-It), took notes (Note-It), comprehended and synthesized the information from multiple sources into maps or graphic organizers (Map-It), and composed expository reports (Write-It) that they then published and shared with their class.

## EVALUATION OF ACCEL

To evaluate the ACCEL project, the curricular strategies were implemented in a number of different settings and contexts. In the first year of data collection, we piloted the ACCEL strategies in English Language Arts and special education classes. The ACCEL program was implemented for 4.5 months. We analyzed students' informational literacy skills on a number of pretest and posttest measures including note taking, highlighting, retelling, and writing performance. The total group included 33 students, with 16 general education students and 17 students with learning disabilities.

We first analyzed students' note-taking skills, as measured by their ability to produce well-organized notes that contained topically related classes of main ideas and details. At the beginning of the year both general education and special education students demonstrated low-level skills rated as "limited." In large part, students copied the source text verbatim and tended to copy only small sections of the text rather than taking notes with sufficient depth and breadth. However, we found significant improvements in students' abilities to produce notes over time. By the end of the project students showed greater reduction and increased use of paraphrasing, and they covered more topical categories. Although general education students surpassed special education students in the organization and quality of their written notes, both groups gained equally from pretest to posttest. In fact, raters who were blind to the time of year were able to distinguish between the pretests and posttests of participating students with 70% reliability.

On the same measure, we required that students retell the passage in writing. Their written retellings were evaluated in terms of the number of ideas that were recalled, as well as the structure of their retellings based on inclusion of superordinate and subordinate categories that paralleled the major ideas in the text. Again our analysis showed significant improvements from the beginning to the end of the study for both groups of students. Students made significant gains in their ability to recall details and to organize their written retellings into chunks of related ideas. On the pretest, general education students recalled only 1 of the 13 possible chunks, and special education students couldn't recall a single complete chunk. On the posttest, students nearly doubled their recall of chunks and details.

Finally, we examined students' ability to synthesize and represent the information from multiple sources into a single organizer or plan, and then to transform that plan into a written expository report. Our analysis revealed that students made significant gains from beginning to end of the year, and that these gains were mostly attributable to their practice in producing well-organized written reports. General education students surpassed special education students, although gains from pretest to posttest were similar across the two groups. From pretest to posttest, students demonstrated gains in their ability to synthesize information from multiple sources in arrangements that were clearly signaled to the reader and that were topically organized by categories of main ideas and details.

## CONCLUSION

We developed ACCEL to encompass an array of strategies and habits of mind that are essential to reading success. In our project these strategies were used recursively and with a number of different representational tools to support thinking and conversations about texts.

ACCEL sought to promote strategy transfer across the curriculum. An organized set of literacy strategies was taught in multiple venues to promote students' abilities to apply the strategies to occasions when they read silently or orally. Likewise, teachers sought to emphasize that the strategies could be applied both with physical tools or scaffolds for representing their understanding or as mental tools.

Based on our evaluation of ACCEL, the results are promising and show that instruction in expository strategies does benefit students in their ability to read and write with greater confidence. Clearly, the expository instruction benefits both general and special education students. As we moved in the 2nd and 3rd years to employ these strategies in the content area curriculum, we maintained the emphasis on teacher think-alouds, combined with the demonstration of the literacy strategies in the context of the pragmatic contexts of the content area discipline. Although it may not seem easy for teachers to develop literacy practices in the content areas, those who are able to utilize effective strategies will help their students become more successful in confronting the complexities of their expository subjects.

### Follow-up Activities

1. Discuss the framing questions presented at the beginning of the chapter. What are indicators of literacy development and strategy enactment in the content areas?

2. Collaborate to develop a plan to engage students in an inquiry process that requires their implementation of a number of strategies involving planning, reading, note taking, mapping, synthesizing, and writing, and that can be taught within and across the school curriculum. How do the strategies vary across the disciplinary subjects of the curriculum? What are the ways that an inquiry process can be used to support literacy and content acquisition?
3. Discuss aspects of research-based components of effective reading/ writing instruction and effective teaching that can be incorporated into your plan to improve literacy outcomes, and consider how these components can be incorporated into the routine instruction of the expository curriculum.

## REFERENCES

Baker, L. (2002). Metacognition in comprehension instruction. In C. Block & M. Pressley (Eds.), *Comprehension instruction: Research-based best practices* (pp. 77–95). New York: Guilford Press.

Baker, S., Gersten, R., & Scanlon, D. (2003). Procedural facilitators and cognitive strategies: Tools for unraveling the mysteries of comprehension and the writing process, and for providing meaningful access to the general curriculum. *Learning Disabilities Research and Practice, 17*(1), 65–77.

Bakhtin, M. M. (1981). *The dialogic imagination: Four essays by M. M. Bakhtin.* Austin: University of Texas Press.

Beck, I., McKeown, M., Hamilton, R., & Kucan, L. (1997). *Questioning the author: An approach for enhancing student engagement with text.* Newark, DE: International Reading Association.

Block, C. C., & Pressley, M. (Eds.). (2002). *Comprehension instruction: Research-based best practices.* New York: Guilford Press.

Block, C. C., Schaller, J. L., Joy, J. A., & Gaine, P. (2002). Process-based comprehension instruction. In C. C. Block & Pressley, M. (Eds.), *Comprehension instruction: Research-based best practices* (pp. 42–61). New York: Guilford Press.

Block, C. C., & Israel, S. E. (2004). The ABCs of performing highly effective think-alouds. *The Reading Teacher, 58,* 154–167.

Bracewell, R. J., & Witte, S. P. (1997, March). The implications of activity, practice, and semiotic theory for cognitive constructs of writing. Paper presented at the annual meeting of the American Educational Research Association. Chicago, IL.

Brown, A., Pressley, M., Van Meter, P., & Schuder, T. (1996). A quasi-experimental validation of transactional strategies instruction with low-achieving second-grade readers. *Journal of Educational Psychology, 88,* 18–37.

Cervetti, G. N., Pearson, P. D., Bravo, M. A., & Barber, J. (2005). *Reading and writing in the service of inquiry-based science.* Berkley: University of California.

Chall, J. S., Jacobs, V. A., & Baldwin, L. E. (1990). *The Reading crisis: Why poor children fall behind*. Cambridge, MA: Harvard University Press.

Cole, M., & Engestrom, Y. (1993). A cultural-historical approach to distributed cognition. In G. Salomon (Ed.), *Distributed cognitions: Psychological and educational considerations* (pp. 1–46). New York: Cambridge University Press.

Cope, B., & Kalantzis, M. (1993). The power of literacy and the literacy of power. In B. Cope & M. Kalantzis (Eds.), *The powers of literacy: A genre approach to teaching writing* (pp. 63–89). Pittsburgh, PA: University of Pittsburgh Press.

Daniels, H. (2001). *Vygotsky and Pedagogy*. New York: Routledge.

Deshler, D. D., Ellis, E. S., & Lenz, B. K. (Eds.). (1996). *Teaching adolescents with learning disabilites* (2nd ed.). Denver, CO: Love Publishing Company.

Deshler, D. D., Schumaker, J. B., Lenz, B. K., Bulgren, J. A., Hock, M. F., Knight, J., et al. (2001). Ensuring content-area learning by secondary students with learning disabilities. *Learning Disabilities Research and Practice, 16*, 96.

Donahue, P. L., Voekl, K., Campbell, J. R., & Mazzeo, J. (1999). *NAEP 1998 report card for the nation and states*. Washington, DC: U.S. Department of Education.

Duffy, G. G. (2002). The case for direct explanation of strategies. In C. C. Block & Pressley, M. (Eds.), *Comprehension instruction: Research-based best practices* (pp. 28–41) New York: Guilford Press.

Dwyer, D. (1994). Apple classrooms of tomorrow: What we've learned. *Educational Leadership, 51*(7), 4–10.

Ellis, E. S. (1993). Integrative strategy instruction: A potential model for teaching content area subjects to adolescents with learning disabilities. *Journal of Learning Disabilities, 26*, 358–383.

Ellis, E. S., & Colvert, G. (1996). Writing strategy instruction. In D. D. Deshler, E. S. Ellis, & B. K. Lenz (Eds.), *Teaching adolescents with learning disabilities* (2nd ed., pp. 127–207). Denver, CO: Love Publishing.

Englert, C. S., & Dunsmore, K. (2004). The role of dialogue in constructing effective literacy settings for students with language and learning disabilities. In E. Silliman & L. Wilkinson (Eds.), *Language and literacy learning in schools* (pp. 201–238). New York: Guilford Press.

Englert, C. S., & Hiebert, E. H. (1984). Children's developing awareness of text structure in expository materials. *Journal of Educational Psychology, 76*, 65–74.

Englert, C. S., Mariage, T. V., & Okolo, C. (2006). *Project ACCEL curriculum materials: Teacher handbook*. East Lansing: Michigan State University, Literacy Achievement Research Center.

Englert, C. S., & Raphael, T. E. (1989). Developing successful writers through cognitive strategy instruction. In J. E. Brophy (Ed.), *Advances in research on teaching* (Vol. l, pp. 105–151). Greenwich, CT: JAI Press.

Englert, C. S., Raphael, T. E., Anderson, L. M., Gregg, S. L., & Anthony, H. M. (1989). Exposition: Reading, writing, and the metacognitive knowledge of learning disabled students. *Learning Disabilities Research and Practice, 5*(1), 5–24.

Gersten, R. (1998). Recent advances in instructional research for students with learning disabilities. *Learning Disabilities Practice, 13*, 162–170.

Gersten, R., & Baker, S. (1998). Real-world use of scientific concepts: Integrating situated cognition with explicit instruction. *Learning Disabilities Research and Practice, 17*(1), 65–77.

Gersten, R., Fuchs, L., Williams, J., & Baker, S. (2001). Teaching reading comprehension strategies to students with learning disabilities: A review of research. *Review of Educational Research, 71,* 279–320.

Goldman, S. R., Hasselbring, T. S., & the Cognition and Technology Group at Vanderbilt. (1996). Achieving meaningful mathematics literacy for students with learning disabilities. *Journal of Learning Disabilities, 30*(2), 198–208.

Graham, S. (2006). Strategy instruction and the teaching of writing. In C. MacArthur, S. Graham, & J. Fitzgerald (Eds.), *Handbook of writing research* (pp. 187–207). New York: Guilford Press.

Graham, S., MacArthur, C. A., & Schwartz, S. S. (1995). The effects of goal setting and procedural facilitation on the revising behavior and writing performance of students with writing and learning problems. *Journal of Educational Psychology, 87,* 230–240.

Harvey, S. (1998). *Non-fiction matters: Reading, writing and reasearch in grades 3–8.* Portland, ME: Stenhouse.

Harvey, S., & Goudvis, A. (2000). *Strategies that work: Teaching comprehension to enhance understanding.* Portland, ME: Stenhouse.

Jitendra, A. K., Hoppes, M. K., & Xin, Y. P. (2000). Enhancing main idea comprehension for students with learning problems: The role of summarization strategy and self-monitoring instruction. *Journal of Special Education, 34* (127–139).

Kim, A., Vaughn, S., Wanzek, J., & Wei, S. (2004). Graphic organizers and their effects on the reading comprehension of students with LD: A synthesis of research. *Journal of Learning Disabilities, 37*(2), 105–118.

Klingner, J. K., & Vaughan, S. (1996). Reciprocal teaching of reading comprehension strategies for students with learning disabilities who use English as a second language. *Elementary School Journal, 96*(3), 275–293.

Klingner, J. K., & Vaughan, S. (1998). Using Collaborative Strategic Reading. *Teaching Exceptional Children, 30*(6), 32–37.

Kolligan, J., & Sternberg, R. J. (1987). Intelligence, information processing, and specific learning disabilities: A triarchic systhesis. *Journal of Learning Disabilities, 20*(1), 8–17.

Kozulin, A. (2003). Psychological tools and mediated learning. In A. Kozulin, B. Gindis, V. S. Ageyev, & S. M. Miller (Eds.), *Vygotsky's educational theory in cultural context* (pp. 15–38). New York: Cambridge University Press.

Mastropieri, M. A., & Scruggs, T. E. (1997). Best practices in promoting reading comprehension in students with learning disabilities: 1976 to 1996. *Remedial and Special Education, 18,* 197–214.

Mehigan, K. (2005). The strategy toolbox: A ladder to strategic teaching. *The Reading Teacher, 58,* 552–566.

Morocco, C., Hindin, A., Mata-Aguilar, C., & Clark-Chiarelli, N. (2001). Building a deep understanding of literature with middle-grade students with learning disabilities. *Learning Disability Quarterly, 24,* 47–58.

Neufeld, P. (2005). Comprehension instruction in the content area classes. *The Reading Teacher, 59,* 302–312.

No Child Left Behind Act of 2001 (NCLB), Pub. L. No. 107-110 (2002). Available online: http://www.ed.gov/policy/elsec/leg/esea02/index.html

Ogle, D., & Blachowicz, C. L. Z. (2002). Beyond literature circles: Helping students comprehend informational texts. In C. C. Block & M. Pressley (Eds.), *Comprehension instruction: Research-based best practices* (pp. 259–274). New York: Guilford Press.

Okolo, C. M., & Ferretti, R. P. (1996). Knowledge acquisition and technology-supported projects in the social studies for students with learning disabilities. *Journal of Special Education Technology, 13*(2), 91–103.

Palincsar, A. S. (1986). The role of dialogue in providing scaffolded instruction. *Educational Psychologist, 21*(1&2), 73–98.

Palincsar, A. S., & Brown, A. L. (1984). Comprehension-fostering and comprehension-monitoring activities. *Cognition and Instruction, 1,* 117–175.

Palincsar, A. S., & Brown, A. L. (1989). Classroom dialogues to promote self-regulated comprehension. In J. E. Brophy (Ed.), *Advances in research in teaching* (Vol. 1, pp. 35–71). Greenwich, CT: JAI Press.

Pearson, P. D., & Duke, N. K. (2002). Comprehension instruction in the primary grades. In C. C. Block & M. Pressley (Eds.), *Comprehension instruction: Research-based best practices* (pp. 247–258). New York: Guilford Press.

Perie, M., Grigg, W. S., & Donahue, P. L. (2005). *The nation's report card: Reading 2005* (NCES 2006-451). Washington, DC: U.S. Department of Education, Institute of Education Sciences, National Center for Education Statistics.

Pressley, M., Brown, R., El-Dinary, P. B., & Afflerbach, P. (1995). The comprehension instruction that students need: Instruction fostering constructively responsive reading. *Learning Disabilities Research and Practice, 10*(4), 215–224.

Raphael, T. (2000). Balancing literature and instruction: Lessons from the Book Club project. In B. M. Taylor & P. van den Broek (Eds.), *Reading for meaning: Fostering comprehension in the middle grades* (pp. 70–94). New York: Teachers College Press.

Raphael, T., Pardo, L., Highfield, K., & McMahon, S. (1997). *Book Club: A literature-based curriculum.* Littleton, MA: Small Planet Communications.

Rose, M. (1999). "Our hands will know": The development of tactile diagnostic skill—teaching, learning, and situated cognition in a physical therapy program. *Anthropology and Education Quarterly, 30*(2), 133–160.

Roth, W.-M. (1998). *Designing communities.* Boston: Kluwer Academic.

Roth, W.-M., & McRobbie, C. (1999). Lifeworlds and the 'w/ri(gh)ting' of classroom research. *Journal of Curriculum Studies, 31,* 501–522.

Scanlon, D., Deshler, D. D., & Schumaker, J. B. (1996). Can a strategy be taught and learned in secondary inclusive classrooms? *Learning Disabilities Research & Practice, 11*(1), 41–57.

Scribner, S. (1997). The Cognitive consequences of literacy. In Tobach, E., Falmagne, R. J., Parlee, M. B., Martin, L. M. W., & Kapelman, A. S. (Eds.), *Mind and social practice: Selected writings of Sylvia Scribner* (pp. 160–189). New York: Cambridge University Press.

Swanson, H. L. (1999). Reading research for students with LD: A meta-analysis of intervention outcomes. *Journal of Learning Disabilities, 32,* 504–532.

Trabasso, T., & Bouchard, E. (2002). Teaching readers how to comprehend text strategically. In C. C. Block & M. Pressley (Eds.), *Comprehension instruction: Research-based best practices* (pp. 176–200). New York: Guilford Press.

Vaughn, S., Gersten, R., & Chard, D. (2000). The underlying message in LD intervention research. *Exceptional Children, 67,* 99–114.

Vaughn, S., Klingner, J. K., & Bryant, D. P. (2001). Collaborative strategic reading as a means to enhance peer-mediated instruction for reading comprehension and content area learning. *Remedial and Special Education, 22*(2), 66–74.

Vygotsky, L. S. (1978). *Mind in society: The development of higher psychological processes* (M. Cole, V. John-Steiner, S. Scribner, & E. Souberman Eds.). Cambridge, MA: Harvard University Press.

Wells, G. (1999). *Dialogic inquiry: Toward a sociocultural practice and theory of education.* New York: Cambridge University Press.

Wertsch, J. V. (Ed.). (1995). *The need for action in sociocultural research.* Cambridge: Cambridge University Press.

Wertsch, J. V. (1998). *Mind as action.* New York: Oxford University Press.

Wertsch, J. V. (2002). *Voices of collective remembering.* Cambridge: Cambridge University Press.

Wertsch, J. V., & Toma, C. (1995). Discourse and learning in the classroom: A sociocultural approach. In L. P. Steffe & J. Gale (Eds.), *Constructivism in education* (pp. 159–174). Hillsdale, NJ: Erlbaum.

Williams, J. P. (2003). Teaching text structure to improve reading comprehension. In H. L. Swanson, K. R. Harris, & S. Graham (Eds.), *Handbook of learning disabilities* (pp. 293–305). New York: Guilford Press.

Wong, B. Y. L. (2000). Writing strategies instruction for expository essay writing for adolescents with and without learning disabilities. *Topics in Language Disorders, 20*(4), 29–44.

Wong, B. Y. L., Wong, R., & Blenkinsop, J. (1989). Cognitive and metacognitive aspects of learning disabled adolescents' composing problems. *Learning Disability Quarterly, 12,* 300–322.

# PART IV

# Effective Schoolwide Practices to Improve All Students' Reading

# CHAPTER 8

# Multiple Tiers of Intervention: A Framework for Prevention and Identification of Students with Reading/Learning Disabilities

Sharon Vaughn
Jeanne Wanzek
Jack M. Fletcher

Taking a prevention orientation, in this chapter we identify how a multitiered approach to instruction creates an opportunity to provide increasingly more intensive interventions for students at risk for reading problems.

Questions for Reflection and Discussion

- How does a prevention model for framing reading problems relate to the current ways in which reading instruction is provided, and what guidelines for change in current practice might occur as a result of implementing a prevention model?
- What framework for implementing effective interventions for students with reading difficulties might be appropriate in your school, and what instructional practices need to occur to assure effective implementation?

How are education and public health related? As early as 1923, Edward A. Winslow described public health as the science of preventing disease and prolonging life: He indicated that public health is based on organized community efforts that improve water and air quality and reduce disease, address the education of the community, and include medical services for diagnosing and treating disease. Only recently has education accepted a

similar view of preventing learning difficulties. Like public health, education has universal and valued goals:

- Providing a comprehensive education for all students
- Identifying students who have difficulties and providing additional
  support
- Developing more intensive interventions, such as special education,
  for students who have persistent difficulties and need long-term support

## THE THREE-TIERED FRAMEWORK
## FOR PUBLIC HEALTH

For almost a century, public health has designed and implemented a
prevention system to reduce the overall precedence of poor health conditions
and to ameliorate the resulting consequences. Largely, the goal was to increase worker productivity by improving overall health. To improve health,
the focus needed to be on all socioeconomic levels with special concentra-
tion on reducing poverty and an ultimate goal of improving national health
and reducing high public expenses associated with poor health (Beaglehole
& Bonita, 1997). The public health approach includes:

1. Specifying through research the risk factors associated with the
   problem
2. Identifying or developing, implementing, and evaluating interventions
   associated with reducing the problem
3. Providing large-scale implementation procedures to provide the intervention to improve health
4. Using ongoing monitoring and assessment of the interventions to
   determine their effectiveness (Schneider, 2000)

These four steps are carried out through a three-tier system that involves three levels of prevention/intervention: primary, secondary, and tertiary. These three levels are intended to provide the appropriate amount of
support based on the increasing level of need at each of the levels (less need
at the primary level to very intensive need at the tertiary level). The inten-
tion is to allow most people to stay healthy through the least intensive level
of prevention.

In public health, a primary prevention/intervention would include ongoing screening of key indicators associated with health for each age and
risk group. For example, blood pressure is used to screen for cardiovascular

difficulties in most individuals from young adult through life. Specific screening practices associated with gender include mammograms for women and prostate screening for men. Furthermore, good primary prevention approaches include providing vaccinations to young children and promoting practices such as good nutrition, appropriate weight maintenance plans, and exercise routines.

Even with good primary prevention practices, individuals get sick and require additional supports or have minor difficulties that require ongoing treatment (e.g., allergies). Through secondary interventions many more people are put on the track to good health. This would include readily available high-quality health care when illness occurs and is either more transient or readily treated (e.g., strep throat, broken bones, treatable high blood pressure). This multilevel approach allows the most intensive intervention (tertiary) to be used only for those few who develop severe or chronic health problems.

Using this as a framework, primary prevention/intervention is provided to everyone to avoid or prevent illness or injury. Secondary intervention is implemented to minimize the severity of illness or injury once risk or illness is identified. These early treatment procedures tend to be less costly, less invasive, and require a shorter period of treatment due to the early detection. Tertiary intervention is implemented to minimize the effects of an identified disability or illness by providing medical care and rehabilitation services. As the most intensive level of the three-tiered approach, tertiary intervention is only required for those persons who develop severe illness or disability despite the efforts of primary and secondary intervention. If primary and secondary intervention programs are effective, fewer individuals require the most extensive tertiary interventions. As a result, the rationale from a public health perspective is that the three-tiered system leads to overall better public health and increased productivity, as well as lower public costs for treatment of illness.

## APPLYING A PREVENTATIVE
## MODEL TO EDUCATION

A framework similar to the public health approach has been used in education in both the behavioral area as well as reading to conceptualize prevention and early intervention for individuals with behavior or reading difficulties. Similar to the field of public health, poor academic performance and behavior problems are of great concern to the public at large and are prognostic of overall low quality of life. The fastest growing jobs in the

United States require education beyond high school (Meeder, 2003). Students who acquire less education than a bachelor's degree are at greater risk for unemployment, overall low income, and even poor health (National Center of Education Statistics, 2005). Reading and appropriate behavior are essential for success in school, opportunity for higher education, and life success.

The goal of a preventative education model is to assure effective instruction and lower the number of students who develop severe academic difficulties. Forness (2005) describes it this way:

> Our field has, however, begun to reconceptualize its interventions for children with emotional or behavioral disorders in terms of primary, secondary, and tertiary prevention and thus brought special education research into a more comprehensive and potentially more effective pubic health model. (p. 323)

Aligned with this view, the National Joint Committee on Learning Disabilities (2005) and the National Association of State Directors of Special Education (2005) have recommended a three-tiered model for implementing a response to intervention (RtI) approach.

## Behavioral Area

For example, in the behavioral area this three-tiered intervention can be found in the Schoolwide Positive Behavior Support model (Sugai & Horner, 2002). The primary level of intervention for preventing behavior problems includes defining behavioral expectations for all students, teaching the expected behaviors to students, implementing procedures for encouraging the expected behaviors and preventing problem behavior, and monitoring student progress and implementation efforts (Sugai & Horner, 2002). Despite the effective implementation of primary behavioral interventions, it is likely that some students will still exhibit behavior difficulties and require more support. These students may receive secondary targeted group or individual interventions. These interventions are implemented based on functional assessments of student behavior. Examples of secondary interventions include social skills clubs and simple student behavior reinforcement plans. The additional support and behavior intervention provided at the secondary level allow more students to get on track with appropriate behavior and as a result these students may never develop severe behavior problems.

Tertiary intervention is provided for those students who develop severe behavior problems despite implementation of primary and secondary interventions. In other words, these are the students who need more intensive support. As a result, specialized, individualized support systems are designed by collaborative school teams in order to meet these students' individual needs.

## Reading and Learning Disabilities

How can a multitier approach be applied to instruction? Perhaps the academic area in which there is the most research on the application of a multitiered approach is reading (Dickson & Bursuck, 1999; Kamps & Greenwood, 2005; McMaster, Fuchs, Fuchs, & Compton, 2005; O'Connor, 2000; O'Connor, Fulmer, Harty, & Bell, 2005; O'Connor, Harty, & Fulmer, 2005; Vaughn, Linan-Thompson, & Hickman, 2003). Until recently schools have been reluctant to identify and provide interventions for all but the most severe cases of reading disabilities in the early grades (McCardle, Scarborough, & Catts, 2001). Within the last few years, researchers have viewed interventions in terms of increasing intensity through reducing group size, increasing time, and/or situating the instruction so that it is even more carefully tailored to the instructional needs of the learner (Fletcher, Denton, Fuchs, & Vaughn, 2005; Vaughn & Linan-Thompson, 2003).

Multitiered instruction combines prevention and intervention through ongoing assessment and implementation of successive levels of support increasing in intensity and specificity to assist students with academic difficulties. Tier 1 (primary intervention) is provided to all students who receive evidence-based reading instruction from well-trained teachers. Students are screened for the presence of risk characteristics that predict a reading problem (e.g., inadequate knowledge of letter sounds) as early as kindergarten. Students identified as at-risk or with an academic deficit who do not respond adequately to primary intervention (classroom-based reading instruction) are provided successive levels of intervention as needed. These levels of intervention function as secondary or tertiary interventions.

## DIMENSIONS OF A MULTITIERED APPROACH TO READING INTERVENTION

To establish the rationale for a multitiered approach to prevention and intervention for students with reading/learning difficulties, we describe five dimensions that characterize different interventions: (1) screening and ongoing progress monitoring, (2) differentiating instruction through small-group instruction or tutoring, (3) increasing the duration of the intervention, (4) targeting instruction to students' specific needs, and (5) determining the content of the instructional approach.

## Screening and Ongoing Progress Monitoring

Fundamental to the effective implementation of any prevention or remedial program is the use of screening measures to identify students at risk and in need of further support. Universal screening of all students is part of Tier 1 (primary intervention) and provides a rapid process of determining competency in the fundamental skills in reading with the sole purpose of identifying students at risk for reading difficulties. The essential feature of a good screening instrument is predictive validity so that students who require additional intervention can be identified (Rathvon, 2004) and so that we are firm about which students are *not* at risk (Foorman & Ciancio, 2005). Since interventions are expensive, it is essential that screening measures precisely target students most in need of supplemental reading practices and interventions (Speece, 2005). After students are identified as at-risk using screening measures, students are provided Tier 2 intervention immediately, and ongoing progress monitoring measures for students identified as at-risk are implemented frequently (every couple of weeks) so that the effectiveness of alternative or supplemental interventions can be documented. The use of schoolwide screening with ongoing progress monitoring is critical to implementing a response-to-intervention approach since screening and progress monitoring are the essential tools for determining who requires secondary intervention and then ultimately whether students' response to secondary intervention is sufficient or whether they require more intensive tertiary interventions.

## Instructional Group Size

Class or schoolwide primary interventions can be effective practices for supporting the reading instruction of a large percentage of students—as many as 90% with effective schoolwide instruction in reading (Fletcher et al., 2005; Lyon, Fletcher, Fuchs, & Chhabra, 2006; Torgesen, 2000). Approaches to improving classroom instruction involve implementation of scientifically based comprehensive reading programs with professional development of teachers and enhanced assessment (e.g., Dickson & Bursuck, 1999; Simmons, Kuykendall, King, Cornachione, & Kame'enui, 2000; Vaughn & Chard, 2006).

Despite the overall effectiveness of schoolwide and classwide efforts (often reducing reading difficulties to below 10%), some students will require additional instruction to either prevent or remediate reading difficulties (Denton & Mathes, 2003; O'Connor, 2000; Torgesen, 2000). For these students, additional instruction typically involves small-group or individual support. We know that interventions provided to students with reading difficulties in large groups (more than eight in a group) are unlikely to be associated with improved outcomes (Elbaum, Vaughn, Hughes, & Moody, 1999,

2000; Foorman & Torgesen, 2001; Swanson, Hoskyn, & Lee, 1999; Torgesen, 2004). Thus small-group or individual tutoring is often provided to accelerate student learning so that the schoolwide and classwide efforts are profitable.

Even with more extensive interventions (Tiers 2 and 3) the numbers of students identified for special education are unlikely to decrease (O'Connor, 2000), and some students who have received individual or very small group intensive interventions have not sufficiently closed the gap between their reading performance and expected reading performance (McMaster et al., 2005; Vaughn et al., 2003). Consistent findings suggest that there are students whose response to reading interventions is low despite highly focused instruction from well-trained adults that is often provided in one-on-one instruction or very small groups (Mathes et al., 2005; McMaster et al., 2005; Torgesen, 2004; Vaughn & Linan-Thompson, 2003). These findings leave open the possibility that "we may be seriously overestimating the effects of our short-term interventions on the long-term trajectory of reading growth" (O'Connor, 2000, p. 53).

## Duration of the Intervention

Another element of instruction that is likely to influence the effectiveness of the intervention is the duration or time allocated to providing the intervention. The time of the intervention can be spread over years (Blachman, Tangel, Ball, Black, & McGraw, 1999; O'Connor, Fulmer, et al., 2005; O'Connor, Harty, et al., 2005), months (Blachman et al., 2004; Lovett et al., 1994), or weeks (Denton, Fletcher, Anthony, & Francis, in press; Torgesen et al., 2001), with the greatest gains realized early in the implementation of the intervention. Duration is also related to the amount of time allocated each day to provide the intervention.

The group size and amount of time allocated to the intervention determine the intensity of the intervention and are related to the outcomes. For example, Iversen, Tunmer, and Chapman (2005) report that when one-on-one tutoring was compared with one-on-two (one teacher and two students) using a modified Reading Recovery format (adding explicit training in phonological awareness and orthographic analogies), results were the same for one-on-one instruction and one-on-two instruction. However, the intervention time increased from 33 minutes per day to 42 minutes per day. Thus twice as many students were provided with effective intervention by minimally increasing the time allocated for intervention.

## Targeting Instruction

We think of targeting instruction as the application of systematic and explicit instruction matched to the instructional needs of students with consideration of those skills that have the highest priority. Critical to the success of targeted instruction is scaffolding instruction that provides increasingly more difficult instruction with many opportunities for success.

Foorman, Francis, Fletcher, Schatschneider, and Mehta (1998) contrasted the effects of reading curriculums that varied in the explicitness of instruction in word recognition for at-risk students receiving Title 1 services in eight schools in Grades 1–2. The students were taught by one of four approaches:

1. *Explicit code*—a basal curriculum, which provided explicit instruction in word recognition, along with instruction in comprehension strategies
2. *Embedded code*—a phonics program (Hiebert, Colt, Calto, & Gary, 1992), which emphasized the learning of phonics concepts within the context of whole words
3. *Implicit code (research)*—a curriculum implemented by the researchers that stressed contextual reading; responses to literature, writing, spelling, and phonics in context; and integration of reading, writing, listening, and speaking, with no decontextualized instruction in phonics
4. *Implicit code (district)*—the district's approach to reading instruction, which was like the implicit code (research) condition, but with no support from the researchers

All students received the same amount of time in their respective programs, with comparable student-teacher ratios. The teachers received professional development and support from the researchers for implementing each of the first three approaches; the district provided support for the fourth approach.

Growth curve analyses were conducted on measures of phonological awareness, word reading, and spelling administered at four time points between September and April. Across a variety of literacy outcomes, students in the explicit code group improved at a faster rate than students who received the implicit code condition, and had significantly higher April scores in word reading, phonological processing, and spelling. The means for students in the embedded code condition were between those of the other two groups. A significantly higher percentage of students in the implicit and embedded code groups than in the explicit instruction group showed little improvement in word reading over the year. In addition, Foorman et al. (1998) found that the relation between phonological analysis and word reading was stronger for explicit code students than for implicit code students, suggesting that the effects of explicit instruction on word reading stemmed from its effects on phonological awareness.

Juel and Minden-Cupp (2000) reported similar findings with first-grade students with reading difficulties who fared better in classrooms where phonics was directly taught and practiced in controlled texts than when trade books were employed. "Specifically, instruction for children who have difficulties learning to read must be more explicit and comprehensive, more intensive, and more supportive than the instruction required by the majority of children" (Foorman & Torgesen, 2001, p. 206). Explicit and systematic instruction is associated with improved outcomes for at-risk learners who are native English speakers (Blachman, Ball, Black, & Tangel, 2000; Hatcher, Hulme, & Ellis, 1994; Vellutino et al., 1996) as well as those who are not (Gunn, Smolkowski, Biglar, Black, & Blair, 2005; Quiroga, Lemos-Britton, Mostafapour, Abbott, & Berninger, 2002; Vaughn, Linan-Thompson, et al., 2006; Vaughn, Mathes, et al., in press).

Targeting instruction also refers to prioritizing the instruction most needed for students at risk for reading problems. Coyne and colleagues (Coyne, Kame'enui, & Simmons, 2001) refer to this as "drawing a line in the sand and mapping backwards" (p. 69). Thus school personnel have clearly articulated goals for students and realize that to reach these goals critical benchmarks along the way need to be reached. For example, while reading comprehension is unquestionably the reading goal for all students—whether they are at risk for reading difficulties or not—the instruction targeted for at-risk students may not be reading comprehension strategies if students are unable to read words. In the very beginning stages of reading acquisition, students with reading difficulties will require extensive and explicit instruction on applying the alphabetic principle (mapping sounds of language to print) through decoding and encoding (Brown & Felton, 1990; Torgesen, et al., 1999). Thus the target of their instruction would be application of the alphabetic principle and word reading.

Scaffolding students' instruction refers to the thoughtful and responsive sequencing of instruction so that students have ample opportunities to succeed and yet new learning is always occurring. Fundamental to instruction that is scaffolded effectively is the interaction between the teacher and the learner that involves questioning, responding, supporting (cognitively and motivationally), and extending new learning. Similarly, methods that involve student reading of a wide range of materials are more effective when the materials are scaffolded to the reading level of the student than when students simply read silently for extended periods (Stahl, 2004). These practices are particularly necessary for students at risk for reading difficulties/disabilities.

## Content of the Instructional Approach

Recently, reading researchers have agreed that the previous debates about the appropriate content of reading instruction have often consisted of simplistic interpretations of whether phonics or whole language were superior. Consensus reports of summaries of research on effective reading instruction and effective practices for teaching students with reading difficulties/disabilities concur that learning to read requires explicit instruction in components of reading involving decoding words effectively, fluency, and comprehension (Biancarosa & Snow, 2004; Donovan & Cross, 2002; National Reading Panel, 2000; RAND Reading Study Group, 2002; Snow, Burns, & Griffin, 1998; Swanson et al., 1999; Vaughn, Gersten, & Chard, 2000). For example, the National Research Council Report, *Preventing Reading Difficulties in Young Children* (Snow et al., 1998), reported that for students to become successful in reading, teachers must *integrate* instruction involving the alphabetic principal (word recognition), teaching for meaning (comprehension), and opportunities to read (fluency). Five essential components for learning to read were identified by the National Reading Panel (2000): phonemic awareness, phonics, fluency, comprehension, and vocabulary.

Research on students identified with learning disabilities reveals that the most effective instruction uses a combination of explicit and strategic instruction in both word recognition and reading comprehension strategies, with scaffolded instruction that provides modeling and feedback to promote internalization and use of the practice through active engagement to build sight word vocabulary and fluency (Foorman & Torgesen, 2001; Swanson, 1999). The message from all these syntheses is that successful reading programs help teachers integrate instruction that involves different domains of reading, prioritizing those domains most essential in the development of proficient reading. Thus even students with severe word recognition problems need to have opportunities to access print, almost from the beginning of reading intervention, and reading must be taught with a goal of understanding, learning from, and appreciating different text types. Denton, Vaughn, and Fletcher (2003) summarize the multiple syntheses on reading difficulties and identify these features as essential to enhance reading development of all students:

- A teacher who has both content and procedural knowledge
- Integration of key instructional elements with emphasis on those elements that are most appropriate developmentally
- Differentiated instruction particularly for students with special needs
- Explicit and systematic instruction
- Making connections between research knowledge and practice

In examining the instructional content of more recent reading intervention studies, successful interventions combine instruction across multiple domains (e.g., integrating word reading with reading for meaning) in different ways. Programs vary considerably in the amount of instructional time devoted to sublexical word recognition skills. For example, Wise, Ring, and Olson (2000) found that a computer-based program that primarily corrected errors was as effective as intervention with a program providing extensive attention to the sublexical component of word recognition. Similarly, another remedial study found relatively little difference between an intense sublexical program and an intervention that provided about 20% explicit instruction in alphabetic principle and 50% time reading and writing connected text (Torgesen et al., 2001). Mathes and colleagues (2005) compared a program that integrated instruction in the alphabetic principle, comprehension, and fluency, including use of highly decodable text in a scripted scope and sequence, with a program based on guided reading principles that included explicit instruction in the alphabetic principle but also emphasized reading and writing of connected text. There were no major differences on the effects of these programs on students' outcomes in reading.

These studies provide evidence that effective reading instructional programs must integrate explicit instruction in word recognition, fluency, and comprehension. Programs may vary in how they do this and in how intensely they teach different components of word recognition, fluency, and comprehension; but it is the integration of these components that appears to be critical. We believe that there is now compelling evidence that there is no one component of reading instruction that in isolation will yield superior results (e.g., either phonics only instruction or literature only). Rather, the issue is how to integrate components of learning to read so that the individual needs of students can be met.

The group for whom we are least confident about the content and ways of integrating instruction are those students who have failed to respond adequately to typically effective interventions (McMaster et al., 2005; O'Connor, Harty, et al., 2005; Vaughn et al., 2003). For example, after 30 weeks of small-group supplemental reading instruction for at-risk students, Vaughn and colleagues (2003) found that almost 25% of these at-risk students were responding at a minimal rate to the intervention. Relatedly, McMaster and colleagues (2005) did not report statistically significant findings for students identified as "nonresponding" to a classwide intervention when they were subsequently provided peer tutoring or tutoring by an adult. O'Connor and colleagues (O'Connor, Harty et al., 2005) followed students from kindergarten through third grade reporting that even students who had participated in multiple tiers of intervention over years—even intensive interventions that provided very small group instruction for 5 days a week—yielded approximately 8% of students who were still significantly behind in reading.

## INITIAL FINDINGS FROM A THREE-TIER FRAMEWORK IN READING

We are in the process of implementing a K–3 reading three-tier framework of primary, secondary, and tertiary interventions in a large urban school district consisting of six Title 1 elementary schools. The research project is a longitudinal design including treatment and comparison groups at each of the three tiers. Student progress over time is being analyzed using multiple reading and language assessments.

During the 1st year of the study, we began with assessment of a historical control group. We assessed this cohort of students beginning in kindergarten and followed them through third grade as they participated in the classroom instruction and interventions typically provided by the schools. We did not provide primary, secondary, or tertiary interventions to this group. During the 2nd year of the study, implementation of the three-tiered intervention model began with the cohort of students who entered kindergarten the year after the historical control group. This group of students comprised our first treatment cohort of students (Cohort 1). We are in the process of following this first treatment cohort of students through third grade while providing primary, secondary, and tertiary intervention as they progress through each grade. Similarly during the third year of the study, we intervened with a second cohort of students beginning in kindergarten (Cohort 2). Again, we are in the process of providing intervention for these students as they progress through the grades.

As students move from one grade to the next, teachers at each successive grade level participate in the primary intervention. With regard to students, the focus is on growth in reading. With regard to teachers, the focus is on improved teaching skills and on perceptions concerning barriers and facilitators related to schoolwide implementation of the model.

Students who do not make adequate progress in the primary intervention (core classroom instruction) qualify for secondary intervention. For this research project, the students qualifying for secondary intervention are randomly assigned to receive either a research-implemented secondary intervention or school-implemented services. Thus a treatment and comparison group of at-risk readers is utilized for examining effects of secondary intervention. Each classroom teacher has students in the secondary intervention treatment and comparison group to control for teacher effects.

Students who do not make adequate progress in secondary intervention are provided a more intensive tertiary intervention. The students qualifying for tertiary intervention continue in their assigned treatment or comparison group allowing for examination of effects over time. Students receive secondary or tertiary intervention (not both at the same time) and continue in their primary intervention program. At each level of the three-tiered model individual characteristics, background, school experiences, and outcomes of students who do and do not make adequate progress in response to intervention are documented.

We currently have complete data for all three cohorts—historical control group, treatment Cohort 1, and treatment Cohort 2 related to primary intervention through their first-grade year. In addition, we have complete data for secondary and tertiary intervention for Cohort 1 through second grade. Below is a summary of preliminary findings for these cohorts of students. Complete data analysis is in process and will be published in full at a later date.

## Primary Intervention

Primary intervention consisted of two elements supported by the research team: ongoing professional development for teachers (approximately 27 hours each year) and application of progress monitoring practices for all students three times per year and for students at risk for reading problems six to eight times per year. Schools continued to use the materials/curricula they were using prior to implementation of the three-tier framework in their schools. In the first treatment year the kindergarten teachers participated in primary intervention (when Cohort 1 was in kindergarten). In the second treatment year the first-grade teachers participated in primary intervention and the kindergarten teachers continued to implement primary intervention (when Cohort 2 was in kindergarten).

Each year we provided professional development in a variety of formats including workshops, in-class support, and grade-level meetings. All of the teachers attended 1–2 full-day introductory sessions during the summer and five 3-hour after-school workshops each year (for 2 years total). The topics related to high-priority, grade-level-specific outcomes including phonics and word recognition, differentiated instruction, vocabulary, comprehension, and the use of data to make instructional decisions. These workshop sessions were followed by in-class support (e.g., demonstration lessons of specific reading content and/or features of effective instruction; assistance with implementing specific content, grouping, or features of effective instruction; assistance with planning and implementation of progress monitoring; and recommendations of resources to supplement instruction) and grade-level meetings to discuss data, instruction for at-risk students, and instructional questions. During the initial year, in-class support was provided approximately twice a month for 30 minutes each session; however support was differentiated according to teacher need. During the follow-up year (the second year we worked with teachers at a specific grade level), in-class support was decreased to approximately once a month or less and most information was shared/discussed at monthly grade-level meetings. Teachers used data collected three times per year on all students and also monitored the progress of at-risk students throughout the school year.

We were particularly interested in the effect of primary intervention on the outcomes for at-risk students. Students were identified as at-risk in winter of kindergarten if they were below grade-level expectations on prereading measures of phonemic awareness and letter knowledge. To examine the effects of primary intervention only, we analyzed the data from at-risk students who were assigned to a comparison group and did not receive the research-implemented secondary or tertiary intervention. We then followed the students' progress through the end of first grade as their kindergarten teachers and first-grade teachers received professional development and began monitoring the progress of the students in their classes.

Preliminary data indicate no significant differences between the historical control group, Cohort 1, and Cohort 2 at the end of first grade on word identification measures. Word attack measures revealed significant differences between Cohort 2 and the historical control group and between Cohort 2 and Cohort 1. There were also significant differences found between the historical control group and Cohort 2 on end-of-first-grade passage comprehension measures. In addition, we found a decrease in the number of at-risk students over time as teachers implemented primary intervention. The at-risk students identified achieved higher levels of reading each year. As a result, primary intervention appears to have reduced the incidence of reading difficulties in this school district.

## Secondary Intervention

In addition to providing primary intervention to all students, secondary intervention was provided to students identified as at risk for reading difficulties. Students were assessed in fall of first grade and the winter of first grade and identified at each time point as at-risk or on-track in reading development. Once identified as at-risk, students were randomly assigned to either a treatment or a comparison group, provided secondary intervention when at-risk status was identified (fall only, spring only, or fall and spring), and followed through the end of second grade.

The students randomly assigned to the treatment group received secondary intervention from the research team. The intervention included daily 30-minute sessions provided in instructional groups of 4–6 students. Students received instruction in phonics and word recognition, fluency, text reading, and comprehension with weekly progress monitoring used to make instructional decisions. The students randomly assigned to the comparison group continued to receive typical school services.

Preliminary results indicate that secondary intervention was sufficient for many of the students to get on track as readers, and they did not qualify for further intervention after first grade. We examined the sample of students who were identified as at-risk during first grade and followed the students through the end of second grade. Of the students who participated in the treatment group, there were 27 students who exited from secondary intervention and did not require further intervention. These 27 students represented 61.4% of the sample assigned to the treatment group. Twenty-five students who participated in the comparison group and received typical school services were able to exit from intervention and did not require further intervention (50% of the sample assigned to the comparison students). The total number of students in the treatment and comparison groups on track with reading after first-grade risk identification was 52 students and represented 15.3% of the total number of students in the cohort. It is important to note that treatment and comparison students differed only with respect to secondary intervention—all students participated in primary intervention. We examined the data for students exiting secondary intervention by the end of first grade in the treatment and comparison groups. Overall, the first-grade treatment group achieved higher levels of reading after receiving secondary intervention, and these gains continued through the end of second grade.

## Tertiary Intervention

Students in the treatment condition who did not respond sufficiently to secondary intervention by the end of first grade were provided tertiary intervention in second grade. For 7 students in the treatment group and 15 students in the comparison group, tertiary intervention was provided after insufficient response to a secondary intervention was provided in both the fall and spring of first grade. These students were the lowest students in secondary intervention demonstrating at-risk status continuously through first and second grade. This tertiary subsample represented 15.9% of the original at-risk treatment sample and 30% of the original at-risk comparison sample. These 22 students qualifying for intervention throughout first and second grade (treatment or comparison group) represented 6.6% of the total number of students in their grade-level cohort. There were also 10 students in the treatment group and 10 students in the comparison group that qualified for tertiary intervention in second grade after receiving one round of sessions of secondary intervention in first grade. These 20 students represented an additional 6% of the total number of students in the grade-level cohort.

Students in the treatment group received 50-minute intervention sessions daily in addition to continued primary intervention. The students were instructed in groups of 2–4 for approximately 13 weeks in the fall and 13 weeks in the spring. Students received explicit instruction in advanced word study, vocabulary, application of word study and vocabulary to text reading, fluency, and comprehension. Students in the comparison group continued to receive typical school services.

Examining the data for students consistently qualifying for intervention through first and second grade, the treatment students ($n = 7$) were reading an average of 46.57 words per minute (median = 48) after one year of tertiary intervention, while the students in the comparison group ($n = 15$) achieved an average of 29.47 words per minute (median = 25). However, there were no students in either the comparison or treatment group that achieved grade-level expectations in oral reading fluency. These students may need sustained intensive interventions in order to continue making progress.

## CONCLUSION

There are no "silver bullets" for effectively teaching all students to read. Approaches to enhancing reading success have been well developed and documented including tutoring approaches (Torgesen et al., 1999; Vellutino et al., 1996; Wasik & Slavin, 1993), using peer partners in learning (Fuchs, Fuchs, & Burish, 2000; Greenwood, Delquadri, & Hall, 1989), and interventions that involve small-group instruction from group sizes of 2 (Iversen et al., 2005) to larger groups of 3–5 students (Mathes et al., 2003; Rashotte, MacPhee, & Torgesen, 2001). Engaging students in active responding often through small groups or pairs with a focus on higher level comprehension questions is associated with improved outcomes (Taylor, Pearson, Peterson, & Rodriguez, 2003). All research-based approaches regardless of intensity yield a small percentage of students whose response to instruction is less than expected. In fact, students' response to intervention may be the most valuable information for identifying students with significant reading disabilities. Vellutino, Scanlon, and Jaccard (2003) examined follow-up data on first-grade students identified as at-risk and provided tutoring. They confirm "that there are small but significant numbers of children who will require intensive and individualized remedial assistance for a period of time beyond that provided by the intervention project in order for them to become functionally independent readers" (p. 117).

We contend that the students whose response to interventions is very low are the students for whom special education is most suited. While numbers vary in research studies from 1.5% to 8% depending upon the age of students and the criteria for response to intervention (e.g., Mathes et al., 2005; McMaster et al., 2005; O'Connor, Fulmer, et al., 2005; O'Connor, Harty, et al., 2005; Vaughn et al., 2003), these are precisely the students for whom additional research on effective interventions is most needed and for whom we have the fewest examples of effective practice (Reschly, 2005). In the spring of 2006, several LD Centers will be funded by the National Institute for Child Health and Human Development to address research issues related to response-to-intervention and students who are minimal responders.

A major need is the development of effective interventions for students who do not respond adequately to primary- and secondary-level interventions. Such students have rarely been specifically isolated, but can only be identified through a multitiered framework in which they emerge as a small subset of inadequate responders. Multiple tiers of instruction hold promise for:

- Identifying students at risk rather than by deficit
- Identifying and treating students with learning difficulties early rather than waiting for more significant and often insurmountable learning problems
- Reducing bias in the identification process
- Linking identification assessment with instructional planning and progress monitoring (Vaughn & Fuchs, 2003).

In addition, using multiple layers or tiers of interventions provides a framework for

- Integrating best practices in reading instruction including screening and progress monitoring
- Differentiating instruction through grouping and tutoring
- Targeting appropriate instructional needs
- Integrating reading content so that students are provided early and effective interventions and students requiring more sustained and intensive interventions can be identified

O'Connor's work exemplifies the positive outcomes afforded when multiple layers of effective interventions are provided to students over time (O'Connor, Fulmer et al., 2005; O'Connor, Harty et al., 2005). Students who are typical achievers benefit, as do students who are struggling. Even students identified as having a learning disability had near-average standard scores on word attack and comprehension compared with controls (also identified as having learning disabilities) whose scores were more than 1 standard deviation below the average.

## Follow-up Activities

1. Consider your responses to the first two questions at the beginning of the chapter. What more would you like to know about prevention approaches to reading difficulties? What about effective secondary and tertiary interventions?
2. Ask each member of your study group to identify an intervention that is used in their school for students with reading difficulties. Discuss the relative merits and challenges with implementing the intervention. Decide what additional elements could be added to make the intervention more effective.
3. Select from the research cited in this chapter or in other chapters about students with reading difficulties. Ask each member of the study group to read one of the articles and to report what they learned. Share and discuss findings as they relate to instructional practice in your school.

## REFERENCES

Beaglehole, R., & Bonita, R. (1997). *Public health at the crossroads: achievements and prospects.* New York: Cambridge University Press.

Biancarosa, G., & Snow, C. E. (2004). *Reading next—A vision for action and research in middle and high school literacy: A report to Carnegie Corporation of New York.* Washington, DC: Alliance for Excellent Education.

Blachman, B. A., Ball, E. W., Black, R., & Tangel, D. M. (2000). *Road to the code: A phonological awareness program for young children.* Baltimore: Brookes.

Blachman, B. A., Schatschneider, C., Fletcher, J. M., Francis, D. J., Clonan, S. M., Shaywitz, B. A. et al. (2004). Effects of intensive reading remediation for second and third graders and a 1-year follow-up. *Journal of Educational Psychology, 96*(3), 441–461.

Blachman, B. A., Tangel, D. M., Ball, E. W., Black, R., & McGraw, C. K. (1999). Developing phonological awareness and word recognition skills: A two-year intervention with low-income, inner-city children. *Reading and Writing: An Interdisciplinary Journal, 11*(3), 239–273.

Brown, I. S., & Felton, R. H. (1990). Effects of instruction on beginning reading skills in children at risk for reading disability. *Reading and Writing: An Interdisciplinary Journal, 2*(3), 223–241.

Coyne, M. D., Kame'enui, E. J., & Simmons, D. C. (2001). Prevention and intervention in beginning reading: Two complex systems. *Learning Disabilities Research and Practice, 16*(2), 62–73.

Denton, C. A., Fletcher, J. M., Anthony, J. L., & Francis, D. J. (in press). An evaluation of intensive intervention for students with persistent reading difficulties. *Journal of Learning Disabilities.*

Denton, C. A., & Mathes, P. G. (2003). Intervention for struggling readers: Possibilities and challenges. In B. Foorman (Ed.), *Preventing and remediating reading difficulties: Bringing science to scale* (pp. 229–252). Baltimore: York Press.

Denton, C. A., Vaughn, S., & Fletcher, J. M. (2003). Bringing research-based practice in reading intervention to scale. *Learning Disabilities Research and Practice, 18*(3), 201–211.

Dickson, S. V., & Bursuck, W. D. (1999). Implementing a model for preventing reading failure: A report from the field. *Learning Disabilities Research and Practice, 14*(4), 191–195.

Donovan, M. S., & Cross, C. T. (Eds.). (2002). *Minority students in special and gifted education.* Washington, DC: National Research Council, National Academy of Sciences.

Elbaum, B., Vaughn, S., Hughes, M. T., & Moody, S. W. (1999). Grouping practices and reading outcomes for students with disabilities. *Exceptional Children, 65*(3), 399–415.

Elbaum, B., Vaughn, S., Hughes, M. T., & Moody, S. W. (2000). How effective are one-to-one tutoring programs in reading for elementary students at risk for reading failure? *Journal of Educational Psychology, 92*(4), 605–619.

Fletcher, J. M., Denton, C. A., Fuchs, L., & Vaughn, S. R. (2005). Multi-tiered reading instruction: Linking general education and special education. In S. O. Richardson & J. W. Gilger (Eds.), *Research-based education and intervention: What we need to know* (pp. 21–43). Baltimore: The International Dyslexia Association.

Foorman, B. R., & Ciancio, D. J. (2005). Screening for secondary intervention: Concept and context. *Journal of Learning Disabilities, 38*(6), 494–499.

Foorman, B. R., Francis, D. J., Fletcher, J. M., Schatschneider, C., & Mehta, P. (1998). The role of instruction in learning to read: Preventing reading failure in at-risk children. *Journal of Educational Psychology, 90*(1), 37–55.

Foorman, B. R., & Torgesen, J. (2001). Critical elements of classroom and small-group instruction promote reading success in all children. *Learning Disabilities Research and Practice, 16*(4), 203–212.

Forness, S. R. (2005). The pursuit of evidence-based practice in special education for children with emotional or behavioral disorders. *Behavioral Disorders, 30*(4), 311–330.

Fuchs, D., Fuchs, L. S., & Burish, P. (2000). Peer-assisted learning strategies: An evidence-based practice to promote reading achievement. *Learning Disabilities Research and Practice, 15*(2), 85–91.

Greenwood, C. R., Delquadri, J. C., & Hall, R. V. (1989). Longitudinal effects of classwide peer tutoring. *Journal of Educational Psychology, 81*(3), 371–383.

Gunn, B., Smolkowski, K., Biglar, A., Black, C., & Blair, J. (2005). Fostering the development of reading skill through supplemental instruction: Results for Hispanic and non-Hispanic students. *The Journal of Special Education, 39*(2), 66–85.

Hatcher, P. J., Hulme, C., & Ellis, A. W. (1994). Ameliorating early reading failure by integrating the teaching of reading and phonological skills: The phonological linkage hypothesis. *Child Development, 65*(1), 41–57.

Hiebert, E. H., Colt, J. M., Calto, S. L., & Gary, E. C. (1992). Reading and Writing of first-grade students in a restructured chapter 1. *American Educational Re-search Journal, 29,* 545–572.

Iversen, S., Tunmer, W. E., & Chapman, J. W. (2005). The effects of varying group size on the Reading Recovery approach to preventive early intervention. *Journal of Learning Disabilities, 38*(5), 456–472.

Juel, C., & Minden-Cupp, C. (2000). Learning to read words: Linguistic units and instructional strategies. *Reading Research Quarterly, 35*(4), 458–492.

Kamps, D. M., & Greenwood, C. R. (2005). Formulating secondary-level reading interventions. *Journal of Learning Disabilities, 38*(6), 500–509.

Lovett, M. W., Borden, S. L., DeLuca, T., Lacerenza, L., Benson, N. J., & Brack-stone, D. (1994). Treating the core deficits of developmental dyslexia: Evidence of transfer of learning after phonologically and strategy-based reading training program. *Developmental Psychology, 30*(6), 805–822.

Lyon, G. R., Fletcher, J. M., Fuchs, L., & Chhabra, V. (2006). Treatment of learning disabilities. In E. Mash & R. Barkley (Eds.), *Treatment of childhood disorders* (3rd ed.). New York: Guilford Press.

Mathes, P. G., Denton, C. A., Fletcher, J. M., Anthony, J. L., Francis, D. J., & Schatschneider, C. (2005). The effects of theoretically different instruction and student characteristics on the skills of struggling readers. *Reading Research Quarterly, 40*(2), 148–182.

Mathes, P. G., Torgesen, J. K., Clancy-Menchetti, J., Santi, K., Nicholas, K., Robinson, C., et al. (2003). A comparison of teacher-directed versus peer-assisted instruction to struggling first-grade readers. *Elementary School Journal, 103*(5), 459–479.

McCardle, P., Scarborough, H. S., & Catts, H. W. (2001). Predicting, explaining, and preventing children's reading difficulties. *Learning Disabilities Research and Practice, 16*(4), 230–239.

McMaster, K. L., Fuchs, D., Fuchs, L. S., & Compton, D. L. (2005). Responding to nonresponders: An experimental field trial of identification and intervention methods. *Exceptional Children, 71*(4), 445–463.

Meeder, H. K. (2003, October). *Policy directions for career and technical education.* Retrieved May 3, 2007, from emsc32.nysed.gov/cte/techprep/docs/stateconf/NCCTE-WEB-CAST-OCT-30-2003-2.ppt

National Association of State Directors of Special Education (NASDSE). (2005). *Response to intervention: Policy considerations and implementation.* Alexandria, VA: Author.

National Center for Education Statistics (NCES). (2005). *The condition of education: Indicator list.* Retrieved December 20, 2005, from http://www.nces.ed.gov/programs/coe/list/i2.asp

National Joint Committee on Learning Disabilities (NJCLD). (2005, June). *Responsiveness to intervention and learning disabilities.* Retrieved March 9, 2006, from http://www.ldonline.org/?module-upload&func-download&field-46/

National Reading Panel (NRP). (2000). *Report of the National Reading Panel: Teaching children to read: Reports of the subgroups* (NIH Publication No. 00-4754). Washington, DC: National Institute of Child Health and Human Development, National Institutes of Health.

O'Connor, R. E. (2000). Increasing the intensity of intervention in kindergarten and first grade. *Learning Disabilities Research and Practice, 15*(1), 43–54.

O'Connor, R. E., Fulmer, D., Harty, K. R., & Bell, K. M. (2005). Layers of reading intervention in kindergarten through third grade: Changes in teaching and student outcomes. *Journal of Learning Disabilities, 38*(5), 440–445.

O'Connor, R. E., Harty, K. R., & Fulmer, D. (2005). Tiers of intervention in kindergarten through third grade. *Journal of Learning Disabilities, 38*(6), 532–538.

Quiroga, T., Lemos-Britton, Z., Mostafapour, E., Abbott, R. D., & Berninger, V. W. (2002). Phonological awareness and beginning reading in Spanish-speaking ESL first graders: Research into practice. *Journal of School Psychology, 40*(1), 85–111.

RAND Reading Study Group. (2002). *Reading for understanding: Toward an R&D program in reading comprehension.* Santa Monica, CA: RAND.

Rashotte, C. A., MacPhee, K., & Torgesen, J. K. (2001). The effectiveness of a group reading instruction program with poor readers in multiple grades. *Learning Disability Quarterly, 24*(2), 119–134.

Rathvon, N. (2004). *Early reading achievement: A practitioner's handbook.* New York: Guilford.

Reschly, D. J. (2005). Learning disabilities identification: Primary intervention, secondary intervention, and then what? *Journal of Learning Disabilities, 38*(6), 510–515.

Schneider, M. J. (2000). *Introduction to public health.* Gaithersburg, MD: Aspen.

Simmons, D. C., Kuykendall, K., King, K., Cornachone, C., & Kame'enui, E. J. (2000). Implementation of a schoolwide reading improvement model: "No one ever told us it would be this hard!" *Learning Disabilities Research and Practice, 15*(2), 92–100.

Snow, C. E., Burns, M. S., & Griffin, P. (1998). *Preventing reading difficulties in young children.* Washington, DC: National Academy of Sciences, National Research Council, Commission on Behavioral and Social Sciences and Education.

Speece, D. L. (2005). A longitudinal study of the development of oral reading fluency in young children at risk for reading failure. *Journal of Learning Disabilities, 38*(5), 387–399.

Stahl, S. A. (2004). What do we know about fluency? Findings of the National Reading Panel. In P. McCardle & V. Chhabra (Eds.), *The voice of evidence in reading research* (pp. 187–212). Baltimore: Brookes.

Sugai, G., & Horner, R. H. (2002). Introduction to the special sciences series on positive behavior support in schools. *Journal of Emotional and Behavioral Disorders, 10*(3), 130–135.

Swanson, H. L. (1999). Instructional components that predict treatment outcomes for students with learning disabilities: Support for a combined strategy and direct instruction model. *Learning Disabilities Research and Practice, 14*(3), 129–140.

Swanson, H. L., Hoskyn, M., & Lee, C. (1999). *Interventions for students with learning disabilities: A meta-analysis of treatment outcomes.* New York: Guilford Press.

Taylor, B. M., Pearson, P. D., Peterson, D. S., & Rodriquez, M. C. (2003). Reading growth in high-poverty classrooms: The influence of teacher practices that encourage cognitive engagement in literacy learning. *Elementary School Journal, 104*(1), 3–28.

Torgesen, J. K. (2000). Individual differences in response to early interventions in reading: The lingering problem of treatment resisters. *Learning Disabilities Research and Practice, 15*(1), 55–64.

Torgesen, J. K. (2004). Lessons learned from research on interventions for students who have difficulty learning to read. In P. McCardle & V. Chhabra (Eds.), *The voice of evidence in reading research* (pp. 355–382). Baltimore: Brookes.

Torgesen, J. K., Alexander, A. W., Wagner, R. K., Rashotte, C. A., Voeller, K. K. S., & Conway, T. (2001). Intensive remedial instruction for children with severe reading disabilities: Immediate and long-term outcomes from two instructional approaches. *Journal of Learning Disabilities, 34*(1), 33–58, 78.

Torgesen, J. K., Wagner, R. K., Rashotte, C. A., Rose, E., Lindamood, P., Conway, T., et al. (1999). Preventing reading failure in young children with phonological processing disabilities: Group and individual responses to instruction. *Journal of Educational Psychology, 91*(4), 579–593.

Vaughn, S., & Chard, D. (2006). Three-Tier Intervention research studies: Descriptions of two related projects. *Perspectives, 32*(1), 29–34.

Vaughn, S., & Fuchs, L. S. (2003). Redefining learning disabilities as inadequate response to instruction: The promise and potential problems. *Learning Disabilities: Research and Practice, 18*(3), 137–146.

Vaughn, S., Gersten, R., & Chard, D. J. (2000). The underlying message in LD intervention research: Findings from research syntheses. *Exceptional Children, 67*(1), 99–114.

Vaughn, S., & Linan-Thompson, S. (2003). What is special about special education for students with learning disabilities? *Exceptional Children, 69*(4), 391–409.

Vaughn, S., Linan-Thompson, S., & Hickman, P. (2003). Response to instruction as a means of identifying students with reading/learning disabilities. *Exceptional Children, 69*(4), 391–409.

Vaughn, S., Linan-Thompson, S., Mathes, P. G., Cirino, P. T., Carlson, C. D., Pollard-Durodola, S. D. et al. (2006). Effectiveness of Spanish intervention for first-grade English language learners at risk for reading difficulties. *Journal of Learning Disabilities, 39*(1), 56–73.

Vaughn, S., Mathes, P. G., Linan-Thompson, S., Cirino, P. T., Carlson, C. D., Pollard-Durodola, S. D. et al. (in press). First-grade English language learners at-risk for reading problems: Effectiveness of an English intervention. *Elementary School Journal.*

Vellutino, F. R., Scanlon, D. M., & Jaccard, J. (2003). Toward distinguishing between cognitive and experiential deficits as primary sources of difficulty in learning to read: A two-year follow-up of difficult-to-remediate and readily remediated poor readers. In B. F. Foorman (Ed.), *Preventing and remediating reading difficulties: Bringing science to scale* (pp. 73–120). Baltimore: York Press.

Vellutino, F. R., Scanlon, D. M., Sipay, E. R., Small, S. G., Pratt, A., Chen, R. et al. (1996). Cognitive profiles of difficult-to-remediate and readily remediated poor readers: Early intervention as a vehicle for distinguishing between cognitive and experiential deficits as basic causes of specific reading disability. *Journal of Educational Psychology, 88*(4), 601–638.

Wasik, B. A., & Slavin, R. E. (1993). Preventing early reading failure with one-to-one tutoring: A review of five programs. *Reading Research Quarterly, 28*(2), 178–200.

Winslow, C. E. A. (1923). *The evolution and significance of the modern public health campaign.* New Haven, CT: Yale University Press.

Wise, B. W., Ring, J., & Olson, R. K. (2000). Individual differences in gains from computer-assisted remedial reading. *Journal of Experimental Child Psychology, 77*(3), 197–235.

# CHAPTER 9

# Toward the Development of a Nuanced Classroom Observational System for Studying Comprehension and Vocabulary Instruction

Russell Gersten
Joseph Dimino
Madhavi Jayanthi

This chapter describes the intricacies of developing a moderate-inference classroom observational measure used to assess the quality of reading comprehension and vocabulary instruction provided to first-grade English-language learners (ELLs). We discuss the dilemmas faced in developing the measure and how the research literature on effective reading comprehension and vocabulary instruction served as a guide in developing the measure's items.

### Questions for Reflection and Discussion

- What are the critical components of effective vocabulary and comprehension instruction?
- What are the similarities and differences between the components of the comprehension and vocabulary instruction described in this article and the instructional design of the core reading program used in your school?

Intuitively, classroom observation is an appealing way to study qualities of instruction and, hopefully, to link observed practices with students' growth in learning. Yet, reliable measurement of important qualities of instruction in a classroom has proved to be an intricate, arduous task. The construct of quality instruction is complex and multidimensional, open to numerous interpretations. Researchers over the years have developed a variety of observational systems for measuring classroom events and behaviors.

An examination of the literature on classroom observations reveals a spectrum of measurement systems. At one end are the high-inference, open-ended qualitative naturalistic observations. In this measurement system, the observer takes detailed notes of the instructional events and behaviors observed in the classroom. The observer later makes an inference regarding the quality of instruction based on the field notes gathered. These subjective interpretations of quality, however, are often colored by the observer's own experiences and beliefs (McIntosh, Vaughn, Schumm, Haager, & Lee, 1994). High-inference systems are thus ideal when the research focus is still exploratory in nature.

These observational systems were widely used in instructional research in the 1990s. In some studies, issues such as nuances and subtleties of instruction and power relationships that exist in classrooms were examined. Many also tried to draw valid inferences using techniques adopted from anthropology and sociology, critical theory, and arguably journalism. These studies attempted to understand the context and uniqueness of each classroom and teacher studied. Researchers talked to teachers before and after observations, attempted to understand their perspective, and created interpretations based on what was observed and what was reported in interviews. Despite the occasionally important qualitative classroom observational study (e.g., Ball, 1990; Rueda & Mehan, 1986), many seemed to be plagued by issues of potential bias and lack of objectivity in reporting. Even though a high-inference system can yield rich descriptive accounts of classroom events, and is useful in learning about issues that had not been fully explored or understood, their applicability is somewhat limited in large-scale replications due to low observer reliability resulting from the subjective nature of the measurement system.

At the other end of the continuum are low-inference, quantitative observation systems like those used by Anderson, Evertson, and Brophy (1979); Foorman, Francis, Beeler, Winikates, and Fletcher (1997); and Stallings and Kaskowitz (1974). Low-inference systems are useful in recording discrete events and behaviors that can be easily defined, observed, and measured. The advantage of these systems is that low inference in needed on the observer's part, as the recording of instructional events and behaviors in a classroom has an objective basis. Low-inference systems are therefore typically associated with high inter-rater reliabilities. However, low-inference systems do not lend themselves well to observing and recording complex instructional events and behavior in a classroom. They are more applicable in answering research questions such as "How much time was spent on teaching vocabulary, word-level reading, or reading connected text?", "How many students were engaged during the phonics segment of the lesson?", and "How much time was devoted to small-group instruction?".

Low-inference systems have been used to study the nature of classroom interactions as well as instructional activities and activity structures. These studies ask questions such as "Does the teacher provide feedback when student responses are incorrect?" and "Does the teacher ask follow-up questions to help students elaborate their responses?" A reasonably large body of research summarized by Brophy and Good (1986) and Rosenshine and Stevens (1986) appeared to demonstrate that certain patterns of teacher-student interaction were consistently linked to growth on standardized achievement tests. This pattern has often been called explicit or direct instruction or instruction with high levels of academic engaged time. Even though this convergence of findings was deemed a major advance in the science of educational research, many remained unsure of how to use this information to improve the quality of teaching. The low-inference systems used by Brophy and Good (1986) or Stallings (1975) did not and could not assess the clarity and richness of teacher explanations or the richness or paucity of content in student responses. Many felt that the measures failed to illuminate the process of teaching in a rich fashion and failed to measure issues such as quality and quantity of scaffolding that are critical for successful teaching (Ball, 1990; Beck, McKeown, Sandora, Kucan, & Worthy, 1996; National Reading Panel [NRP], 2000).

At the middle of the spectrum of measurement systems are the moderate-inference measures such as inferential rating scales that are part qualitative and part quantitative in nature. This middle-of-the-road measure has allowed researchers to combine some of the advantages of both high-inference and low-inference observation systems. They can produce inter-rater reliabilities (unlike qualitative field notes), but the reliabilities tend to be lower that those of the aforementioned systems (Gersten, Baker, Haager, & Graves, 2005). They are also not nearly as limiting as the low-inference measures in the type of behaviors and events that can be measured.

Moderate-inferential rating scales are useful in assessing more complex aspects of teaching such as quality of teacher modeling, clarity of explanations, and how vocabulary concepts are taught. We and other researchers (e.g., Edmonds & Briggs, 2003; Gersten, Fuchs et al., 2005; Haager, Gersten, Baker, & Graves, 2003) have used rating scales to evaluate quality of reading instruction in classrooms in California and Texas. Rating scales have also played a role in the complex observation system developed by Foorman and colleagues (Foorman & Schatschneider, 2003).

Typically, scores on rating scales often have much stronger correlations with growth in outcomes than variables generated from low-inference systems (Gersten, Carnine, Zoref, & Cronin, 1986; Schatschneider, Fletcher, Francis, Carlson, & Foorman, 2004; Stoolmiller, Eddy, & Reid, 2000). However, even with these advantages, the use of moderate-inference measures in large-scale studies is of concern. Despite their high face validity, difficulties in development of standardization procedures and clear-cut definitions have been of issue (Kennedy, 1999). In addition, rating scales are prone to halo effects; consequently, a high internal-consistency reliability coefficient could mean either that an observational scale measures a construct reliably or that the observational scale is marred by halo effects. Such problems of interpretation do not arise with scales that require fewer global judgments and fewer inferences.

## DILEMMAS FACED IN DEVELOPING THE MEASURE

In our multiple-site, randomized, controlled trials study of professional development, our goal was to assess the extent to which teachers implemented the approaches for teaching comprehension and vocabulary that experimental research consistently supported as being sophisticated. We needed a classroom observation system that was suitable for assessing the quality of reading comprehension and vocabulary instruction for ELLs in sites across the country. Our measure therefore had to be sensitive to the various nuances and fine distinctions that epitomize classroom teaching. As we embarked on our study, the limitations of the various classroom observation systems were foremost in our minds.

Clearly, a low-inference quantitative measure would not be able to capture the nuances of the various features that characterize and define quality instruction. On the other hand, a high-inference qualitative measure would capture the complexities of classroom teaching, but present reliability issues, especially given that multiple sites and observers were to be involved. We also did not want to resort to the middle-of-the-road rating scale approach used in our earlier research for several reasons. The first is that inter-rater reliability, though respectable for a high-inference measure, is lower than desired (Gersten, Fuchs et al., 2005). The second is fear of potential halo effects. The third is that we wanted a measure that could be used by a larger set of trained observers across the nation and not just by a few well-qualified reading experts who have the know-how to make highly evaluative judgments about the quality of teacher instruction. We wanted a system that requires lower levels of inference and that presents a more precise, objective picture of what really happens during classroom reading instruction in first-grade classrooms in Reading First schools.

The only solution we could envision was to attempt to measure *quality* of instruction by considering *quantity* as a reasonable surrogate. We hypothesized that the quality of reading comprehension and vocabulary instruction can be estimated by the number of times an evidence-based instructional behavior is seen. We were aware that in some areas—for the number of literal questions asked per lesson or the number of interactions centered on activating background knowledge—quantity would not necessarily serve as an estimate of quality. In fact, based on earlier experiences in observational research, we thought that too much time spent on activation activities might have a dampening effect on comprehension. However, for the majority of variables of interest we thought that quantity might serve as a reasonable means to assess quality of comprehension and vocabulary instruction in an objective fashion. These include variables such as number of teacher models of compare-contrast or story grammar elements, the number of times definitions were provided with multiple examples, and the amount of practice in "finding the gist" of a section of a story. It is therefore logical to assume that the higher the frequency of highly valued research-supported teaching behaviors, the greater will be the quality of reading instruction in that classroom.

We operationalized this concept of quantity as a surrogate for quality through a 12-month iterative process of extensive field testing and ongoing refinement of the measure. We used a cadre of recently retired teachers or program facilitators as our key observational staff. We fine-tuned the measure on the basis of the input we received from these veterans and the observational notes collected by our research staff (primarily the coauthors of this chapter). Our goal was to develop clear definitions of the subtle teaching practices described by NRP (2000). The items in the measure came from experimental research (as opposed to direct observations of classroom practices), and researchers sometimes use different terms to refer to similar teaching strategies. For both these reasons, creating operational definitions so that each item was mutually exclusive was an arduous and time-intensive task.

Through the use of tapes and debriefing on issues raised during live observations, we were able to develop a code book that defines each variable and provides examples and coding rules. As will be demonstrated, we were able to develop an observation system of adequate reliability with at least some of the richness and nuance that was required to seriously study comprehension and vocabulary instruction. In the next section, we provide a brief review of the research base used to develop the measure.

## RESEARCH THAT GUIDED
## DEVELOPMENT OF THE MEASURE
## OF COMPREHENSION INSTRUCTION

After observing more than 4,000 minutes of classroom reading instruction, Durkin (1978–79) reported that only 20 minutes—less than one percent of the total time—were devoted to comprehension. Durkin found that in a typical comprehension section of a reading lesson, teachers initially mentioned a skill or strategy (e.g., identifying the main idea), then asked students to practice the skill (often through workbook exercises), and finally assessed whether students used the skill successfully (often by providing "right/wrong feedback"). Missing from this approach of "comprehension instruction" was any guidance for students on how to come to an understanding of difficult text.

Over the past three decades, research has established that teaching students to use comprehension strategies leads to active construction of the texts they read (NRP, 2000). Sifted from the literature in the report is a set of specific strategies that have been demonstrated to be effective for improving comprehension:

- Summary and prediction
- Question generation (for e.g., Pressley et al., 1992; Wong & Jones, 1982)
- Understanding of text structures for both narrative and expository text
- Use of graphic organizers

In addition, evident from the NRP (2000) report and a review of intervention research for students with reading disabilities (Gersten, Fuchs, Williams, & Baker, 2001) is that, in general, interventions that teach flexible use of multiple strategies to improve comprehension tend to produce high effect sizes. Furthermore, a good deal of research emphasizes the importance of asking students to justify or explain how they reached an answer to a question (Gersten, 1996a) and teaching them to "question the author" (Beck et al., 1996). All these variables served as a basis for the comprehension component of our measure.

For the vocabulary domain, we relied heavily on the syntheses by Baumann and Kame'enui (1991), Beck, McKeown, and Kucan (2002), and Graves (2006). These syntheses stress that vocabulary instruction needs to include

- Clear, student-friendly definitions with multiple examples, including nonexamples of the concept or term

- Many opportunities for students to use the words (e.g., during reading, writing, and oral language activities)
- Practice with new vocabulary words over a period of several days

## THE CIERA OBSERVATIONAL SYSTEM

The Center for the Improvement of Early Reading Achievement (CIERA) observational system, developed by Taylor, Pearson, Peterson, and Rodriguez (2003), also influenced our thinking. Taylor et al. present a solid conceptual foundation for framing their observational system. They note that the National Reading Panel (2000) report has been useful in specifying the *content*, or the *what*, of reading instruction. However, they also felt that significant gains in student reading outcomes were directly linked to effective instructional practices in the area of reading, that is, the *how* of reading. Taylor and her colleagues emphasized the critical importance of earlier seminal research on effective reading instruction from the 1970s (e.g., Brophy & Good, 1986; Stallings & Kaskowitz, 1974). They concluded that the

> more effective teachers focused on academics, had high numbers of pupils on task, and provided direct instruction that included making learning goals clear, asking students questions as part of monitoring their understanding of what was being covered, and providing feedback to students about their academic progress. (p. 45)

Taylor and her colleagues also concurred with our reasoning that, as Langer (1999) found, effective teachers "explicitly taught students strategies for thinking about ideas and completing activities" (p. 45).

## THE RCV OBSERVATIONAL MEASURE

Our goal was to develop a measure that is well aligned with the current beliefs and findings from the extant literature on effective reading instruction. Consequently, in our measure, we focused not only on the *what* of reading instruction, but also on the *how* of the reading instruction. We wanted to capture, in our measure, a variety of effective teaching/instructional behaviors, some of which would be present for most teachers (e.g., previewing a reading selection, asking literal questions). Others would help differentiate the best from the average and the poor teachers (e.g., modeling how to make inferences, and thinking-aloud a character analysis to make overt the cognitive thinking processes).

With these objectives in mind, we developed the Reading Comprehension and Vocabulary (RCV) Observational Measure. The measure focuses on two reading domains: comprehension and vocabulary (see Figures 9.1 and 9.2). The comprehension component has 29 items (i.e., teaching behaviors), of which 20 are frequency items, wherein the observer tallies the number of times an item is seen, and the remaining 9 items have a Yes/No answer format. The vocabulary component has 7 items, all of which are frequency items.

Data is recorded in 15-minute intervals. A 90-minute classroom observation therefore translates to 6 intervals. After each 15-minute interval, the observer turns the page and continues tallying the appropriate items on a new protocol. There are areas throughout the measure for observers to write field notes to help them confirm their tallying and provide examples of the instructional practices they observed. Observers are encouraged but not mandated to write field notes whether they be in the space provided or on a note pad.

The items in the RCV Observational Measure essentially reflect two major pedagogical aspects of effective teacher instruction: explicitness of instruction and nature of the interactive corrective instruction (i.e., the amount of scaffolded student practice and feedback provided). In the ensuing section, we discuss these instructional tenets and some of the items that help measure them.

## Explicit Instruction

The National Reading Panel and the majority of reading researchers stress the importance of clear, systematic, explicit instruction in the areas of comprehension strategies and vocabulary. During explicit instruction, the purpose of the target strategy is clarified to the students before it is taught. The teacher models and makes the thinking process public for students. Through comprehensible explanations, clear demonstrations, and multiple examples, the teacher builds students' ability to implement the steps of, for example, a main idea strategy resulting in a concise sentence that represents the most important idea in the paragraph. Students also learn the conditions when use of the strategy is appropriate. For example, while reading, students reread paragraphs to make sense out of a portion of the text they do not understand.

### Comprehension Items

These items capture the degree to which the teacher models strategies before, during, and after reading. Prior to reading a selection, the observer tallies each time the teacher models any of the strategies listed in Item A1 (see Figure 9.1). For example, if a teacher actually thinks through how she or he would develop a prediction for what will happen in the story, she or he would receive one tally for modeling and thinking aloud, a preparatory activity. Other activities that are coded include relating text to students' experience (i.e., previous reading and/or background knowledge), discussing

**Figure 9.1.** Comprehension component of the RCV Observational Measure Comprehension—1st Interval

| | Tally Total (Max=15) | Notes |
|---|---|---|
| **A. Explicitness of Instruction** | | |

*Prior to reading, teacher*
1. Conducts preparatory activities: relating text to student experiences/ previous readings, background knowledge, discussing pictures, title/ author, browsing (book cover, spine, TOC), predicting story content.

*During or after reading, teacher*
2. Models the use of following (includes think-alouds)

   a.  Text cues to interpret text: pictures, subheadings, captions, graphics

   b.  Visualize events, clarify, re-read.

   c.  Evaluate predictions

   d.  Generate questions about text

   e.  Make text-to-text connections

   f.  Make inferences, summarize/find main ideas—theme, character analysis

   g.  Retell, sequencing—what's happening, what happened first

   h.  Story grammar elements—except for theme, character analysis    N    Y

   i.  Compare-contrast or cause-effect text structure    N    Y
3. Reiterates or reinforces concepts that highlight the meaning of text.

| | Tally Total (Max 15) | Notes |
|---|---|---|
| ***B. Student Practice*** | | |

*Prior to reading, teacher*
1. Gives students practice in preparatory activities: relating text to student experiences, previous readings, background knowledge; discussing pictures, title/author, browsing (book cover, spine, TOC); predicting story content.

*During or after reading, teacher*
2. Gives students practice in the following:

   a.  Text cues to interpret text—pictures, subheadings, captions, graphics

   b.  Visualize events, clarify, reread

   c.  Evaluate predictions

   d.  Generate questions about text

   e.  Make text-to-text connections    N    Y

   f.  Summarize/find main ideas    N    Y

   g.  Retell, Sequencing—what's happening, what happened first    N    Y

   h.  Story grammar elements    N    Y

   i.  Compare-contrast or cause-effect text structure    N    Y
3. Asks students to answer literal recall questions from the text. (Specific questions).
4. Asks students questions requiring inferences based on text.
5. Asks students to justify or elaborate their responses.
6. Teacher keeps students thinking for 2+ seconds before calling on a student for response.
7. Teacher gives independent practice in answering comprehension ques- N    Y tions or applying comprehension strategy(ies) with expected product.

| | Tally Total (Max 15) | Notes |
|---|---|---|
| ***C. Corrective feedback: Teacher*** | | |
1. Communicates clearly what student(s) did correctly about the strategy.
2. Reinstructs when student makes a mistake by encouraging child to try again or reminding student about comprehension strategy.

***D. Uses a graphic organizer before, during, or after lesson***    N    Y

**Figure 9.2.** Vocabulary component of the RCV Observational Measure
Vocabulary—1st Interval

| A. Explicitness of Instruction | Tally Total (Max=15) | Notes |
|---|---|---|

Teacher
1. Provides an explanation, a definition, and/or an example.
2. Elaborates using multiple examples.
3. Elaborates using contrasting example(s) to pinpoint definition.
4. Uses visuals, gestures, facial expressions, pictures, or demonstrations
   to teach word meanings. (gestures are related to word meaning)

| B. Student Practice | Tally Total (Max=15) | Notes |
|---|---|---|

Teacher
1. Asks students to answer questions or participate in activities that
   require knowledge of words—e.g., define words; make sentences; find
   words based on clues; show me how you would look if you were cross;
   raise your hand if I say something that is enormous.
2. Gives students opportunity to apply word-learning strategies—using
   context clues, word parts, root meaning.
3. Teacher further pinpoints the definition by extending or elaborating
   students' responses.

pictures, stating the title and author, and predicting story content or browsing the selection. Preparatory activities are not hypothesized to necessarily enhance comprehension and thus, although recorded, do not enter in the comprehension scale computed for each observation.

During- and after-reading items are the key items under explicitness (see Items A2a–A2i and A3 in Figure 9.1). They address specific reading comprehension strategies that are supported by a body of experimental research. The observer tallies every time the teacher demonstrates how to use a comprehension strategy or thinks aloud for the students. For example, a teacher would receive a tally for showing students how the information from the story was used to help generate an inference about a character. Items in this section of the measure also determine whether text structures are modeled and the number of times the teacher reinforces or explains critical concepts that highlight the meaning of the text.

Vocabulary Items

In Figure 9.2, Items A1 to A4 attempt to describe key features of effective vocabulary instruction. In Item A1, the teacher receives a tally for each word that is taught using an explanation, definition, and/or example. Although at first we attempted to differentiate student-friendly definitions (Beck et al., 2002) from the more formal, less comprehensible definitions that often appear in reading series or dictionaries, we could not develop a method for doing so reliably, especially given the rapidity with which teachers often provide "off the cuff" definitions. Item A2 assesses a teacher's use of multiple examples to teach the meaning of a word. For example, while teaching the word *pleasant*, the teacher can provide multiple examples to present the various nuances such as "a day can be pleasant" or "a person can be pleasant."

Item A3 tallies a teacher's use of contrasting examples. The vocabulary research literature consistently suggests that contrasting examples are linchpins of strong vocabulary instruction. Contrasting, discriminating examples help pinpoint the meaning of the word by providing instances where the definition does not apply. Contrasting examples help to solidify meanings and prevent misconceptions by explicitly telling students the attributes that are not part of the word's connotation. For example, when teaching the word *clutch*, the teacher would explain that *clutch* means to hold something very tightly because one is afraid something might happen to it. The contrasting example would involve explaining why swinging a backpack back and forth while walking down the street is *not* an attribute of the word.

Item A4 is tallied when teachers use visuals, gestures, facial expressions, pictures, or demonstrations to teach word meaning. This adds a critical and effective dimension to the instruction, especially for English-language learners (Echevarria, Vogt, & Short, 2000; Gersten, Keating, Yovanoff, & Harniss, 2001). Therefore, an item capturing the number of times this teaching method is used has been incorporated into the measure although to date there is no solid research support for this practice.

## Nature of Interactive Instruction: Student Practice and Corrective Feedback

Interactive teaching of reading, often called "scaffolded instruction," is critical for successful teaching. In order for students to independently apply strategies taught and learn the meanings of words, they must be afforded practice opportunities to apply the strategy with teacher support and scaffolding. We attempted to measure the teacher's skill in building on students' responses and ideas to help students use the strategies in a thoughtful fashion. Scaffolded instruction entails providing questions or prompts that enable students to correct an error or formulate an answer to a question that may be difficult. For example, if a student is having difficulty answering an inferential question, the teacher would use scaffolding by asking a series of simpler leading questions that guide the student to answering the question correctly.

### Comprehension Items

The strategies in this section are, quite intentionally, the same as those in explicitness of Instruction. We also probe qualities of interactive instruction deemed to be related to gains in achievement. These include student practice questions requiring inferences based on information from the text (Taylor et al., 2003), and prompting to justify or elaborate on their responses (Beck et al., 1996; Gersten, 1996a, 1996b) and the use of wait time to ensure that students have a couple of seconds to really think through an answer.

The Corrective Feedback items (Figure 9.1, Items C1 and C2) refer to effective practices that can be used to correct students' responses or guide a student or group to a more accurate or richer response. Specifically, when a student makes an error, the teacher confirms any part of the response that is correct, guides the student through the steps of the strategy to help him logically generate the correct answer, reminds him about the comprehension strategy, and/or encourages him to try again.

Providing appropriate feedback when the students respond incorrectly to a question is a daunting task. Often when a student responds incorrectly to an inferential question, teachers continue to call on other students until the question is answered correctly. A better practice would be to provide corrective feedback to the student who has answered incorrectly. The two corrective feedback items were developed to record instances where teachers effectively respond to students who have difficulty answering questions by communicating what the student did correctly and/or reinstructing the student by guiding him or her through the strategy.

### Vocabulary Items

Students must have multiple meaningful exposures for words to become part of their listening, speaking, reading, and writing vocabularies. The first item in section B (see Figure 9.2) highlights this essential student practice aspect of vocabulary instruction by tallying the number of times the teacher involves students in activities that require them to demonstrate their knowledge of words. This includes defining, using a word in a sentence, using facial expressions or gestures to demonstrate a word's meaning, and distinguishing between examples and contrasting examples. The second item reflects the number of times students have the opportunity to apply context clues, affixes, and base words to determine the meaning of a word.

## Postobservation Component

At the end of the observation, the observer completes 13 items aimed at providing a global sense of the teaching practices (see Figure 9.3). Six of these items have a Yes/No response format; the remaining are rated on a Likert scale. Researchers have often found that Likert scale ratings actually demonstrate higher criterion-related validity (i.e., linkages to growth in achievement) than the much more reliable estimates of rates of behaviors gained

**Figure 9.3.** Post-observation component of the RCV Observational Measures

**Answer the following questions at the end of your observation:**

**A. During comprehension instruction,**

1. Teacher gave inaccurate and/or confusing explanations while modeling strategies.    N   Y
2. Teacher missed opportunity to correct or address error, or provided confusing or inaccurate feedback.    N   Y
3. Teacher called individually on about half or more of students.    N   Y

**B. During vocabulary instruction,**

1. Teacher gave definition, explanation, and/or example that is inaccurate and/or confusing    N   Y
2. Teacher missed opportunity to correct or address error, or provided confusing or inaccurate feedback.    N   Y
3. Teacher called individually on about half or more of students.    N   Y

**C. Based on your overall judgment, how would you rate the quality of each domain you observed?**

|  | *Not observed* | *Minimal/ Erratic* | *Partially Effective* | *Good* | *Excellent* |
|---|---|---|---|---|---|
| Comprehension | NO | 1 | 2 | 3 | 4 |
| Vocabulary | NO | 1 | 2 | 3 | 4 |

**D. Please rate management/responsiveness to students on the following 4-point scale.***

|  | *Minimal/Poor* | *Fair* | *Good* | *Excellent* |
|---|---|---|---|---|
| 1. The instructional routines appear to be | 1 | 2 | 3 | 4 |
| 2. The teacher maximizes the amount of time available for instruction (e.g., brief transitions). | 1 | 2 | 3 | 4 |
| 3. The teacher manages student behavior effectively in order to avoid disruptions and to provide productive learning environments. | 1 | 2 | 3 | 4 |

**E. How would you rate student engagement today?**

|  | *Few students seem engaged during the lesson.* | *Many students seem engaged much of the time.* | *Most students are engaged all of the time.* |
|---|---|---|---|
| 1. Students are engaged during the *first 45 minutes* of the reading block | 1 | 2 | 3 |
| 2. Students are engaged during the remainder of the reading block. | 1 | 2 | 3 |

\* Items are adapted from Teacher Competency Checklist (Foorman & Schatschneider, 2003).

from low-inference observational systems (e.g., Foorman & Schatschneider, 2003; Stoolmiller et al., 2000).

This provided the rationale for developing two items to record observers' judgments of the overall quality of comprehension and vocabulary instruction. In Item C a four-point Likert scale was used to rate the quality of instruction as minimal/erratic (little quality occurred); partially effective (there were some moments of quality interspersed with weak instruction); good (generally quality practices throughout the lesson); excellent (outstanding example of quality and consistently throughout the lesson).

Classroom management and the teachers' responsiveness to students was addressed by Items D1–D3 that were adapted from the Teacher Competency Checklist (Foorman & Schatschneider, 2003). These items address whether there are clear classroom routines, if the teacher maximizes the use of instructional time, and whether the overall classroom management is such that disruptions are minimized thus creating a productive learning environment. The items are rated on a four-point rating scale (1 = Minimal/Poor, 2 = Fair, 3 = Good, 4 = Excellent).

Summary Items E1–E2 required the observers to rate student engagement. Observers estimated the number of students who appear to be engaged during the first 45 minutes and during the remainder of the reading block using a three-point scale: 1 = few seem engaged, 2 = many seem engaged, 3 = most seem engaged. We noted that in the long (90 to 150 minutes) literacy blocks commonly used in American schools, engagement rates during the latter part of the lesson can go down dramatically. Another two items (A3 and B3) address whether the teacher gives at least half of the students an opportunity to respond individually during the literacy block. One item (D3) asks for a general appraisal of how well teachers monitor independent work.

Problematic instruction observed in the classroom was also recorded. Items A1 and B1 address whether the teacher gives inaccurate and/or confusing explanations that may contribute to students' misunderstanding of critical concepts and strategies. Although, as we expected, this rarely occurred, we thought this would be highly problematic and might well be a negative correlate of achievement growth. Analogous Items A2 and B2 were used to determine whether the teacher missed an opportunity to correct or address an error, or if students received confusing and/or inaccurate feedback to their responses.

## UNIQUENESS OF THE RCV OBSERVATIONAL MEASURE

The RCV Observational Measure includes some items that reflect teaching practices that go beyond routine pedagogy. We now draw attention to two of those items that highlight instructional variables that help raise the bar of effective reading instruction in classrooms.

## Evaluating Predictions

Modeling how to make predictions or asking students to make predictions is a common practice. Often, however, the most important aspect of making predictions—evaluating them for accuracy—is overlooked (Hansen, 1981). In Figure 9.1 the purpose of Items A2c and B2c is to determine the frequency with which teachers ask students to confirm or amend their predictions before and/or after reading a selection. Making predictions helps students set a purpose for reading. Since students enjoy finding out if their predictions are correct, knowing they are going to evaluate their predictions piques their interest and enhances their motivation to read the selection.

## Making Text-to-Text Connections

Items A2e and B2e, in Figure 9.1, are about making text-to-text connections. This strategy challenges children to think critically by asking them to make connections between the selection they are reading and previously read selections. It is important to dispel the "we've finished that story" mind-set, where once a selection is read, it is not discussed or referred to again. Students must understand that neither the narrative nor expository selections they read exist in a vacuum and that the selections they have read previously may help them make sense out of what they are currently reading. Text-to-text connections provide an ideal venue to teach the compare/contrast text structure and its application to writing.

## CONCLUSION

This chapter describes the process we used to develop a moderate-inference observation measure that reflects the current research on effective comprehension and vocabulary instruction. A critical issue for successful implementation of this measure is the observers' qualifications. The observers for this study were experienced teachers who were familiar with the research upon which the measure was based. High inter-rater reliabilities were obtained by the combination of qualified observers, intensive, high-quality training conducted by the developers, and follow-up practice observations in first-grade classrooms with master coders. The time and effort spent in this effort resulted in a measure that captured the effects of a professional development intervention on classroom instruction.

## Follow-up Activities

1. Compare your list of critical components to those addressed in this chapter and in the National Reading Panel report. Make revisions to your list as you identify the components.
2. Discuss the similarities and differences between these components and the instructional design of the vocabulary and comprehension instruction in your core reading program.
3. Choose a selection in the core reading program that you will be teaching within the next 2 weeks. Decide which components are present in the lesson. Work with a colleague to revise the lesson to include the critical instructional components. Teach the lesson to your students.
4. Discuss the advantages and disadvantages of low-, moderate-, and high-inference observation measures.

# APPENDIX: RELIABILITY AND VALIDITY OF RCV OBSERVATIONAL MEASURE

## Inter-Rater Reliability

We calculated inter-rater reliability for the comprehension and vocabulary components of the measure. As some of the observed behaviors had a low base rate (more so in the case of comprehension than vocabulary), the likelihood of overinflating agreements based on unobserved behaviors is very high. To prevent this overinflation and present an objective picture of reliability that is grounded in observed classroom teaching events, we limited our calculation of inter-rater reliability to only active (15-minute) intervals. For an interval to be active, at least one observer has to record data. Intervals with no observed data were excluded from the reliability calculations. Reliability was calculated in the following manner. First, agreements and disagreements were noted for each item in the active intervals. Then, agreements and disagreements from all the active intervals were totaled, and reliability was calculated using the following formula: agreements divided by agreements plus disagreements times 100. Inter-rater reliability was collected on 22 observations and included both experimental and control teachers. Inter-rater reliability for comprehension is 94% (range = 90–96%) and for vocabulary is 89% (range = 85–91%).

## Internal Consistency

We created a vocabulary and a comprehension subscale for possible use in data analyses. As we attempted to create a measure with adequate internal consistency, we confronted some problems particularly in the area of comprehension. First, many of the items were low-base-rate teaching practices, that is, measures with relatively little variance as most teachers received a score of 0. This is not surprising in that, although we encouraged teachers to utilize multiple strategies, it was unlikely they would use more than one or two during a given lesson. Yet, our measure attempted to assess the full range of possible strategies. Second, several items used a Yes/No format (e.g., use of story grammar to help frame questions or use of graphic organizers), and it made little sense to attempt to reliably assess frequency of use as Yes/No items have a very restricted range (either 0 or 1) precluding high item-to-total correlations. The final issue, especially in the area of comprehension was that we included some items that we did not think necessarily reflected best practice, but rather typical practice. These items were intentionally included to obtain a richer picture of comprehension instruction and also to help reduce possible halo effects in that observers were blind as to which these items were.

The internal consistency reliability (Cronbach's alpha) for the comprehension scale is .67. In many cases, the low base rates for the items likely caused several low item-to-total correlations; yet the composite score demonstrates adequate internal consistency measure (Shadish, Cook, & Campbell, 2002). In developing this scale, we intentionally excluded items that dealt with discussion of background knowledge such as A1 and B1 in Figure 9.1. Based on our pilot observations, we noted that these discussions rarely were directly relevant to the text to be read and did not seem to be aligned with research based comprehension instruction. The comprehension scale has 35 items—26 items from the main comprehension part of the measure (excluding A1, B1, and A2c in Figure 9.1) and 9 items from the postobservation component (i.e., in Figure 9.3, ratings on global comprehension, management, and student engagement).

In the domain of vocabulary, there were fewer low-base-rate items. The vocabulary scale has a Cronbach's alpha of .74, which is more than suitable for a dependent measure (Shadish et al., 2002). The vocabulary scale consists of 12 items—6 items from the vocabulary component of the measure (excluding B1 in Figure 9.2) and 6 items from the postobservation component of the measure (i.e., in Figure 9.3 global vocabulary, management, and student engagement ratings). These appear to be a set of critical practices that typify high quality, interactive vocabulary instruction. Note that Item B1, while a necessary part of vocabulary instruction, is of limited value without the explicit teacher instruction that is the essence and soul of explicitness items (A1–A4) or without the scaffolding that is the basis of Item B3.

## Construct Validity: Sensitivity to Intervention

One key component of construct validity is sensitivity to intervention. This aspect of validity was particularly important to us in that we designed this measure to be one of several outcomes in a study of professional development for first-grade teachers of ELLs. The intervention, described elsewhere in detail (Gersten, Dimino, Jayanthi, & Santoro, 2006), focused on how to translate principles from the research on comprehension and vocabulary into daily use. Teachers worked on applications using the unit in their core reading program that they would be covering the following week and reported back on successes and failures. Our goal was to improve observed teaching practice in these domains.

We calculated descriptive statistics on the observational measure for the experimental and comparison samples during the first year (first round) of a three-round randomized controlled trials study. For the comprehension domain, the mean frequency for the experimental and control group are 1.86 and 1.07, respectively. Similarly, for the vocabulary domain, mean frequency for the experimental group is 5, whereas the mean for control group is 2.67. Although these data are preliminary, we conducted a MANOVA and found significant differences between the groups on both the set of comprehension items and the set of vocabulary items. Thus it does appear that the measure is sensitive to interventions geared toward enhancing teachers' use of select research-based strategies in teaching reading and vocabulary.

## REFERENCES

Anderson, L., Evertson, C., & Brophy, J. (1979). An experimental study of effective teaching in first-grade reading groups. *Elementary School Journal, 79,* 193–223.

Ball, D. L. (1990). Reflections and deflections of policy: The case of Carol Turner. *Educational Evaluation and Policy Analysis, 12,* 247–259.

Baumann, J. F., & Kame'enui, E. J. (1991). Research on vocabulary instruction: Ode to Voltaire. In J. Flood, D. Lapp, & J. R. Squire (Eds.), *Handbook of research on teaching the English language arts* (pp. 604–632). Upper Saddle River, NJ: Merrill/Prentice Hall.

Beck, I. L., McKeown, M. G., & Kucan, L. (2002). *Bringing words to life: Robust vocabulary instruction.* New York: Guilford Press.

Beck, I. L., McKeown, M. G., Sandora, C., Kucan, L., & Worthy, J. (1996). Questioning the author: A yearlong classroom implementation to engage students with text. *Elementary School Journal, 96,* 385–414.

Brophy, J., & Good, T. L. (1986). Teacher behavior and student achievement. In

M. Witrock (Ed.), *The third handbook of research on teaching* (pp. 328–375). New York: McMillan.

Durkin, D. (1978–79). What classroom observations reveal about reading comprehension instruction. *Reading Research Quarterly, 14,* 481–533.

Echevarria, J., Vogt, M., & Short, D. J. (2000). *Making content comprehensible for English language learners: The SIOP model.* Boston: Allyn & Bacon.

Edmonds, M., & Briggs, K. L. (2003). *The instructional content emphasis instrument: Observations of reading instruction.* Baltimore: Brookes.

Foorman, B. R., Francis, D. J., Beeler, T., Winikates, D., & Fletcher, J. (1997). Early interventions for children with reading problems: Study designs and preliminary findings. *Learning Disabilities: A Multi-Disciplinary Journal, 8,* 63–71.

Foorman, B. R., & Schatschneider, C. (2003). Measurement of teaching practices during reading/language arts instruction and its relation to student achievement. In S. R. Vaughn & K. L. Briggs (Eds.), *Reading in the classroom: Systems for the observation of teaching and learning.* Baltimore: P. H. Brookes.

Gersten, R. (1996a). The double demands of teaching English language learners. *Educational Leadership, 53,* 18–22.

Gersten, R. (1996b). Literacy instruction for language-minority students: The transition years. *Elementary School Journal, 96,* 227–244.

Gersten, R., Baker, S., Haager, D., & Graves, A. (2005). Exploring the role of teacher quality in predicting reading outcomes for first-grade English learners: An observational study. *Remedial and Special Education, 26,* 197–206.

Gersten, R., Carnine, D., Zoref, L., & Cronin, D. (1986). A multifaceted study of change in seven inner city schools. *Elementary School Journal, 86,* 257–276.

Gersten, R., Dimino, J., Jayanthi, M., & Santoro, L. (2006, June). *Research on coaching and teacher study groups as a means of professional development.* Paper presented at the 14th annual Pacific Coast Research Conference (PCRC), Coronado, CA.

Gersten, R., Fuchs, L. S., Compton, D., Coyne, M. D., Greenwood, C., & Innocenti, M. (2005). Quality indicators for group experimental and quasi-experimental research in special education. *Exceptional Children, 71,* 149–164.

Gersten, R., Fuchs, D., Williams, J., & Baker, D. (2001). Teaching reading comprehension strategies to students with learning disabilities. *Review of Educational Research, 71,* 279–320.

Gersten, R., Keating, T., Yovanoff, P., & Harniss, M. (2001). Working in special education: Factors that enhance special educators' intent to stay. *Exceptional Children, 67,* 549–567.

Graves, M. F. (2006). *The vocabulary book: Learning & instruction.* New York: Teachers College Press.

Haager, D., Gersten, R., Baker, S., & Graves, A. (2003). The English-language learner classroom observation instrument: Observations of beginning reading instruction in urban schools. In S. R. Vaughn & K. L. Briggs (Eds.), *Reading in the classroom: Systems for observing teaching and learning.* Baltimore: Brookes.

Hansen, J. (1981). The effects of inference training and practice on young children's reading comprehension. *Reading Research Quarterly, 16,* 391–417.

Kennedy, M. M. (1999). Approximations to indicators of student outcomes. *Educational Evaluation and Policy Analysis, 21*, 345–363.

Langer, J. (1999). Examining background knowledge and text comprehension. *Reading Research Quarterly, 19*, 468–481.

McIntosh, R., Vaughn, S., Schumm, J. S., Haager, D., & Lee, O. (1994). Observations of students with learning disabilities in general education classes. *Exceptional Children, 60*, 249–261.

National Reading Panel (NRP). (2000). *Report of the National Reading Panel; Teaching children to read* (NIH Publication No. 00-4769). Washington, DC: National Institute of Child Health and Human Development, National Institutes of Health.

Pressley, M., El-Dinary, P. B., Gaskins, I., Schuder, T., Bergman, J., Almasi, J. et al. (1992). Beyond direct explanation: Transactional instruction of reading comprehension strategies. *Elementary School Journal, 92*, 511–554.

Rosenshine, B., & Stevens, R. (1986). *Teaching functions.* In M. C. Wittrock (Ed.), *Handbook of research on teaching* (3rd ed., pp. 376–391). New York: MacMillan.

Rueda, R., & Mehan, H. (1986). Metacognition and passing: Strategic interactions in the lives of students with learning disabilities. *Anthropology and Education Quarterly, 17*, 145–165.

Schatschneider, C., Fletcher, J., Francis, D. J., Carlson, C. D., & Foorman, B. (2004). Kindergarten prediction of reading skills: A longitudinal comparative analysis. *Journal of Educational Psychology, 96*, 265–282.

Shadish, W. R., Cook, T. D., & Campbell, D. T. (2002). *Experimental and quasi-experimental designs for general causal inference.* Boston: Houghton Mifflin.

Stallings, J. (1975). Implementation and child effects of teaching practices in follow through classrooms. *Monographs of the Society for Research in Child Development, 40*, (7–8, Serial No. 163).

Stallings, J., & Kaskowitz, D. (1974). *Follow through classroom observation evaluation 1972–1973* (SRI Project URU-7370). Menlo Park, CA: Stanford Research Institute.

Stoolmiller, M., Eddy, J. M., & Reid, J. B. (2000). Detecting and describing preventative intervention effects in a universal school-based randomized trial targeting delinquent and violent behavior. *Journal of Consulting and Clinical Psychology, 68*, 296–306.

Taylor, B., Pearson, P. D. Peterson, D., & Rodriguez, M. C. (2003). Reading growth in high-poverty classrooms: The influence of teacher practices that encourage cognitive engagement in literacy learning. *Elementary School Journal, 104*, 3–28.

Wong, B. Y. L., & Jones, W. (1982). Increasing metacomprehension in learning disabled and normally achieving students through self-questioning training. *Learning Disability Quarterly, 5*, 228–238.

# CHAPTER 10

# Scaling Up a Reading Reform in High-Poverty Elementary Schools

Barbara M. Taylor
Debra S. Peterson
Monica Marx
Michelle Chein

This chapter focuses on the need for an ongoing, collaborative, schoolwide reading improvement effort to substantially improve the reading abilities of students in diverse, high-poverty schools. Sound classroom reading instruction and research-based reading interventions in word recognition, vocabulary, and comprehension are essential, but not sufficient. One successful model of schoolwide reading improvement is described in this chapter.

## Questions for Reflection and Discussion

- The School Change Framework focuses on 3 goals in which teachers and administrators (1) improve the schoolwide delivery of reading instruction, (2) work collaboratively to teach reading and to improve reading instruction, and (3) use research on effective teaching practices, school reform, effective schools, and effective teachers to guide their efforts. What are the challenges and benefits of working toward each of these goals?
- How can you get better at looking closely at your own teaching practices to enhance students' reading abilities?

This chapter is adapted from *The Impact of the School Change Framework in Twenty-Three REA Schools*, by B. M. Taylor and D. S. Peterson (Minneapolis: University of Minnesota, Minnesota Center for Reading Research, 2006). Reprinted by permission of the authors and the publisher.

One important way to help struggling readers in high-poverty schools is through systemic, schoolwide reading reform. Because many of the children in high-poverty schools may be reading below grade level, a single reading intervention, or even a series of reading interventions at different grade levels, will not suffice. A teaching staff in which some teachers, but not all, strive to improve the effectiveness of their reading instruction will not suffice either.

This chapter describes the impact of the School Change Framework for Reading Instruction used by 23 high-poverty schools participating in a state-wide reading reform effort. The School Change Framework is structured around the belief that by working collaboratively and relentlessly, teachers can increase the effectiveness of their reading instruction and thus students' reading abilities.

Today we hear a great deal about the importance of researched-based practices in shaping school improvement efforts in reading (Learning First Alliance, 1998; National Reading Panel, 2000; "Put reading first," 2001). There exists a large body of research identifying what effective schools and accomplished teachers can do to promote students' reading growth and achievement (Charles A. Dana Center, 1999; Designs for Change, 1998; Langer, 2000; Lein, Johnson, & Ragland, 1997; Taylor, Pearson, Clark, & Walpole, 2000). The National Reading Panel Report (2000) has been one of the most influential reports on effective reading instruction, highlighting important curricular components of effective reading programs including

- Phonemic awareness instruction
- Explicit systematic phonics instruction
- Repeated oral reading practice with feedback and guidance
- Direct and indirect vocabulary instruction
- Comprehension strategies instruction

Other studies have focused on effective teachers of reading with the idea that *how* we teach may be as important as *what* we teach (Duffy et al., 1987; Pressley et al., 2001; Taylor, Peterson, Pearson, & Rodriguez, 2002). Taylor, Pearson, Peterson and Rodriguez (2003) developed a model of effective reading instruction maximizing students' cognitive engagement in literacy learning that evolved from an analysis of teaching behaviors correlated to students' growth in reading. The model is related to the work of Knapp (1995) on teaching for meaning and the engagement construct of Guthrie et al. (2000). The cognitive engagement framework contains four teaching dimensions:

1. Supporting higher level thinking through talk and writing about text
2. Encouraging independent use of word-recognition and comprehension strategies while reading

3. Using a student-support stance with coaching and modeling in addition to a teacher-directed stance (e.g., telling information or conducting recitations)
4. Promoting active engagement in literacy activities with every child reading, writing, sharing with a partner, or manipulating as opposed to more passive learning such as turn taking

Teachers who provide instruction that maximizes students' cognitive engagement in literacy activities, have seen higher student growth in reading than other teachers (Taylor, Pearson et al. 2003).

A third area of research on effective reading instruction has examined the characteristics of effective schools and successful reading reform efforts (Taylor, Pressley, & Pearson, 2002). Key elements of effective schools include

- Improved student learning is a schoolwide priority
- Strong building leadership
- Strong staff collaboration
- Ongoing professional development and the implementation of research-based practices
- Systematic use of student assessment data
- Strong schoolwide efforts to reach out to parents as partners

Clearly, research has informed educators about what needs to occur within schools and classrooms for students to achieve in reading. Importantly, teachers must collaborate and schools must develop ownership over their reform efforts (Fullan, 1999; Little, 2002; Newmann, 2002). However, implementing effective practices remains difficult; an external change agent cannot simply inform a school staff of what they must do. With this sobering reality in mind, the School Change Framework was designed to assist high-poverty schools that were engaged in schoolwide reading reform efforts (Taylor, Pearson et al., 2003; Taylor, Pearson, Peterson, & Rodriguez, 2005). Specifically, the framework focuses on teachers within schools:

1. Improving their reading program based on local needs and data
2. Working collaboratively in their delivery of reading instruction and with a focus on instructional reflection and improvement in their professional development activities
3. Using research-based knowledge of effective practices related to reading instruction, school reform, effective schools, and effective teachers to guide their efforts

Initial research on this model in 13 high-poverty elementary schools across the United States has demonstrated its effectiveness (Taylor et al.,

2005), with the score a school received for implementing elements of the reform explaining a substantial proportion of the between-school variance in reading comprehension growth. The teachers in high-reform-effort schools used more effective reading instruction practices than teachers in low-reform-effort schools and made more research-based changes in their reading instruction. This chapter describes a replication of the earlier research on this model, based on use by 23 Minnesota schools participating in the Minnesota Reading Excellence Act Program from 2002–04. (For more information, see Taylor & Peterson, 2006.)

## PROGRAM COMPONENTS

At the start of the project, teachers learned about effective reading instruction, characteristics of effective schools, and effective school improvement. Teachers also were reminded about the essential components of the School Change Framework for improving reading (see Taylor et al., 2005). Specifically, at least 80% of the teachers within a building must have voted in favor of using the model, the school must have a literacy coordinator/coach, there must be a leadership team (principal, literacy coordinator, and teacher leaders), and the school must receive outside expertise from an external facilitator.

Additionally, throughout the reform process, all teachers who provide reading instruction in Grades K–3 within the school engage in hour-long study group meetings three times a month. Within study groups, teachers learn about research-based reading practices, reflect on their reading instruction, and apply these practices to improve their reading instruction. The literacy coordinator spends most of her time in classrooms, modeling lessons and providing support and suggestions for improved reading instruction.

Once a month, all K–3 teachers meet in a large group to share study group activities and to discuss issues related to their schoolwide delivery of reading instruction. As a school and individually, teachers examine data on students' reading abilities as well as data on their teaching of reading and on school leadership, collaboration, and parent partnerships as pertains to their reading program. They use the data to make positive changes where needed.

Teachers use the data on students' reading abilities to monitor progress, modify instruction, and place students who are struggling in research-based interventions that will meet individual needs. All struggling readers receive 20–30 minutes a day of an intervention that serves as an "extra shot of quality instruction" at their instructional level designed to accelerate their learning to read. Also, teachers use student assessment data to provide all students with challenging, supplemental lessons in vocabulary and comprehension based on reading material at their instructional level.

Details about the research method and results of the School Change Framework project are provided in the appendix at the end of the chapter.

## IMPACT OF REFORM EFFORT

Based on analyses of the data we collected, we found that schools in the project had the most success with

- Meeting weekly in study groups
- Meeting in cross-grade study groups
- Meeting once a month in a large group to share across study groups and to deal with schoolwide issues
- Sticking with substantive study group topics over time
- Effectively using their external facilitator as a resource

Schools had the least success with

- Reflecting on instruction in study groups
- Being guided by their action plans
- Having an effective internal leadership team

Also, about half the schools had not yet turned to the reform component of working with parents as partners.

Growth curve analysis (Taylor & Peterson, 2006) was conducted to look at the impact of reform effort on individual students' reading comprehension growth across the 2 years of the project. On average, looking across Grades 1–3, students had significant growth (+2.2 normal curve equivalents or NCEs per time point) in comprehension across the 2 years. At the same time, grade level was negatively related to comprehension scores (–1.0 NCEs per grade-level increase per time point). The analysis also revealed that the reform effort made a significant contribution to students' growth in comprehension scores across the 2 years. More specifically, the schools that did a better job of implementing the School Change Framework in Year 2 saw accelerated growth in students' reading comprehension scores. Forty-six percent of the variance in growth in comprehension across the 2 years was between schools, and reform effort accounted for 20% of this variance. For every 1-point increase in the reform effort score, a school's mean NCE increased beyond the average increase of .51 NCEs per time point, or 1.53 NCEs per one-point increase in reform effort score across the 2 years.

One of the most powerful indications of the impact of the School Change Framework comes from comments that teachers and administrators made about the changes they saw in their schools because of the reform effort. One teacher stated:

> Communication and collaboration have increased 100% since starting the grant. Observation feedback and attending study groups have been wonderful. I feel that I have improved my teaching skills tremendously. I always thought I was a good teacher, but now I know that I have improved when I see what my students are doing. I feel good about what is happening at our school.

A teacher at another school confirmed this sentiment by saying, "This project has seriously changed the way we are teaching and we see kids engaged in ways we have never seen before. I get so many good ideas from people I wish it could continue." Another teacher at a third school remarked:

> Nobody is scared to ask for help and nobody looks down on anyone asking for help. There is so much talking among teachers, sharing of ideas, working on problems. There's a lot of positive feedback. Many teachers will never teach reading the same as prior to this.

In follow-up interviews a year after the completion of the grant, we heard positive responses such as:

> I made monumental changes. I do more high-level thinking questions, more coaching and modeling rather than telling. I think that my expectations for the children increased; I raised the bar. . . . What I learned is a part of *all* of my instruction, not just my reading instruction. . . . The School Change Project made a huge difference in respect to our expectations of the children and our collaboration across grade levels.

Important aspects transparent in these teachers' comments are the reflection on and improvement of teaching, increased expectations for students and delight with increased student success, the concept of "we" not just "I", and the idea that what teachers have learned will stay with them for the rest of their teaching careers.

## IMPACT OF CLASSROOM INSTRUCTION

Within each grade level, we used HLM analyses (Raudenbush & Bryk, 2002) to investigate relationships between students' spring reading scores (after controlling for fall scores) and the reading instruction variables (described in the appendix). The significant findings reflect classroom practices related to students' growth in reading between the beginning and end of the school year. Below we will report on significant findings; however, it is important to remember that the findings are correlational, not causal. More detailed reporting of results can be found in Taylor and Peterson (2006).

Teachers were encouraged to interpret their own data by looking at the mean scores and standard deviations for teacher practices for all schools by grade. If a particular practice is positively related to reading achievement, but a school falls below the mean for all schools, teachers may wish to engage in professional development activities that might increase the frequency of the practice. In contrast, if a particular practice is negatively related to achievement, but a school is above the mean for all schools, teachers may wish to decrease (but not eliminate) the prevalence of the practice. Overall, however, teachers in the project were reminded that balance in instruction is of utmost importance.

## Grouping Practices

In Grades 1–3 there was more growth in students' comprehension and vocabulary in classrooms with relatively high levels of whole-group instruction (e.g., observed from 30–60% of the time). In Grades 2–3, there was the least growth in students' fluency in classrooms with relatively high levels of small-group instruction (e.g., observed from 90–100% of the time). These data suggest that in Grades 1–3, students benefit from reading blocks in which whole-group and small-group instruction are balanced. If a teacher is only providing small-group reading instruction, it may be the case that students, in general, are spending too much time working at their seat or in centers (when not with the teacher in small-group instruction) and are not engaged in productive literacy activities during this independent work time.

## Instructional Activities

In Grades 2 and 3, a high incidence of higher level questioning was related to students' comprehension and vocabulary growth. This finding is consistent with Knapp (1995) and our previous research findings (Taylor & Pearson, 2004). In short, high-level questioning is an important factor to consider when focusing on the improvement of classroom reading instruction to increase reading achievement.

In Grade 1, a high incidence of comprehension skill instruction was negatively related to students' reading growth. One interpretation of this finding is that low-level mentioning of or drilling on comprehension skills does little to challenge students' thinking and thus takes valuable time away from more useful instruction. On the other hand, a relatively high level of comprehension strategy instruction was positively related to reading growth in Grades K–3. This finding is compatible with the NRP Report (2000) that stressed the importance of comprehension strategy instruction.

A high level of phonics instruction was not useful for students in general in Grades 2–3. This finding is compatible with research reported in the NRP Report (2000). Furthermore, a high level of phonics instruction was found to be negatively related to reading growth in Grades 2–5 in an earlier School Change study (Taylor, Pearson et al., 2003). Collectively, the findings suggest that teachers in Grades 2–3 must be selective about the amount of explicit phonics instruction needed for different students. Students who read at a mid-second-grade level or higher will probably need relatively little explicit phonics instruction. In a related vein, the NRP Report (2000) has recommended that most phonics instruction occur in Grades K–1.

In kindergarten, students in the current study showed less growth in phonemic awareness in classrooms of teachers at the high end of the continuum for frequency of phonemic awareness instruction (e.g., 25–35% of the time). While this may seem puzzling, it is actually compatible with the NRP report finding that 5–20 hours of phonemic awareness is sufficient. Phonemic awareness instruction is important, but so is balance. A supplementary analysis of the observations in the current study of teachers who were particularly high in providing phonemic awareness activities revealed that most of the instruction was in rhyme and alliteration (beginning sounds). This suggests that an overemphasis on phonemic awareness instruction, especially on aspects other than phoneme blending and segmentation, may not be beneficial to students' literacy development.

## Teacher and Student Actions

A high level of recitation was negatively related to students' fluency growth in Grade 1 and students' vocabulary growth in Grades 2–3. Coaching was positively related to growth in decoding in Grade 1 and phonemic awareness development and letter-sound knowledge in kindergarten. A high incidence of students on task was positively related to students' growth in fluency in Grade 1.

In earlier studies, the teacher practice of telling (e.g., the teacher engaged in a lot of talking) was negatively related to students' literacy growth (Taylor, Peterson et al., 2002; Taylor, Pearson et al., 2003). In the current project, a surprising finding was that a reasonably high amount of telling (e.g., 50–70% of the time), was positively related to vocabulary growth in Grades 2–3. However, it makes sense that when focusing on unfamiliar, high-utility words (e.g., Tier 2 words; see Beck, McKeown, & Kucan, 2002), a teacher would initially provide specific information about these words (e.g., tell them). Another finding in the current study was that recitation was negatively related to Grade 2–3 students' vocabulary growth. Results do not suggest that a teacher should refrain from engaging in recitation. However, results do suggest that if teaching is very top-down (e.g., heavily teacher directed), with too much recitation or telling, children may not be actively engaged in learning and their reading growth may suffer. Shifting from a heavily teacher-directed stance toward instruction to a stance that includes more student support (e.g., modeling, coaching, watching, and giving feedback) as students are actively engaged in literacy lessons may enhance students' reading growth.

## Materials

In Grades K–3, the use of informational text was seldom observed. In contrast, narrative text was coded with great regularity. A similar finding on the low usage of informational texts was recently reported by Duke (2000) in a study of first-grade classrooms. Increased use of informational text during reading instruction, especially in Grades 2 and 3, is a practice that some teachers may wish to consider.

## AN EXAMPLE OF EFFECTIVE
## READING PRACTICES

One limitation of quantitative analyses is that these results can seem distant from the real-life work of classroom teachers. To offer a clearer picture of what effective reading practices identified in this study actually look like in a classroom, we describe a lesson of a teacher who had been participating in the School Change Framework for 2 years. Mr. Larson (a pseudonym) was a kindergarten teacher in a very high poverty, urban school in Minnesota. One third of the 21 students in his full-day kindergarten class did not speak English as a first language. Mr. Larson began his 2-day lesson by reading *Geraldine's Big Snow* by Holly Keller to his students and explaining that they would be talking about an important theme from the story— anticipation. To develop students' understanding of the word *anticipation*, the class completed a vocabulary word map. Definitions the children gave for "anticipation" were "to be excited about," "to look forward to," "to be hopeful or eager," and "to want something to happen." Each child wrote a sentence and drew a picture about something he or she anticipated. The next day, Mr. Larson reminded students of the important theme and the meaning of the word "anticipation." He explicitly stated:

Our purpose is to construct meaning from the story, to understand what it means to anticipate something. We're going to do this by stopping along the way to ask and answer questions. Good readers do this to gain meaning. Just reading the words is not enough. We need to know what the story is about. We also want to make connections to our own lives. We will do this by doing a Think-Pair-Share and then we'll be writing in response to the story.

Mr. Larson asked high-level questions to help the students make connections between the story and their lives. For example, he asked, "In the story, Mr. Peters wants to read a lot of books during the big snow. What would you like to do during a big snow, and why would you want to do that?" The children had time to think about the question, and then Mr. Larson asked them to turn to a partner to share their responses. This involved every child in active responding instead of only one or two students being called on to share. While the children were talking in pairs, Mr. Larson walked around and coached children to elaborate on their answers. One boy shared that he would like to make a snow fort and snowballs in the big snow. Mr. Larson asked him, "Why do you think this would be fun?" The student responded with more detail, "I would build a humongous snow fort so I could hide and throw snowballs at my brother and smack him!"

Following the read-aloud, Mr. Larson told the group they would write about an activity that they had anticipated. They would describe the activity by saying when and where it happened, who was there, and what they had hoped would happen. They would also write about how they felt during the activity and explain why they felt that way. Then Mr. Larson explicitly demonstrated and modeled how he would respond. He said he was going to do a "think-aloud" to help them see how he would organize his thoughts before writing. Mr. Larson talked about how he had anticipated adopting his son, and how he was feeling as he prepared for parenthood. He specifically modeled how to elaborate on ideas using details and how to reread the question to ensure a complete answer.

As a prewriting activity, Mr. Larson had children do a Think-Pair-Share. The children who were able to start writing returned to their seats, while Mr. Larson worked with a small group of children who needed additional support. In the small group, Mr. Larson coached students to write more and elaborate on their thoughts. For example, one girl said she was really happy. Mr. Larson asked her, "What were you happy about?" She responded, "I was happy that my dad was going to bake a cake." After she had written that sentence, Mr. Larson asked her, "Why was your dad baking a cake? Was it for a special occasion?" She elaborated by describing her brother's birthday and how they prepared for the special event.

After students who needed more support were all writing, Mr. Larson walked around the room to coach and give feedback to other students. He reminded students to use the tools available around the room to help them with their writing. These tools included the Word Wall with high-frequency words and other sight words; a quality-work rubric developed by the class to self-check their work; short vowel charts; alphabet charts; sound boards; and student dictionaries. When a child asked for help writing the word *friends*, Mr. Larson asked him, "Where can you find the word *friends*?" The child went to the Word Wall. When students asked how to spell various other words, Mr. Larson encouraged them to say words slowly and to write the sounds they heard.

All students wrote multiple sentences about the activity they anticipated. They concluded the lesson by reading their responses to three peers in the classroom. In summary, this lesson demonstrated a balance between whole- and small-group instruction, high-level questioning with both talking and writing about text, active responding, and teacher coaching and modeling.

## CONCLUSION

The School Change Framework for Reading Improvement was effective in project schools. Almost all schools saw growth in students' reading scores, and those schools that did a better job of implementing the School Change Framework saw accelerated growth. Importantly, this finding on the effectiveness of the School Change Framework within a school leading to accelerated reading growth replicates research from an earlier study (Taylor et al., 2005).

Essential components of this reading reform model include a high degree of teacher buy-in to implement the reform; use of data on students' reading and teachers' teaching to provide effective reading instruction to all students; a constant effort by all teachers to reflect on and improve their reading instruction; and a conscious attempt by teachers to come together as a school community. Teachers learn that they needed to focus on teaching reading well rather than on jumping from one hot topic to another or looking for a silver bullet.

Change is a long, slow process. All school staff members who are involved in this process need to keep the faith and to remain patient and supportive of one another through the natural ups and downs of a reform effort. School leaders need to help school members maintain commitment and perseverance. But by working together and providing excellent teaching throughout a school, almost *all* students can become good readers and thinkers. It is particularly exciting to see this happening in high-poverty schools where we have a moral imperative to make a substantial, positive difference in children's education.

## Follow-up Activities

1. Discuss the two framing questions at the beginning of the chapter. What more would you like to know about the research on effective schoolwide reading improvement?
2. Read and discuss additional research on schoolwide reading improvement and develop an initial, tentative plan for schoolwide improvement in reading.
3. Develop a timetable for developing a complete, detailed schoolwide reading improvement plan to be implemented in your school.

# APPENDIX: METHOD AND RESULTS

## Scaling Up a Reading Reform

In the 2003–04 school year there were 23 Minnesota schools using the School Change Framework. Fifteen of these schools were very high poverty schools, with 70–98% of their students on subsidized lunch. Three were high-poverty schools with 50–69% of students on subsidized lunch, and five were moderately high poverty schools with 44–49% of students on subsidized lunch. Fifteen of these schools had moderate to high percentages (20–49%) of ELL students. Fifteen of these schools were in urban school districts, four were in suburban districts, and four were in small town/rural districts.

## Student Assessments

All children in K–3 regular education classrooms were tested in the fall and spring by data collectors who had been elementary teachers. At relevant grades, children were tested individually in phonemic awareness, phonics, and fluency. Students in Grades 1–3 were assessed in vocabulary and/or comprehension on the Gates MacGinitie test, which was administered in a group setting by their classroom teacher.

## Reform Effort Rubric

The notes from study group meetings and the action plans, as well as information from teacher and principal interviews, comprised the artifacts analyzed to determine which aspects of the School Change Framework were being implemented within schools. A composite scale was created on 10 essential aspects of the reform effort. Each school's set of artifacts was scored by one of seven people using the reform effort rubric. A second person scored all school sets of artifacts. The inter-rater agreement was 93%. The reform effort rubric included the following dimensions:

- Meeting 1 hour per week in study groups
- Meeting in cross-grade study groups
- Reflecting on instruction and student work
- Considering research-based practices
- Being guided by action plans
- Sticking with substantive topics for 3–4 months or more
- Meeting once a month as a whole faculty to share and to discuss issues
- Working on a plan to involve parents as partners
- Taking advantage of the services of the external facilitator
- Having an effective internal leadership team.

## Classroom Observation Data

On three occasions, classroom teachers in Grades K–3 were observed for an hour during reading instruction. In some schools specialists were observed if they were the main reading teacher for a group of students. The purpose of these observations was to provide schools and individual teachers with data related to teaching including their grouping practices, literacy activities, materials, interaction styles, expected student responses to the literacy events, and students' engagement rate. Teachers received their observation data along with questions for self-reflection. They were encouraged to interpret their data with colleagues to improve classroom reading instruction with the understanding that the best benchmarks for interpreting data from a particular school were the means and standard deviations for all of the project schools on the various aspects of instruction by grade level (K, 1, 2, 3) and the significant relationships of various practices with students' growth in reading during the year.

The observation includes a description of what the teacher and children are saying and doing in 5-minute segments as well as a record of the number of children on task. The written description is coded so that instructional data can be statistically analyzed. The codes indicate who provided the instruction (Level 1), the grouping pattern (Level 2), the type of literacy instruction—reading, writing, or language (Level 3), the three or four most salient literacy activities (Level 4), the materials (Level 5), the teacher interaction styles (Level 6), and the expected responses of the students (Level 7).

An example of a 5-minute observation segment is provided below. The observation scheme is further described in Taylor, Pearson et al., 2003; Taylor et al., 2005.

### Sample of Observational Notes

9:15 A small group of first graders is silently reading a book *The Perfect Pet* at the table. Teacher (T) is listening to one child (S) at a time read aloud softly. S: "It's a turtle!" T: "Did you think that when you were reading earlier?" S: "No, I thought that it was a lizard. And here's a turtle and there is one on the back of the book, too." T: "Yes, there is. Keep reading." Ss continue reading silently. T listens to another S. When he stops on a word, T says: "That's a hard word. The middle sound is /ou/." S: "Loud." T: "You're right." S continues reading and stops at another word. T: "The 'i' is saying its name because of the magic 'e'." S: "Wide." T: "Right." Ss have finished reading. T: "What were some of the hints that Mrs. Green gave the children?" S: "It can get out by itself. It doesn't make noise." T: "Right, it doesn't make noise, because it was quiet."

5/5 OT (On Task)[1]
*Codes*   c/s/r    r/n/l/r    wr/n/c/or-tt   m1/n/r/or-tt
*Levels*   1/2/3   4/5/6/7   4 /5/6/7     4 /5/6/7

Observers (*n* = 19) received training and demonstrated that they could score a practice observation with at least 80% agreement at all 7 Levels of the coding scheme before they began observations. The inter-rater agreement on actual observations was as follows: 99% at Level 2, 99% at Level 3, 86% at Level 4, 91% at Level 5, 88% at Level 6, 85% at Level 7.

## Students' Reading Scores

Reading scores in Year 1 and Year 2 are presented in Tables 10.1–10.4. In all instances, comparable scores were higher for students in Year 2 than in Year 1.

Importantly, Grade 2 students also demonstrated substantial movement, and Grade 3 students some movement, out of the lowest third in terms of comprehension scores based on national percentiles. There was also movement into the highest third in both grades (see Table 10.5). Based on the assumption that most of the students in the lowest third were likely to be struggling readers, there were relatively fewer struggling readers in Grades 2 and 3 at the end of Year 2 than at the end of Year 1 in the schools in this study.

**Table 10.1.** Summary of year 1 and 2 student scores, grade K

|  |  | Letter Sounds (total = 23) | Phonemic Awareness (total = 12) |
|---|---|---|---|
| All schools Fall, Year 1 | $M$ | 5.27 |  |
|  | $(SD)$ | (6.00) |  |
|  | $N$ | 1302 |  |
| All schools Spring, Year 1 | $M$ | 16.66 | 6.12 |
|  | $(SD)$ | (5.57) | (4.32) |
|  | $N$ | 1302 | 935 |
| All schools Fall, Year 2 | $M$ | 6.37 |  |
|  | $(SD)$ | (6.30) |  |
|  | $N$ | 1153 |  |
| All schools Spring, Year 2 | $M$ | 17.49 | 6.78 |
|  | $(SD)$ | (4.83) | (4.42) |
|  | $N$ | 1160 | 1252 |

*Note. M* = Mean score, *(SD)* = Standard deviation, *N* = Number of students.

**Table 10.2.** Summary of year 1 and 2 student scores, grade 1

|  |  | Phonemic awareness (total = 12) | Words correct per minute (spring target= 60)* | Gates Comprehension normal curve equivalent score |
|---|---|---|---|---|
| All schools Fall, Year 1 | $M$ | 5.45 |  |  |
|  | $(SD)$ | (4.13) |  |  |
|  | $N$ | 1417 |  |  |
| All schools Spring, Year 1 | $M$ |  | 53.01 | 47.85 |
|  | $(SD)$ |  | (34.50) | (20.43) |
|  | $N$ |  | 1361 | 1366 |
| All schools Fall, Year 2 | $M$ | 6.38 |  |  |
|  | $(SD)$ | (4.29) |  |  |
|  | $N$ | 1409 |  |  |
| All schools Spring, Year 2 | $M$ |  | 58.75 | 49.20 |
|  | $(SD)$ |  | (35.84) | (20.07) |
|  | $N$ |  | 1383 | 1228 |

*Target score from Johns, J. C., & Berglund, R. L. (2005). *Fluency strategies and assessment (2nd ed.).* Dubuque, IA: Kendall Hunt.

**Table 10.3.** Summary of year 1 and 2 student scores, grade 2

|  |  | Words correct per minute (spring target = 90)* | Gates MacGinitie Reading Test Vocabulary— normal curve equivalent score | Gates MacGinitie Reading Test Comprehension— normal curve equivalent score |
|---|---|---|---|---|
| All schools | M | 58.08 | 42.26 | 42.57 |
| Fall, Year 1 | (SD) | (37.70) | (19.70) | (20.05) |
|  | N | 1285 | 1218 | 1220 |
| All schools | M | 91.79 | 42.97 | 44.52 |
| Spring, Year 1 | (SD) | (38.42) | (19.27) | (19.62) |
|  | N | 1285 | 1218 | 1220 |
| All schools | M | 61.38 | 44.27 | 44.85 |
| Fall, Year 2 | (SD) | (37.25) | (20.25) | (20.53) |
|  | N | 1143 | 1149 | 1147 |
| All schools | M | 93.62 | 43.94 | 45.32 |
| Spring, Year 2 | (SD) | (37.53) | (19.54) | (20.63) |
|  | N | 1143 | 1149 | 1147 |

* Target score from Johns, J. C., & Berglund, R. L. (2005). *Fluency strategies and assessment (2nd ed.).* Dubuque, IA: Kendall Hunt.

**Table 10.4.** Summary of year 1 and 2 student scores, grade 3

|  |  | Words Correct per Minute (spring target = 110)* | Gates MacGinitie Reading Test Vocabulary— normal curve equivalent score | Gates MacGinitie Reading Test Comprehension —normal curve equivalent score |
|---|---|---|---|---|
| All schools | M | 91.93 | 38.12 | 42.01 |
| Fall, Year 1 | (SD) | (37.95) | (20.48) | (18.64) |
|  | N | 1361 | 1367 | 1368 |
| All schools | M | 112.61 | 42.49 | 43.97 |
| Spring, Year 1 | (SD) | (39.31) | (20.48) | (20.28) |
|  | N | 1361 | 1367 | 1368 |
| All schools | M | 96.58 | 40.13 | 43.81 |
| Fall, Year 2 | (SD) | (38.94) | (20.77) | (18.86) |
|  | N | 1170 | 1178 | 1179 |
| All schools | M | 115.96 | 44.17 | 44.19 |
| Spring, Year 2 | (SD) | (38.79) | (21.35) | (20.63) |
|  | N | 1170 | 1178 | 1179 |

* Target score from Johns, J. C., & Berglund, R. L. (2005). *Fluency strategies and assessment (2nd ed.).* Dubuque, IA: Kendall Hunt.

**Table 10.5.** Percentage of students falling into the lowest, middle, and highest thirds in comprehension on the Gates-MacGinitie, based on national norms

| Grade | National Percentile Band | Fall Year 1 | Spring Year 1 | Fall Year 2 | Spring Year 2 |
|---|---|---|---|---|---|
| 2 | Lowest 1/3 | 50 | 43 | 44 | 42 |
| 2 | Middle 1/3 | 30 | 31 | 32 | 30 |
| 2 | Highest 1/3 | 20 | 26 | 24 | 28 |
| 3 | Lowest 1/3 | 51 | 45 | 49 | 46 |
| 3 | Middle 1/3 | 30 | 32 | 31 | 32 |
| 3 | Highest 1/3 | 19 | 23 | 20 | 22 |

## NOTES

1. Code meanings are as follows:
Level 1:  c = classroom teacher
Level 2:  s = small group
Level 3:  r = reading focus
Level 4:  r = reading connected text
        wr = [using] word recognition strategies
        m1 = [answering] lower-level comprehension questions
Level 5:  s = [using] worksheet
        n = [using] narrative text
Level 6:  r = [teacher leading] recitation
        c = [teacher] coaching
Level 7:  r = [students]reading text
        or-tt = [students participating in] oral turn-taking

## REFERENCES

Beck, I. L., McKeown, M. G., & Kucan, L. (2002). *Bringing words to life: Robust vocabulary instruction.* New York: Guilford Press.

Charles A. Dana Center, University of Texas at Austin.(1999). *Hope for urban education: A study of nine high-performing, high-poverty urban elementary schools.* Washington, DC: U.S. Department of Education, Planning, and Evaluation Service.

Duffy, G. G., Roehler, L. R., Sivan, E., Rackliffe, G., Book, C., Meloth, M. S. et al. (1987). Effects of explaining the reasoning associated with using reading strategies. *Reading Research Quarterly, 20,* 347–368.

Duke, N. (2000). 3.6 minutes per day: The scarcity of informational texts in first grade. *Reading Research Quarterly, 35*, 202–224.

Fullan, M. (1999). *Change forces: The sequel.* Philadelphia: Falmer.

Guthrie, J. T., Cox, K. E., Knowles, K. T., Buehl, M., Maxxoni, S. A. et al. (2000). Building toward coherent instruction. In L. Baker, M. J. Dreher, & J. T. Guthrie (Eds.), *Engaging young readers: Promoting achievement and motivation* (pp. 1–16). New York: Guilford Press.

Knapp, M. S. (1995). *Teaching for meaning in high-poverty classrooms.* New York: Teachers College Press.

Langer, J. A. (2000). Excellence in English in middle and high school: How teachers' professional lives support student achievement. *American Educational Research Journal, 37*, 397–439.

Learning First Alliance. (1998). Every child reading: An action plan of the Learning First Alliance. *American Educator, 22*(1–2), 52–63.

Lein, L., Johnson, J. F., & Ragland, M. (1997). *Successful Texas schoolwide programs: Research study results.* Austin: Charles A. Dana Center, University of Texas at Austin.

Little, J. (2002). Professional communication and collaboration. In W. Hawley (Ed.), *The keys to effective schools* (pp. 43–55). Thousand Oaks, CA: Corwin Press.

National Reading Panel (NRP). (2000). *Report of the National Reading Panel: Teaching children to read* (NIH Publication No. 00-4769). Washington DC: National Institute of Child Health and Human Development, National Institutes of Health.

Newmann, F. (2002). Achieving high-level outcomes for all students: The meaning of staff-shared understanding and commitment. In W. Hawley (Ed.), *The keys to effective schools* (pp. 28–42). Thousand Oaks, CA: Corwin Press.

Pressley, M., Wharton-McDonald, R., Allington, R. L., Block, C. C., Morrow, L., Tracey, D. et al. (2001) A study of effective first-grade literacy instruction. *Scientific Studies of Reading, 5*, 35–58.

*Put reading first.* (2001). Washington, DC: National Institute for Literacy.

Raudenbush, S. W., & Bryk, A. S. (2002). *Hierarchical linear models: Applications and data analysis methods* (2nd ed.). Thousand Oaks, Ca: Sage.

Taylor, B. M., & Pearson, P. D. (2004). Research on learning to read—at school, at home, and in the community. *Elementary School Journal, 105*, 167–181.

Taylor, B. M., Pearson, P. D., Clark, K., & Walpole, S. (2000). Effective schools and accomplished teachers: Lessons about primary grade reading instruction in low-income schools. *Elementary School Journal, 101*, 121–165.

Taylor, B. M., Pearson, P. D., Peterson, D. S., & Rodriguez, M. C. (2003). Reading growth in high-poverty classrooms: The influence of teacher practices that encourage cognitive engagement in literacy learning. *Elementary School Journal, 104*, 3–28.

Taylor, B. M., Pearson, P. D., Peterson, D. S., & Rodriguez, M. C. (2005). The CIERA school change framework: An evidence-based approach to professional development and school reading improvement. *Reading Research Quarterly, 40*(1), 40–69.

Taylor, B. M., & Peterson, D. S. (2006). *The impact of the school change framework in twenty-three Minnesota REA schools.* Minneapolis: University of Minnesota: Minnesota Center for Reading Research.

Taylor, B. M., Peterson, D. S., Pearson, P. D., & Rodriguez, M. C. (2002). Looking inside classrooms: Reflecting on the "how" as well as the "what" in effective reading instruction. *The Reading Teacher, 56,* 70–79.

Taylor, B. M., Pressley, M. P., & Pearson, P. D. (2002). Research-supported characteristics of teachers and schools that promote reading achievement. In B. M. Taylor & P. D. Pearson (Eds.), *Teaching reading: Effective schools, accomplished teachers* (pp. 361–374). Mahwah, NJ: Erlbaum.

# CHAPTER 11

# Schoolwide Reading Improvement to Meet All Students' Needs

Barbara M. Taylor
Debra Peterson

In Chapter 1 we stated that this book on educational interventions for struggling readers would highlight instructional factors that contribute to students' success as readers. We have focused on schools reducing reading difficulties through effective instruction because this is where educators can make substantial, positive contributions.

All of the chapters in this book provide excellent, research-based suggestions on how to provide good classroom reading instruction and interventions. Chapters 3–7 focus on effective classroom instructional techniques in the areas of word recognition, vocabulary, and comprehension. Chapters 2 and 8 focus on providing intensive reading interventions. Chapters 8–10 focus on how teachers within schools can effectively work together to maximize all students' success as readers in the elementary grades. We will highlight key points from these chapters before describing a framework a school staff can use to translate these research-based ideas into practice.

In Chapter 3 Chambers and associates discuss the effectiveness of multimedia techniques embedded within explicit phonics lessons in the classroom to enhance primary-grade students' word recognition abilities. Teachers use brief animated video segments as a supplement to their instruction to provide students with memorable demonstrations of letter-sound correspondences and letter-sound blending strategies to decode words. Chambers et al. have found that multimedia enhancements hold promise for improving beginning readers' success in learning to read.

In Chapter 4 Graves outlines a sound program of classroom vocabulary instruction. The four-part program includes extensive experiences with language, instruction in specific words, instruction in strategies to determine word meanings, and development of students' interest in words around them. Graves suggests that about an hour a week devoted to this four-part program would suffice for elementary students in general; however, he recommends about 30 minutes a day for students who are struggling readers or who are English-language learners.

August and Snow in Chapter 5 add to Graves' description of effective vocabulary instruction by presenting research-based information on effective vocabulary instruction for English-language learners. They report on effective modifications for teachers to use with English-language learners such as pictures and demonstrations to illustrate word meanings, use of cognates or students' first language when appropriate, and use of discussion about texts read to develop students' oral language abilities. They also point out that vocabulary instruction will need to vary for students who are newcomers versus those who are moderately proficient in English.

In Chapter 6 Santoro and associates focus on techniques to enhance first-grade students' comprehension of stories based on teacher read-alouds. In their project, teachers used lesson guides to engage students in prereading discussions about concepts in stories or informational texts, in during-reading discussions about events or information in these texts, and in post-reading retelling of the stories or informational texts that were read aloud. Teachers learned about the value of incorporating intentional and strategic talk about texts into their instruction to positively impact students' comprehension.

In Chapter 7 Englert and associates discuss an effective instructional program to develop middle-grade students' comprehension of content area reading. General and special education students were found to benefit from learning to integrate reading strategies and writing about text across multiple content areas. Through ongoing professional development, teachers developed a common language to teach students how to use various strategies such as note taking, questioning, mapping, synthesizing, and reporting about what was read.

In Chapter 8 Vaughn and associates describe a 3-tier model of providing interventions to struggling readers. This is a schoolwide effort that includes good classroom reading instruction at Tier 1, focused small-group interventions at Tier 2 for students for whom good classroom instruction is not enough to help them succeed as readers, and intensive small-group or one-on-one interventions at Tier 3 for students for whom Tier 2 interventions are not sufficient. Vaughn and associates point out that the integration of explicit instruction in word recognition, fluency, and comprehension is a critical element of effective interventions. They conclude that more needs to be learned about how to provide maximally effective integrated instruction to students who do not respond well to Tier 3 interventions.

Morris in Chapter 2 describes important components of successful Tier 3 interventions. He also concludes that it is not materials or programs but teacher expertise that is the key to preventing reading failure in the primary grades. He stresses that substantial teacher training is essential for teachers to develop this expertise.

In Chapters 8–10, the focus is on schoolwide collaboration in the development and delivery of sound reading instruction for all students. As noted above, in Chapter 8, Vaughn and associates describe an approach to effective reading instruction based on the response-to-intervention (RTI) model that includes a 3–tiered system of providing interventions to struggling readers. In Chapter 9 Gersten and associates discuss an observation tool that can be used to help teachers reflect on the effectiveness of their vocabulary and comprehension instruction. In Chapter 10 Taylor and associates focus on the transition of all teachers into maximally effective teachers of reading and the schoolwide leadership and professional development needed for a school to revamp its schoolwide reading program.

In the remainder of this final chapter, we describe a process that schools can use to learn how to implement instructional suggestions offered in Chapters 1–10 of this book. These action steps explain how a school leadership team can initiate and monitor a reading reform plan. The process for schoolwide reading improvement is based on the framework for change used in the Minnesota School Change in Reading Project described in Chapter 10. Three studies have found this approach to be effective in enhancing students' reading growth (Taylor, Pearson, Peterson, & Rodriguez, 2005; Taylor & Peterson, 2006a; Taylor & Peterson 2006b). Throughout the chapter we refer readers to the appendix, which lists resources organized by the topics discussed.

## Questions for Reflection and Discussion

- Do you as a school have the administrative and teacher leadership capacity and would you have sufficient teacher buy-in to succeed with a significant schoolwide reading improvement effort such as the one outlined in this chapter?
- Do you feel energized by the concept of collaborative, school-based, intellectually stimulating, reflective professional development? Why or why not?

# IMPLEMENTING A SCHOOLWIDE PLAN
# FOR READING IMPROVEMENT *

## A School Leadership Team Initiates Reform

A group of committed teachers and administrators who want to see a significant reading improvement effort unfold at their school form a leadership team and take a first pass at developing a general reading improvement plan. This gives others some idea of the purpose of and process for such an effort. The group reviews the research on effective school improvement, collaboration, and shared leadership (see the appendix; see also Taylor, Pressley, & Pearson, 2002; York-Barr, Sommers, Ghere, & Montie, 2006), as well as the research on effective reading instruction and effective teachers of reading (National Reading Panel, 2000; Pressley, 2006; Taylor et al., 2002).

The group obtains and studies data on students, quality of reading instruction, school collaboration, leadership, and parent partnerships to determine needs for improving the school reading program and student abilities in reading. The group considers student performance in relation to standards, growth and achievement goals, the effectiveness of current classroom reading instruction and intervention instruction, the sufficiency of time spent on reading instruction, and the degree to which there is balanced reading instruction across the school. Then the group discusses the following questions:

- How can the teachers and administrators in our school develop or improve upon a collaborative approach to leadership?
- How can we make the reading achievement of our students a schoolwide priority in which teachers feel a shared responsibility for all students' success?
- How can we develop a plan to ensure that all teachers are monitoring students' progress using a variety of assessments and using these data to inform their instruction?
- How can we develop a schoolwide reading plan that supports teachers in the implementation of a high-quality, balanced reading program that develops students as thinkers as well as readers?
- How will we foster relationships and partnerships with parents and the community in the effort to improve the reading achievement of our students?

---

*The remainder of this chapter is adapted from Taylor, Frye, Peterson, & Pearson (2003).

Successful schools have an ongoing professional development program and a strong sense of community. Thus the leadership team uses the data and reflections from the steps listed above to develop a tentative plan for professional development that addresses how teachers will be provided with opportunities to learn about effective research-based practices in order to increase their effectiveness as teachers of reading.

## Embarking on a Plan

The leadership team presents a tentative plan for professional development to teachers and makes modifications based on teachers' input. The school then moves forward with a revised plan that at least 80% of teachers have voted to accept. As the school embarks on this plan, the leadership team members help all staff understand that developing a culture of learning based on ongoing professional development with a strong teacher leadership component takes time and patience. Necessary resources need to be allocated, and the entire staff needs to make a commitment and remain focused on the plan that the school has developed.

At the start of the actual improvement process, roles of members of the leadership team are clarified. Additional members are added to the team so that all teachers within the school feel that they are represented. The leadership team meets regularly (at least once a month) to keep the improvement effort moving forward and to provide leadership to the ongoing professional development program. If economically feasible, an external facilitator is hired on a consultant basis to help keep the leadership team and entire school on a path to success. Also, the school should avoid being tempted by other new initiatives that may be proposed in the first several years of a substantial schoolwide reading improvement effort.

It is vital that there is a reading coach who is appointed at least half-time to visit classrooms and provide support, model lessons, and serve as a peer coach for all teachers. This person should be respected by colleagues and be comfortable teaching demonstration lessons of effective practices as requested by teachers.

Members of the leadership team, especially the principal, work with teachers who are not on board with the school-endorsed improvement effort. This requires that leaders be good listeners who take the time to hear reluctant teachers' concerns and recommendations before problem solving occurs.

The leadership team takes responsibility for encouraging all teachers to continue to examine data on students, teaching of reading, school climate, collaboration, leadership, and parent partnerships. From this data, the leadership team determines strengths as well as further changes that are needed.

Also, grade-level teams look at student assessment data regularly to determine progress and to decide where instructional change is needed. Teachers reflect on data on their own reading instruction: *what* is being taught, *how* are lessons being taught, *how much* time is spent on different aspects of reading instruction, what are *strengths* to share with others, and what are further *changes* that are needed to help all children succeed.

Under the direction of the leadership team at monthly whole-group meetings, staff members periodically evaluate the schoolwide reading improvement plan. Adjustments are made as needed.

## Improving Parent Partnerships

The leadership team discusses the strengths and weaknesses of their school's current involvement with parents, keeping in mind that what is important is the larger concept of parent partnerships, not simply parent involvement (see the resources in the appendix). Parents are surveyed or interviewed to assess what they feel is needed to help them become more involved in their children's schooling. Then a plan is developed with parents to improve parent-school partnerships. Later, the leadership team evaluates the effectiveness of the parent-school partnership plan by seeking feedback from parents and teachers. For example, the leadership team might study data from parent and teacher questionnaires or from parent attendance at scheduled events to determine which aspects of the program have been successful and which have not.

## Participating in Intellectually Stimulating and Reflective Professional Development

Teachers plan study groups with specific foci. Study group activities include reading and talking about research-based practices as well as reflecting on and changing teaching within the classroom (see resources in the appendix). Between study group meetings, members of a study group try out the same set of new teaching techniques. It is important that all try out the same things so they can share common experiences. At subsequent meetings and based on new techniques being implemented, study group members engage in the following:

- Examination of student work to improve teaching
- Study of lesson plans with an eye toward good instructional choices being made
- Discussion of effective instruction based on classroom visits or video viewing of 30 or so minutes of an exemplary reading lesson

- Participation in video sharing in which study group members share their own instruction to help all members discuss, reflect on, and improve practice

Study groups meet for an hour once a month, and members take turns filling the roles of leader, timekeeper, and recorder. The group develops an action plan that includes data on students' progress and teachers' successes and keeps meeting notes that are shared with the rest of the school (e.g., posted in a central location). Members get support from a reading coach, another peer from within the school, or an external facilitator who provides peer coaching and demonstration teaching opportunities.

A study group remains on a specific topic, technique, or set of related techniques for at least 6 sessions. Thus it is important for members to select a topic, technique, or set of techniques that warrant a minimum of 6–8 sessions of study.

Periodically, each study group needs to evaluate the process: What went well? What needs to be done to make the study group more productive? A study group also regularly reflects on strengths in their own teaching as well as areas of instruction in need of improvement that they notice, a crucial aspect of study groups that is often overlooked. Study group members ask questions such as: How has my teaching improved based on my study group work? How is my study group work helping my students improve in reading? Group members continually look at student data to identify progress and to identify areas of instruction in need of further attention. Study groups add new techniques to their area of study as members feel ready for new challenges. However, a common mistake that many study groups make is to move on to an entirely new topic too readily before substantial changes are seen in teachers' teaching or in students' performance.

## IMPROVING READING INSTRUCTION ACROSS THE SCHOOL

### Making Adjustments to a Schoolwide Reading Program

The leadership team encourages the staff to consider and propose adjustments in time devoted to reading instruction, blocks of time for reading instruction, collaboration in delivery of reading instruction, use of push-in or pull-out models for supplemental instruction, placement of instructional aides, interventions for struggling readers, and high expectations and challenge for all students. The larger group considers alignment across state and/or district standards, instruction, and assessments in reading. Whole-staff, grade-level, and cross-grade-level meetings are regularly scheduled to discuss the schoolwide reading program (see resources in the appendix).

## Learning About Effective Reading Instruction and Effective Teachers of Reading

Teachers collectively review relevant research on effective reading instruction and effective teachers of reading (see resources in the appendix). They use data on students' and teachers' needs to select foci for several different study groups into which teachers self-select.

In study groups and with in-class support from a literacy coach, teachers learn, implement, and reflect on the effectiveness of new research-based techniques in a particular focus area. Individuals ask questions to reflect on their own teaching that deal with content, process, purpose, timing, and meeting individual needs. Examples of questions include the following:

### Content

- What new technique am I trying?
- Am I teaching important aspects of X?
- Am I using research-based processes to teach X?

### Purpose of lesson

- Why am I teaching this?
- How will it help my students develop their ability in X?

### Process of teaching of lesson

- What is my plan for teaching?
- To be more effective in my teaching, how could I have taught differently, provided more scaffolding as students were engaged in activities, or had students more actively involved?

### Timing of lesson

- Am I spending the right amount of time on X?
- Am I spending the right amount of time on different parts of my reading lesson so that valuable time is not wasted and I am getting through all parts of my lesson?
- Am I spending too much time on certain activities for certain students?

### Individual student needs

- Am I meeting individual needs related to X?
- Are there parts of my lesson that actually won't help students advance in their literacy abilities?

Teachers should continue to implement and reflect on the effectiveness of one or several related research-based techniques in their study group over multiple months (at least 6 sessions) and regularly assess students' progress to inform teaching. Examples of questions for ongoing reflection include:

### Students' progress

- How are my students doing in X (one of the dimensions of reading such as phonemic awareness, word recognition, fluency, vocabulary, or comprehension)?
- What do I need to do differently to help some students be more successful?

### Content, process, and purpose of teaching

- How should I adjust what I teach?
- What have I learned or observed in the study group that will help me make these changes?
- Am I getting better at being guided by my teaching purposes?

### Meeting individual needs

- What data am I looking at to assess students' progress and make instructional adjustments as needed?
- For which students do I need to adjust my instruction to meet their needs.
- What should I do to provide additional support to some students to meet their needs?

Study group members continue to implement and reflect on the effectiveness of new research-based technique or set of techniques over multiple months. However, they also move to a new technique within the same focus area as the group feels ready for new challenges. Examples of questions for reflection:

- Are we ready to focus on learning a new technique to teach X?
- What do we do next to refine our abilities to use this new technique in our teaching?
- How will this new technique improve our teaching?

## CONCLUSION

If we can offer any words of wisdom from years of working with teachers within schools and researching the process described above, it would be as follows: Make sure study groups are intellectually challenging, focus on research-based ideas, reflect on and discuss your own teaching, make changes based on this reflection, and stay the course. Don't jump to try something new too readily. Remember that there are no quick fixes. Work collaboratively with colleagues, put the children first, and maintain high expectations for students' learning.

By working together, sharing expertise, and using data as a friend, not an enemy, teachers within schools can make important changes in or modifications to their teaching of reading that can have a major impact on students' reading abilities. The thousands of teachers with whom we have worked over the last 10 years have told us repeatedly that the process described in this chapter is rewarding, and most important, that they see exciting improvements in students' reading achievement. Also we often hear teachers tell us, "I have changed the way I teach forever." This is sure to have a positive, lasting impact on many, many students over the years.

### Follow-up Activities

1. Discuss the two framing questions at the beginning of the chapter. Do you have the "right stuff" to begin on such a reading improvement effort as outlined in this chapter? What else do you need to know to decide?
2. If the answer to the first question above is affirmative, divide teachers and administrators into groups to learn more about leadership and school change; parent-school partnerships; successful professional learning; and effective reading programs, teachers of learning, reading instruction, and interventions to assist struggling readers. Consult the resources in the appendix. Use your new expertise to develop a schoolwide reading program.

## APPENDIX: RESOURCES

### Leadership and School Change

Fullan, M. (2005). *Leadership and sustainability: Systems thinkers in action.* Thousand Oaks, CA: Corwin Press.

Hasbrouck, J., & Denton, C. (2005). *The reading coach: A how-to manual for success.* Boston: Sopris West.

Hawley, W. D. (Ed.). (2002). *The keys to effective schools: Educational reform as continuous improvement.* Washington, DC: National Education Association.

Taylor, B. M., Pearson, D. P., Peterson, D. S., & Rodriguez, M. C. (2005). The CIERA School Change Framework: An evidence-based approach to professional development and school reading improvement. *Reading Research Quarterly, 40*(1), 40–69.

## Parent Partnerships

Christenson, S. L., & Sheridan, S. M. (2001). *Schools and families: Creating essential connections for learning.* New York: Guilford Press.

Edwards, P. A. (2004). *Children's literacy development: Making it happen through school. Family, and community involvement.* Boston: Pearson/Allyn & Bacon.

Epstein, J. L., Sanders, M. G., Simon, B. S., Salinas, K. C., Jansorn, N. R., & van Voorhis, F. L. (2002). *School, family, and community partnerships: Your handbook for action* (2nd ed.). Thousand Oaks, CA: Corwin Press.

## Professional Learning

Hasbrouck, J., & Denton, C. (2005). *The reading coach: A how-to manual for success.* Boston: Sopris West.

Murphy, C., & Lick, D. (2001). *Whole-faculty study groups: Creating student-based professional development* (2nd ed.). Thousand Oaks, CA: Corwin Press.

Walpole, S., & McKenna. M. C. (2004). *The literacy coach's handbook: A guide to research-based practice.* New York: Guilford Press.

York-Barr, J., Sommers, W. A., Ghere, G. S., & Montie, J. (2006). *Reflective practice to improve schools: An action guide for educators* (2nd ed.). Thousand Oaks, CA: Corwin Press.

## Schoolwide Reading Program

Morrow, L. M. (2003). *Organizing and managing the language arts block: A professional development guide.* New York: Guilford Press

New Standards Primary Literacy Committee. (1999). *Reading and writing grade by grade.* Washington, DC: National Center on Education and the Economy (NCEE).

Taylor, B. M., Peterson, D. S., Marx, M., & Chein, M. (2007). Scaling up a reading reform in high-poverty elementary schools. In this volume, Chapter 10.

Vaughn, S., Wanzek, J., & Fletcher, J. M. (2007). Multiple tiers of intervention: A framework for prevention and identification of students with reading/learning disabilities. In this volume, Chapter 8.

Walpole, S., & McKenna, M. C. (2004). *The literacy coach's handbook: A guide to research-based practice.* New York: Guilford Press.

## Effective Teachers and Schools

Block, C. C., & Mangieri, J. N. (2003). *Exemplary literacy teachers: Promoting success for all children in grades K–5.* New York: Guilford Press.

Gersten, R., Dimino, J., & Jayanthi, M. (2007). Toward the development of a nuanced classroom observational system for studying comprehension and vocabulary instruction. In this volume, Chapter 9.

Morrow, L. M., Gambrell, L. B., & Pressley, M. P. (2003). *Best practices in literacy instruction* (2nd ed.). New York: Guilford Press.

Taylor, B. M., & Pearson, P. D. (Eds.). (2002). *Teaching reading: Effective schools/ accomplished teachers.* Mahwah, NJ: Erlbaum.

Taylor, B. M., Pearson, P. D., Peterson, D. S., & Rodriguez, M. C. (2003). Reading growth in high-poverty classrooms: The influence of teacher practices that encourage students' cognitive engagement in literacy learning. *Elementary School Journal, 104,* 3–28.

Taylor, B. M., Peterson, D. S., Marx, M., & Chein, M. (2007). Scaling up a reading reform in high-poverty elementary schools. In this volume, Chapter 10.

## Phonemic Awareness and Emergent Literacy

McCormick, C. E., Throneburg, R. N., & Smitley, J. M. (2002). *A sound start: Phonemic awareness lessons for reading success.* New York: Guilford Press.

National Reading Panel. (2000). *Report of the National Reading Panel: Teaching children to read: Reports of the subgroups* (NIH Publication No. 00-4754). Washington, DC: National Institute of Child Health and Human Development, National Institutes of Health.

Rog, L. J. (2001). *Early literacy instruction in kindergarten.* Newark, DE: International Reading Association.

## Phonics, Word Recognition, and Fluency

Carnine, D. W., Silbert, J., Kame'enui, E. J., & Tarver, S. G. (2004). *Direct instruction reading* (4th ed.). Upper Saddle River, NJ: Pearson.

Chambers, B., Cheung, A., Madden, N. A., Slavin, R. E., & Gifford, R. (2007). Embedded multimedia: Using video to enhance reading outcomes in Success for All. In this volume, Chapter 3.

Gaskins, I. W., Ehri, L. C., Cress, C., O'Hara, C., & Donnelly, K. (1996). Procedures for word learning: Making discoveries about words. *The Reading Teacher, 50,* 312–327.

National Reading Panel. (2000). *Report of the National Reading Panel: Teaching children to read: Reports of the subgroups* (NIH Publication No. 00-4754). Washington, DC: National Institute of Child Health and Human Development, National Institutes of Health.

Rasinski, T. V. (2000). Speed does matter in reading. *The Reading Teacher, 54*(2), 146–151.

Samuels, S. J., & Farstrup, A. (Eds.). (2006). *What research has to say about fluency instruction* (3rd ed.). Newark, DE: International Reading Association.

Stahl, S. A., & Kuhn, M. R. (2002). Making it sound like language: Developing fluency. *The Reading Teacher, 55*(6), 582–584.

Taylor, B., Short, R., Frye, B., & Shearer, B., (1992). Classroom teachers prevent reading failure among low-achieving first-grade students. *The Reading Teacher, 45,* 592–597.

## Vocabulary

August, D., & Snow, C. (2007). *Developing vocabulary in English-language learners: A review of the experimental research.* In this volume, Chapter 5.

Bauman, J. F., & Kamen'eui, E. J. (Eds.). (2004). *Vocabulary instruction: Research to practice.* New York: Guilford Press.

Beck, I. L., McKeown, M. G., & Kucan, L. (2002). *Bringing words to life: Robust vocabulary instruction.* New York: Guilford Press.

Graves, M. F. (2007). *Conceptual and empirical bases for providing struggling readers with multifaceted and long-term vocabulary instruction.* In this volume, Chapter 4.

National Reading Panel. (2000). *Report of the National Reading Panel: Teaching children to read: Reports of the subgroups* (NIH Publication No. 00-4754). Washington, DC: National Institute of Child Health and Human Development, National Institutes of Health.

## Comprehension Strategies

Block, C., & Pressley, M. (Eds.). (2002). *Comprehension strategies: Research-based practices.* New York: Guilford Press.

Duke, N. K., & Bennett-Armistead, V. S. (2003). *Reading and writing informational text in the primary grades: Research-based practices.* New York: Scholastic.

Englert, C. S., Mariage, T. V., Okolo, C. M., Courtad, C. A., Shankland, R. K., Moxley, K. D., Billman, A., & Jones, N. (2007). Accelerating expository literacy in the middle grades: The ACCEL project. In this volume, Chapter 7.

National Reading Panel. (2000). *Report of the National Reading Panel: Teaching children to read: Reports of the subgroups* (NIH Publication No. 00-4954). Washington, DC: National Institute of Child Health and Human Development, National Institutes of Health.

Raphael, T. E., Highfield, K., & Au, K. H. (2006). *QAR now.* New York: Scholastic.

Santoro, L. E., Baker, S. K., Chard, D. J., & Howard, L. (2007). The comprehension conversation: Using purposeful discussion during read-alouds to promote student comprehension and vocabulary. In this volume, Chapter 6.

## Comprehension: High-Level Talk and Writing About Text

Beck, I. L., & McKeown, M. G. (2002). Text talk: Capturing the benefit of read-aloud experience for young children. *The Reading Teacher, 55*(1), 10–20.

Beck, I. L., McKeown, M. G., Hamilton, R. L., & Kucan, L. (1997). *Questioning the author*. Newark, DE: International Reading Association.

Day, J. P., Spiegel, D. L., McLellan, J., & Brown, V. B. (2002). *Moving forward with literature circles*. New York: Scholastic.

Santoro, L. E., Baker, S. K., Chard, D. J., & Howard, L. (2007). The comprehension conversation: Using purposeful discussion during read-alouds to promote student comprehension and vocabulary. In this volume, Chapter 6.

Raphael, T. R., & McMahon, S., (1994). Book Club: An alternative framework for reading instruction. *The Reading Teacher, 48*(2), 102–116.

Wood, K. D., Roser, N. L., & Martinez, M. (2001). Collaborative literacy: Lessons learned from literature. *The Reading Teacher, 55*(2), 102–111.

## Balanced Reading Instruction and Assessment

McKenna, M., & Stahl, S. (2003). *Assessment for reading instruction*. New York: Guilford Press.

Morrow, L. M. (2003). *Organizing and managing the language arts block: A professional development guide*. New York: Guilford Press.

Pressley, M. (2006). *Reading instruction that works: The case for balanced teaching* (3rd ed.). New York: Guilford Press.

## Meeting Individual Needs

Au, K. (2006). *Multicultural issues and literacy achievement*. Mahwah, NJ: Erlbaum.

August, D., & Shanahan, T. (Eds.). (2006). *Developing literacy in second-language learners: Report of the National Literacy Panel on Language-Minority Children and Youth*. Mahwah, NJ: Erlbaum.

Gaskins, I. W. (2004). *Success with struggling readers: The Benchmark School approach*. New York: Guilford Press.

McCormick, R. L., & Paratore, J. R. (Eds.). (2005). *After early intervention, then what?: Teaching struggling readers in grades 3 and beyond*. Upper Saddle River, NJ: Pearson.

McCormick, S. (2007). *Instructing students who have literacy problems* (5th ed.). Upper Saddle, NJ: Pearson.

Morris, D. (2007). One-to-one reading intervention in the primary grades: An idea that must evolve to survive. In this volume, Chapter 2.

Vaughn, S., Wanzek, J., & Fletcher, J. M. (2007). Multiple tiers of intervention: A framework for prevention and identification of students with reading/learning disabilities. In this volume, Chapter 8.

# REFERENCES

Fullan, M. (2005). *Leadership and sustainability: Systems thinkers in action.* Thousand Oaks, CA: Corwin.

Hawley, W. D. (Ed.). (2002). *The keys to effective schools: Educational reform as continuous improvement.* Washington, DC: National Education Association.

National Reading Panel (NRP). (2000). *Report of the National Reading Panel: Teaching children to read: Reports of the subgroups* (NIH Publication No. 00-4754). Washington, DC: National Institute of Child Health and Human Development, National Institutes of Health.

Pressley, M. (2006). *Reading instruction that works: The case for balanced teaching* (3rd ed.). New York: Guilford Press.

Taylor, B. M., Frye, B. J., Peterson, D. S., and Pearson, P. D. (2003). *Steps for school-wide reading improvement.* Washington, DC: National Education Association.

Taylor, B. M., Pearson, D. P., Peterson, D. S., & Rodriguez, M. C. (2005). The CIERA School Change Framework: An evidence-based approach to professional development and school reading improvement. *Reading Research Quarterly, 40*(1), 40–69.

Taylor, B. M, & Peterson, D. S. (2006a). *The impact of the School Change Framework in twenty-three REA schools.* Minneapolis: University of Minnesota, Minnesota Center for Reading Research.

Taylor, B. M, & Peterson, D. S. (2006b). *Year 3 report of the Minnesota RF1 school change project.* Minneapolis: University of Minnesota, Minnesota Center for Reading Research.

Taylor, B. M., Pressley, M., & Pearson, P. D. (2002). Research-supported characteristics of teachers and schools that promote reading achievement. In B. M. Taylor & P. D. Pearson (Eds.) *Teaching reading: Effective schools, accomplished teachers* (pp. 361–374). Mahwah, NJ: Erlbaum.

York-Barr, J., Sommers, W. A., Ghere, G. S., & Montie, J. (2006). *Reflective practice to improve schools: an action guide for educators* (2nd ed.). Thousand Oaks, CA: Corwin Press.

# About the Editors
# and the Contributors

**Barbara M. Taylor** is a Guy Bond Professor of Reading Education at the University of Minnesota, where she has been on the faculty since 1978. She received a B.A. in English from Tufts University, a M.Ed. from Georgia State University, and an Ed.D. from Virginia Tech. Her research interests focus on school-wide reading improvement, early reading intervention, and school and teacher factors contributing to children's success in reading. She directed a large national study on school change in reading in high-poverty schools, and she is currently helping 28 Reading First schools in Minnesota implement the School Change Framework to improve students' reading achievement in grades K–3. She is also Director, Center for Reading Research at the University of Minnesota. With co-authors David Pearson, Debra Peterson, and Michael Rodriguez, Taylor received the 2005 Albert J. Harris Award for research from the International Reading Association, the 2005 Outstanding Teacher Educator Award from the International Reading Association, and she is a member of the Reading Hall of Fame. She has published numerous books, book chapters, and articles, and her work has appeared in journals including *Reading Research Quarterly, Journal of Reading Behavior, The Reading Teacher, Journal of Educational Psychology, Elementary School Journal,* and *Educational Researcher.*

**James E. Ysseldyke** is Birkmaier Professor of Educational Leadership in the Department of Educational Psychology at the University of Minnesota. From 1983–1989 Ysseldyke was Director of the Minnesota Institute for Research on Learning Disabilities and from 1990–1999 he was Director of the National Center on Educational Outcomes. Ysseldyke teaches courses in Minnesota's School Psychology Program, and from 1988–1993 was Director of the Program.

Professor Ysseldyke's research and writing have focused on issues in assessing and making decisions about students with disabilities. He is an author of major textbooks including *Assessment: In Special and Inclusive Education, Critical Issues in Special Education,* and *Testing Students with Disabilities: Practical Strategies for Complying with State and District*

*Requirements.* He has published many book chapters, articles in professional journals, an instructional environment scale (*Functional Assessment of Academic Behavior: An evidence-based assessment of a student's instructional environment*), and *Strategies and Tactics for Effective Instruction*, a system of practical tips and tactics teachers use in planning, managing, delivering, and evaluating instruction.

Ysseldyke has received awards for his research from the School Psychology Division of the American Psychological Association, the American Educational Research Association, and the Council for Exceptional Children. The University of Minnesota presented him a distinguished teaching award, and he received a distinguished alumni award from the University of Illinois. From 1986–1992 Ysseldyke served as Editor of *Exceptional Children*, the main journal of the International Council for Exceptional Children.

**Diane August** is currently a Senior Research Scientist at the Center for Applied Linguistics as well as an independent consultant located in Washington, DC. Her research focuses on the development of literacy in language minority children. Recently she was Principal Investigator for the National Literacy Panel on Language Minority Children and Youth. For 10 years she was a public school teacher in California, specializing in literacy programs for language minority children in grades K–8 and subsequently served as Legislative Assistant in the area of education for a U.S. Congressman from California, worked as a Grants Officer for the Carnegie Corporation of New York, and was Director of Education for the Children's Defense Fund. She has been a Senior Program Officer at the National Academy of Sciences where she was study director for the Committee on Developing a Research Agenda on the Education of Limited English Proficient and Bilingual Students. Dr. August has also worked for many years as an educational consultant in the areas of literacy, program improvement, evaluation and testing, and federal and state education policy. In 1981, she received her Ph.D. in education from Stanford University, and in 1982 completed a postdoctoral fellowship in psychology also at Stanford. She has published widely in journals and books.

**Scott K. Baker** is the Director of Pacific Institutes for Research in Eugene, Oregon. He specializes in early literacy measurement and instruction in reading and mathematics. Dr. Baker is co-Principal Investigator on two grants funded by the Institute of Education Sciences and he is the co-Director of the Oregon Reading First Center. Dr. Baker's scholarly contributions include conceptual, qualitative, and quantitative publications on a range of topics related to students at risk for school difficulties and students who are English-language learners.

**Alison K. Billman** is a doctoral candidate at Michigan State University. Her work focuses on children's language and literacy development in primary grades particularly in relationship to inquiry and project-based instruction. Billman's research interests emerge from extensive classroom experiences with children. Her teaching was marked by innovative practices involving complex inquiry projects in which primary student researchers accessed resources in the community and in universities across the nation.

**Bette Chambers** is currently Vice President of Research at the Success for All Foundation, where she oversees the Foundation's research and directs the development and dissemination of the preschool, kindergarten, embedded multimedia, and computer-assisted tutoring programs. Dr. Chambers is also a professor in the Center for Research and Reform in Education at Johns Hopkins University. She received her B.A. in Early Childhood Education from Concordia University in 1981 and her Ph.D. in Educational Psychology in 1990 from McGill University. Dr. Chambers has authored or co-authored numerous articles, books, and practical guides for teachers, including *Let's Cooperate: Interactive Activities for Young Children* and *Classroom Connections: Understanding and Using Cooperative Learning.*

**David J. Chard** is an Associate Professor at the University of Oregon, College of Education where he serves as Associate Dean for Curriculum and Academic Programs and Major Director of Special Education. Dr. Chard is a principal investigator on three federal research projects on reading, reading comprehension instruction and mathematics. He also serves as a Co-Principal Investigator to a federally funded center on school-wide models of preventing reading difficulties.

**Michelle Chein** is a doctoral student in literacy education at the University of Minnesota. Her research interests include reading comprehension, struggling readers, school-wide reading improvement, and teacher professional development. She is currently working at the Minnesota Center for Reading Research at the University of Minnesota. Her work involves supporting Reading First schools in Minnesota.

**Alan C. K. Cheung** is an Associate Professor in the Department of Educational Policy and Administration at the Hong Kong Institute of Education. He received his B.A. in English from Brigham Young University-Hawaii in 1995, and his M.Ed. and Ph.D. in Educational Policy from Brigham Young University. His areas of specialization include large-scale assessment, research reviews, research methodology, and private education. Currently Dr. Cheung directs several research projects in Hong Kong, including a large scale, territory-wide survey on curriculum reform in Hong Kong commissioned by the Hong Kong Education and Manpower Bureau. Dr. Cheung has published over 30 professional papers, including book chapters, peer-reviewed journal articles, and technical reports.

**Carrie Anna Courtad** is a doctoral student in Special Education and a Special Education Technology Scholar (SETS) Besides working on Project ACCEL: Accelerating Expository Literacy To Improve School Outcomes, she also works on the Virtual History Museum, a web-based history learning environment. Her research areas are varied with a general focus on literacy, technology, and the preparation of future educators. Prior to attending Michigan State University, she taught at Central Michigan University and in the public school systems as a special education teacher in Austin, Texas, and Shepherd, Michigan.

**Joseph A. Dimino** has had experience as a general education teacher, special education teacher, administrator, behavior consultant, and researcher. He has extensive experience working with teachers, parents, administrators, and instructional assistants in the areas of instruction and early literacy, reading comprehension strategies and classroom and behavior management in urban, suburban, and rural communities. He is the coordinator of a national research project investigating the impact of Teacher Study Groups as a means to enhance the quality of reading instruction for first graders in high poverty schools. He is also involved in a national evaluation investigating the effectiveness of reading comprehension programs.

**Carol Sue Englert** is a professor at Michigan State University in the Department of Counseling, Educational Psychology and Special Education. She received her Master's Degree in special education from the University of Missouri at Columbia, and her doctoral degree in special education from Indiana University at Bloomington. Since 1985, she has directed many federally funded projects in order to study and improve literacy instruction for children with disabilities. Her research interests include expository literacy instruction for students with disabilities, instructional scaffolds, interactive discourse, and instructional technologies in the improvement of literacy performance.

**Jack M. Fletcher** is a Distinguished University Professor of Psychology at the University of Houston. For the past 30 years, Dr. Fletcher, a child neuropsychologist, has completed research on many issues related to learning disabilities and dyslexia, including definition and classification, neurobiological correlates, and intervention. He was the 2003 recipient of the Samuel T. Orton award from the IDA and a co-recipient of the Albert J. Harris award from the International Reading Association in 2006.

**Russell Gersten** is Executive Director of Instructional Research Group, a non-profit educational research institute, and President of RG Research Group. He also is Professor Emeritus in the College of Education at the University of Oregon. He also serves as Director of Research for the Regional Educational Laboratory: Southwest, overseeing the development and refinement of large scale randomized controlled trials. Main areas of expertise include instructional research on English Learners, reading comprehension research, mathematics research, and research methodology. He has published over 150 articles in prestigious journals and serves on 10 editorial boards. In March 2006, he was appointed to the presidentially appointed National Mathematics Panel. He currently serves as Principal Investigator for the *What Works Clearinghouse* on the topic of instructional research on ELLs. He received the AERA Distinguished Special Education researcher in 2002.

**Richard Gifford** is project manager for technology and a reading curriculum developer for the Success For All Foundation in Baltimore, Maryland. He is also the author of several volumes of short stories, articles, and reading activities developed for older reading disabled students. Mr. Gifford holds a Bachelor of Arts in English Literature from the University of Texas and a Master of Arts in Teaching from Johns Hopkins University.

**Michael F. Graves** is a member of the Center for Reading Research and a Professor Emeritus of Literacy Education at the University of Minnesota. Graves received his Ph.D. in Education from Stanford University and his M.A. and B.A. in English from California State College at Long Beach, and joined the University of Minnesota faculty in 1971. His research, development, and writing focus on vocabulary learning and instruction, comprehension development, and effective instruction. His recent books include *Teaching Reading in the 21st Century* with Connie Juel and Bonnie Graves (2007), *Reading and Responding in the Middle Grades* with Lee Galda (2007), and *The Vocabulary Book* (2006). Dr. Graves has served as the Editor of the *Journal of Reading Behavior* and as the Associate Editor of *Research in the Teaching of English* and is a member of the Reading Hall of Fame. He has served or is serving on the Editorial Review Boards for *Reading Research Quarterly*, *Journal of Reading Behavior*, *Research in the Teaching of English*, *National Reading Conference Yearbook*, and *Journal of Reading*. He has published more than 100 books, book chapters, and articles; his work has appeared in a range of journals including *Reading Research Quarterly, Research in the*

*Teaching of English, Journal of Reading Behavior, The Reading Teacher, Journal of Adolescent and Adult Literacy, Journal of Educational Psychology, Elementary School Journal, Child Development, American Educator,* and *Educational Leadership.* He currently serves as a consultant for Seward Inc. on comprehension strategies, for SRA/McGraw Hill on vocabulary instruction, and for World Book Encyclopedia on text difficulty.

After many years as a regular education, special education, and Title 1 teacher, **Lisa Howard** currently works as a Research Assistant at the Pacific Institutes for Research in Eugene, Oregon. She also provides professional development to K–3 teachers as a reading consultant and coach. Ms. Howard is a co-author of *Read Well,* a primary reading curriculum.

**Madhavi Jayanthi, Ed.D.,** is a Research Associate at Instructional Research Group, Long Beach, CA. Her research interests include effective instructional techniques for students with disabilities and at-risk learners, both in the area of reading and mathematics.

**Nathan Jones** is a doctoral student in special education and education policy. His research interests include the mentoring and induction of beginning special education teachers, teacher labor markets, and the overrepresentation of minority students in special education.

**Nancy A. Madden** is currently President of the Success for All Foundation. She received her B.A. in Psychology from Reed College in 1973, and her Ph.D. in Clinical Psychology from American University in 1980. From 1980–1998, she was a research scientist at the Center for Research on the Education of Students Placed at Risk at Johns Hopkins University, where she directed the development of the reading, writing, language arts, and mathematics elements of Success for All. Dr. Madden is the author or co-author of many articles and books on cooperative learning, mainstreaming, Chapter 1, and students at risk, including *Effective Programs for Students at Risk* (1989) and *Every Child, Every School: Success for All* (1996).

**Troy Mariage** is an Associate Professor in the Department of Counseling, Educational Psychology, and Special Education at Michigan State University. His research interests are in the area of informational reading and writing for students with mild disabilities. Related interests include the provision of concurrent academic and social support in classrooms, with attention towards the role that social mediation plays in the construction of meaning, identity, and ways of knowing. He has recently completed a 6-year participant study of school re-culturing in one of the lowest performing schools in

Michigan. He completed his doctoral studies in special education at Michigan State University.

**Monica Marx** is a doctoral student in literacy education at the University of Minnesota. Her research interests include reading comprehension, development of literacy for English language learners, school-wide reading improvement and teacher professional development. Recently, she worked at the Minnesota Center for Reading Research at the University of Minnesota.

**Darrel Morris** is Professor of Education and Director of the Reading Clinic at Appalachian State University in Boone, North Carolina. He began his college teaching career at National-Louis University in Evanston, Illinois. There, he established the Howard Street Tutoring Program, which has since become a model for volunteer tutoring programs throughout the country. Since moving to Appalachian State in 1989, he has directed the Masters program in Reading, researched the beginning reading and spelling processes, and helped school districts in eight states set up early reading intervention programs. Dr. Morris has published extensively in both research and practitioner journals and is the author of two books: *The Howard Street Tutoring Manual* and *Every Child Reading* (with Robert Slavin). He and several co-authors recently received the International Reading Association's *Dina Feitelson Research Award* for an outstanding empirical study in the area of beginning reading.

**Kathleen D. Moxley** is a doctoral student in Teacher Education and Literacy at Michigan State University. Her research interests include K–8 literature-based instructional approaches, reading comprehension and writing strategies at the secondary level, the impact of communities of practice on teacher professional development and the challenges and influences of teachers making instructional changes.

**Cynthia M. Okolo** is a professor of Counseling, Educational Psychology, and Special Education at Michigan State University, where she teaches courses in instructional methods and directs a doctoral program in assistive technology. Prior to obtaining her Ph.D. at Indiana University, she was a special education resource room teacher at the elementary and middle school levels. Her research has focused on improving teaching and learning for understanding in inclusive classrooms, particularly in the areas of literacy and historical understanding. Technology-based instructional experiences and tools have been key elements in her investigations and in the curricular units she and her colleagues have developed. Her work has been funded by grants from the United States Department of Education and has been published in a variety of journals and books in the fields of special education and educational technology. She can be contacted at: okolo@msu.edu

**Debra S. Peterson** is the Assistant Project Director for the Minnesota REA/ Reading First Professional Development Program. She has worked with elementary teachers and schools to improve reading instruction and implement school-wide reform for the past 5 years. Current publications include articles in *Reading Research Quarterly, Elementary School Journal,* and *The Reading Teacher.* Awards include the Albert J. Harris Award for research presented by the International Reading Association. She received her doctorate in Literacy Education from the University of Minnesota and is currently an instructor in the Department of Curriculum and Instruction at the University of Minnesota. She has been an elementary and preschool teacher for almost 20 years. Her research interests include emergent literacy, school reform in reading, and effective professional development in reading.

**Lana Edwards Santoro** currently works as a research associate with the Pacific Institutes for Research in Eugene, Oregon and the Instructional Research Group in Long Beach, California. She is a principal investigator on a series of Institute for Educational Sciences (IES) funded research on teaching reading comprehension to first grade students during classroom read alouds. Of particular focus is her work to develop supplemental interventions for students at-risk of early reading difficulties, students with vocabulary and language deficits, and English-language learners. Dr. Santoro has published work on the effects of research-based strategies on student reading. Topics of focus include spelling, vocabulary, reading comprehension, and content area instruction.

**Rebecca K. Shankland** is a doctoral student in literacy and special education at Michigan State University. Research interests include strategies for reading comprehension and writing, the connection between reading fluency and comprehension, communities of practice in support of teacher learning and change, and implementation of best practice in schools. Current research projects span several areas of literacy including reading fluency and comprehension, informational literacy, writing across the curriculum, and cohesiveness of literacy services in urban versus suburban schools.

**Robert E. Slavin** is currently Director of the Center for Data-Driven Reform in Education at Johns Hopkins University and Chairman of the Success for All Foundation. He received his B. A. in Psychology from Reed College in 1972, and his Ph.D. in Social Relations in 1975 from Johns Hopkins University. Dr. Slavin has authored or co-authored more than 200 articles and

20 books, including *Educational Psychology: Theory into Practice, Cooperative Learning: Theory, Research, and Practice, Show Me the Evidence: Proven and Promising Programs for America's Schools, Effective Programs for Latino Students,* and *One Million Children: Success for All.* He received the American Educational Research Association's Raymond B. Cattell Early Career Award for Programmatic Research in 1986, the Palmer O. Johnson award for the best article in an AERA journal in 1988, the Charles A. Dana award in 1994, the James Bryant Conant Award from the Education Commission of the States in 1998, the Outstanding Leadership in Education Award from the Horace Mann League in 1999, and the Distinguished Services Award from the Council of Chief State School Officers in 2000.

**Catherine Snow** is the Henry Lee Shattuck Professor of Education in the Human Development and Psychology Department at the Harvard Graduate School of Education. She received her Ph.D. in psychology from McGill and worked for several years in the linguistics department of the University of Amsterdam. Her research has encompassed studies of language development, literacy development, social and familial influences on literacy development, acquisition of English and bilingualism in language minority children, and literacy acquisition in a second language. She is currently working on issues of adolescent literacy, and on the prerequisites for improving literacy instruction in middle and secondary schools. She chaired the committees that produced *Preventing Reading Difficulties in Young Children, Reading for Understanding: Towards an R&D Agenda,* and *Knowledge to Support the Teaching of Reading.* For more information: http://gseweb.harvard.edu/~snow/

**Sharon Vaughn** holds the H. E. Hartfelder/Southland Corp. Regents Chair in Human Development, University of Texas at Austin. She was the Editor-in-Chief of the *Journal of Learning Disabilities* and the Co-Editor of *Learning Disabilities Research and Practice.* She is the recipient of the AERA Special Education SIG distinguished researcher award and the author of numerous books and research articles that address the reading and social outcomes of students with learning difficulties. She is currently the Principal Investigator or Co-Principal Investigator on several Institute for Education Science, National Institute for Child Health and Human Development, and Office of Special Education Programs research grants investigating effective interventions for students with reading difficulties and students who are English language learners.

**Jeanne Wanzek** is a research associate at the University of Texas at Austin in the Vaughn Gross Center for Reading and Language Arts. She currently coordinates two research projects examining student response to intervention at the elementary and middle school levels. Her research interests include effective instructional design and beginning reading instruction. Before moving to Texas, Jeanne taught both second and third grade as well as elementary special education in Illinois.

# Index

261